MW00984000

"The perfect book for those who waited for tl
over and return to the fun of the B-movie."

"*Death on the Cheap* is the goods. Rich in facts, history, and lore of some of the most exciting—and over-looked—low budget films ever made, it is also a wealth of behind-the-scenes insights and trivia that kept me glued to the pages. Written with the sure hand of a gifted novelist, Arthur Lyons has opened an entertaining treasure chest that will have you racing to your local video rental joint!"
—*Robert Crais*

"*Death on the Cheap* is a terrific piece of work, the definitive book on its subject, and a body slam of nostalgia that knocked me out of my chair more than once."
—*Dean Koontz*

"At last, a book on film noir written not by a university professor but by a practitioner of the craft. In *Death on the Cheap*, Arthur Lyons provides an entertaining and refreshingly new look not only at film noir but the B movie in general."
—*Steve Shagan, author of* Save the Tiger *and* Voyage of the Damned

"In *Death on the Cheap: The Lost B Movies of Film Noir*, Arthur Lyons shines a bright light of insight, information, and analysis on a hitherto dark subject. Not only is it interesting material to read, it's written in a style that flows and keeps the reader comfortably swimming through facts and references that could easily have been delivered in a dry, scholarly fashion. The reader feels he or she is on a true journey of discovery. You keep looking for glue on the pages because you can't put it down. This is simply put: *a really good book.*
—*Andrew Neiderman, author of* The Devil's Advocate

"Arthur Lyons' approach to film noir is grounded in a thorough knowledge of the old Hollywood studio system and analyzed from the perspective of a highly respected crime writer well-versed in the elements of story-telling. More importantly, his 'take' on some of these old 'B' films will bring a grin to your face. A great read."
—*Sue Grafton*

THE LOST B MOVIES OF
FILM NOIR

BY **ARTHUR LYONS**

PREFACE BY **GERALD PETIEVICH**

DA CAPO PRESS

Library of Congress Cataloging-in-Publication Data
Lyons, Arthur.
    Death on the cheap : the lost B movies of film noir / by Arthur Lyons
        p.   cm.
    Includes bibliographical references and index.
    ISBN 0-306-80996-6 (pbk.)
    1. Film noir—United States—History and criticism.   2. B films—United States—History
and criticsm.   I. Title.

PN1995.9F54 L96   2000
791.43'655—dc21
                                                                                          00-043164

Published by Da Capo Press
A Member of the Perseus Books Group
http://www.perseusbooksgroup.com

1 2 3 4 5 6 7 8 9 10—03 02 0 1 00

This book is dedicated to my wife Barbara, my greatest love, and to the memory of Asta, my friend for sixteen years

CONTENTS

PREFACE

The classic film noir period covered roughly the 1940s and 1950s. It took audiences into a world of crime and corruption, of cynical self-interest and cold-blooded murder. In recent years, there has been a revival of interest in the genre with highfalutin' cinematic analysis of film noir's existential and social roots. What much of this criticism has ignored, and what Arthur Lyons documents, is that the true roots of film noir were in the so-called hard-boiled stories and novels of the thirties and arose from the pragmatic forces and economic restraints within the movie industry itself.

Lyons asserts, correctly, that film noir was an outgrowth of the B crime film and that it became recognized as a genre only when critics began to notice the similarities among the films themselves. Although they were known for a certain look—wet streets, foreboding shadows, nightmarish urban landscapes—it was the dark thematic content rather than just the visual style that caught the attention of the critics. Modern noir filmmakers have also focused on this aspect of the films. Film noir is a child of itself, the creation of a genre where none existed before.

These films–especially the Bs–although wrapped in an expressionistic visual style, were Hollywood's first attempt to present a real view of the underworld. Up to that time, criminal activity had been, for the most part, glamorized in film. The B films, copying from one another, managed to capture the obsessions and inexplicable self-destructiveness of criminals that I found so compelling in real life when I was a U.S. Secret Service agent chasing counterfeiters in Los Angeles and Paris. I knew that the counterfeiter I arrested today would be passing twenties again as soon as he got out of prison.

Whereas some audiences were shocked at the rawness of film noir, most loved it, as evidenced by the fact that film noir remained popular for twenty years and is finding a strong revival today. The genre gives audiences an entertaining escape into a dark world into which they would never venture. At the same time, it provides a measure of identification for some who, like the noir protagonists, feel trapped and victimized by their circumstances.

Most books on the subject of film noir cover only well-known films noir in their filmographies, such as *The Maltese Falcon, Double Indemnity, Out of the Past, The Postman Always Rings Twice,* and *Laura.* However, these were all A productions. Those B films the books do cover are usually titles that have been previously rehashed ad nauseam. Arthur Lyons, in contrast, has dusted off those B films that have been sitting on studio shelves, those that rarely, if ever, appear on television even at three in the morning, and he has some fun doing it. Thankfully, the terms *mise-en-scene, aesthetic reversals,* and *rhetorical form* do not appear in his text.

Having had two of my crime novels made into motion pictures, I have become aware of the reverence in which many of today's leading directors hold the film noir genre. With its entertaining, fresh approach, this book is an excellent way to learn something new about a fascinating, controversial film subject.

Gerald Petievich

INTRODUCTION

In recent years, there has been an incredible resurgence of interest in film noir among both film historians and filmmakers themselves. Dozens of books have been published on the subject by academics and critics who have put forth their own explanations as to what film noir is and how it came about. International film festivals canonizing the genre have been held in the United States and Europe. The 1990s saw an explosion of "neonoir" films produced by young filmmakers. Several (*Pulp Fiction*, 1994; *The Usual Suspects*, 1995; *Fargo*, 1996; and *L.A. Confidential*, 1997) were nominated for or won Academy Awards. Showtime cable network produced its own series of original *noir* films, entitled *Fallen Angels*, and the BBC has done documentaries on the subject. Carly Simon put out her album *Film Noir*, resurrecting songs from some old films noirs as well as adding original songs. American Movie Classics cable network held its own "Tribute to Film Noir," honoring several noir icons including Lauren Bacall, Kirk Douglas, and the late Robert Mitchum.

So what is film noir, how did it come about, and why this latest fetishizing of a period of film history that lasted roughly twenty years, from 1939 to 1959? At least one writer on the subject declares that the recent interest is not only deserved but long overdue, saying that film noir "represented an outburst of artistic maturity, style and meaning which is still unappreciated today."

Film historians attribute the rise of film noir to a coalescence of influences: A flood of foreign auteurs fled Europe with the rise of Hitler and brought with them to America the artistic style of German expressionism; American directors were exposed to French poetic realism; Orson Welles utilized a variety of slick new optics in *Citizen Kane*, opening up a whole new cinematic world; Hollywood recognized and played on the popularity of the "hard-boiled" writers of the 1930s by putting their novels and short stories on film; soldiers returning home from World War II brought with them a postwar cynicism and hardened views of violence; and public paranoia about The Bomb grew with the advent of the Cold War.

Some or perhaps all of these factors likely exerted an influence on what came to be known as film noir. But many academic critics ignore—probably to avoid the more banal explanation of film as a product and representation of history and a snapshot of the American character frozen in time—that film noir was not just a product of history but also a product of Hollywood, a town less known for its artistic maturity than its penchant for imitation. In Hollywood, necessity is often the mother of invention, especially when wartime economic constraints on movie budgets put severe limits on production values.

A few years before his death, Robert Mitchum succinctly put the matter in perspective for me over a two-hour lunch in his dressing room trailer. When I brought up the large number of film noir he had acted in during his career, he sneered: "Hell, we didn't know what film noir was in those days. We were just making movies. Cary Grant and all the big stars [at RKO] got all the lights. We lit our sets with cigarette butts."

Even though films now called film noir by critics have been made in Hollywood since 1939, film noir as a genre did not exist until 1946. In that year an exhibition of American movies was held in Paris, and French film critics got their first look at what had been going on in Tinseltown since the advent of World War II. Among the films shown were *Laura*; *The Maltese Falcon*; *Murder, My Sweet*; *Double Indemnity*; and *The Woman in the Window*.

Those five films shared enough traits that critic Nino Frank gave them a new classification: *film noir*, or literally, "black film." The traits they shared were both stylistic and thematic. They were dark in both look and mood. Their primary action took place at night on rain-swept city streets, in narrow ash-can alleys, in claustrophobic diners, and in dingy, shadowy hotel rooms with neon signs flashing outside the windows, rooms in which, as hard-boiled author Nelson Algren once put it, "every bed you rent makes you an accessory to somebody else's shady past."

The characters in these films were bookies, con men, killers, cigarette girls, crooked cops, down-and-out boxers, and calculating, scheming, and very deadly women. The well-lit, singing and tap-dancing, happy-ending world of the thirties had in ten short years become a hostile, orderless place in which alienation, obsession, and paranoia ruled. The universe seemed to conspire to defeat and entrap the inhabitants who wandered blindly through it. They were victims of fate, their own worst enemies who, looking for a score, ended by defeating themselves. They were people unwired to anything and for whom nobody prayed. Bradford Galt, who in *The Dark Corner* finds himself framed for murder, speaks for all of them: "I feel all dead inside. I'm backed up in a dark corner and I don't know who's hitting me."

The angst and desperation of the films' protagonists is evident in the films' titles: *Framed, Convicted, Abandoned, The Accused, They Won't Believe Me, Railroaded!, Fear, Cornered, Sudden Fear, Desperate, I Walk Alone, I Died a Thousand Times.* Their world was far from the sunny light of day: *The Dark Past, Dark Passage, The Dark Mirror, Nightmare, Night Runner, Night Editor, So Dark the Night, Somewhere in the Night, The City That Never Sleeps, In a Lonely Place.* They were obsessed with sex and violence, to the point that the two became almost synonymous: *Human Desire, Crime of Passion, Kiss of Death, Kiss the Blood Off My Hands, Kiss Me Deadly, A Kiss Before Dying.*

The five films mentioned earlier that were shown at the 1946 exhibition were the ones the French critiqued. These high-budget studio productions most commonly come to the public's mind when the word *noir* is mentioned because of the repeated play they receive on television and because they are cited most often in the spate of contemporary books that have recently been published on the subject. But the noir cycle, although kick-started by the success of those high-budget productions, actually had its roots in the B movie, in particular, in the B crime movie.

As part of its 1999 celebration of film noir, *The Dark Days of Summer*, Turner Classic Movies presented a roundtable interview of four actresses often associated closely with film noir: Audrey Totter, Marie Windsor, Jane Greer, and Coleen Gray. When asked if they knew at the time that the movies they were playing in were film noir, they all replied unequivocally no, that they had heard the term only in the past ten years. When asked what kind of movies they thought they were playing in, they immediately answered, "B movies." (In fact, Marie Windsor said she was known in certain Hollywood circles at the time as "Queen of the Bs.") As writer and director Paul Schrader puts it, "Film noir was ideally suited to the low budget 'B' film and many of the best noir films were 'B' films."

Film noir was made to order for the B, or low-budget, part of the movie double bill. It was cheaper to produce because it required less lighting and smaller casts and usually entailed story lines that required limited-scale sets. Film noir was character-driven, and its story lines, which were unusual and compact, could often be told in the 60 to 80 minutes required of B pictures. Schrader, in his 1972 essay "Notes on Film Noir," cites this association between noir and B films as one reason American film critics largely ignored noir until the 1970s, when interest began to resurge both within the critical community and among modern filmmakers.

Suddenly, almost forty years after most critics cite as the end of the classic noir cycle, noir was artistically rehabilitated to the point that studios began to advertise films as noir, intimating that the term made those films somehow more classy than they would have been if they had been billed as regular old crime or cops-and-robbers movies. It is undeniably true that many B noir films of the 1940s and 1950s embodied more artistic style and originality than a majority of the studios' B fare and even quite a lot of their A fare, but in the 1990s, the allure of the genre for Hollywood's new generation of writers, directors, producers, and actors remained the same as it had been forty years before. As Bryan Singer, director of the modern noir *The Usual Suspects*, puts it, "Film noir, especially the heist film, is a cheap way to make an action movie. That's what makes it attractive to new filmmakers." The resurgence in interest in film noir among young, low-budget filmmakers, then, is in reality a return to the roots of the genre: the B movie.

The purpose of this book is not to repeat the same material that has appeared and reappeared in the dozens of recent books on film noir but to fill in some gaps left by that body of literature. The first part of this book is an attempt to define in some understandable way what film noir was and is, the subject of much wrangling by film critics and authors, as well as to pinpoint its origins and association with B film production. I have expanded my investigation beyond the boundaries of noir and looked at the development of the B movie in general because it is important to understand that film noir developed as a style within the B crime film genre and ultimately developed into a genre itself.

The second part of the book is a filmography of B films noirs that have been neglected by most books on the genre and therefore may be considered lost, at least by the general public. Although I tried to compile a list of titles that are comparatively unknown, I have also included several dozen films that appear in one or the other of two books on the subject that have by far the most exhaustive listings of films noirs, Spencer Selby's *Dark City: The Film Noir* (1984) and *Film Noir: An Encyclopedic Reference to the American Style* (1992) by Alain Silver and Elizabeth Ward. I have chosen these titles for various reasons; they are notable because of the significance of the writers, directors, or cast or because of the studios that released them.

Many of the B movies in the filmography in this book have probably been ignored by critics because they were simply bad. Others may have slipped through the cracks or been the victims of "economic snobbery," as Paul Schrader puts it. "High-budget trash is considered (in some critical circles) more worthy of attention than low-budget trash," Schrader contends, "and to praise a 'B' film is somehow to slight (often unintentionally) an 'A' film."

I must confess without any embarrassment to being subject to no such snobbery, being not only an avid fan and student of film noir but also a great fan of B movies. In fact, my snobbery probably works in reverse. It is hard to imagine how anyone could spend $50 million on the making of an A movie and have it come out bad, although many filmmakers have accomplished just that. It is much more interesting—at least to me—to see what moviemakers could put together for less than $100,000 and how really good some of it is.

Some critics may dispute the inclusion of some of the titles in the filmography as not being true film noir for one reason or another—not surprising considering the disagreement within scholarly film circles as to what constitutes a noir film. (One critic absurdly includes the horror movie *King Kong*, sci-fi such as *The Day the Earth Stood Still*, the western *High Noon*, and the social protest film *The Grapes of Wrath* as being films noirs.) By the time the reader gets to the filmography section of this book, I hope my reasons for including particular films will be clear.

This book is not a scholarly dissertation on film noir; there have been more than enough of those published in recent years. I wrote it out of a passion for film noir and, indeed, B movies in general, and because tracking down these largely ignored films was akin to that excitement a paleontologist must feel dusting off a rock and discovering a dinosaur bone. I had the thrill of exploring territory others have previously explored and discovering something new in it. I hope that you, the reader, have as much fun discovering these obscure films as I did.

Welcome, then, to the lost world of B film noir.

1

FILM NOIR:
IT'S ALL IN THE STORY

What exactly is film noir? That question has been debated strenuously in the past twenty years with the proliferation of literature on the subject. It has alternatively been described as a movement, a genre, a cycle, a mood and sensibility, and a universe. Some critics and filmmakers have defined it as an American film form confined to a specific period, most often 1940–1959; others have argued that noir never died, that the volume of production simply varied, declining in the 1960s and 1970s and exploding in the 1980s and 1990s with filmmakers' rediscovery of the genre.

The truth is that film noir did not originate as a genre but as a faddish way of packaging the crime film. It is only critical analysis and modern self-conscious attempts to resurrect the style of the films noirs of the forties and fifties that have succeeded in creating a definite genre where one did not exist before. In 1944, if you'd asked Billy Wilder or Edward Dmytryk what kind of films they were making when they were in production with *Double Indemnity* or *Murder, My Sweet*, they probably would have said a crime melodrama or detective whodunit. By contrast, ask a filmmaker making a similar type of film today and the answer would be unequivocal: film noir.

In general, historians have agreed on the essential qualities of film noir, such as its dark, brooding visual style typified by deep-focus photography, chiaroscuro lighting, odd camera angles; the presence of crime in the plot, particularly murder; an urban setting; and the free use of voice-overs and narrative flashbacks.

The problem with that analysis is that many films of the forties and fifties ex-hibited stylistic qualities that were common to film noir but were clearly not noir. Conversely, all of those stylistic elements, either singly or in combination, have been absent in many well-recognized films noir. Many films noir were shot in a rel-atively flat style and were not particularly dark (at least in a cinematic sense)—films such as *High Sierra* (1941), *Impact* (1949), *The Capture* (1950), *The Strip* (1951), *Jeopardy* (1953), *Cause for Alarm* (1953), and *While the City Sleeps* (1956). Although film noir is popularly associated with black-and-white film, some direc-tors during the classic noir period experimented with color in such films as *Leave Her to Heaven* (1945), *Rope* (1948), *The Man on the Eiffel Tower* (1949), *Niagara* (1953), *Rear Window* (1954), *I Died a Thousand Times* (1955), *Hell's Island* (1955), *House of Bamboo* (1955), *Slightly Scarlet* (1956), and *Vertigo* (1958). Noirs that do not occur in an urban setting include *Ace in the Hole* (1950), *Deep Valley* (1947), *The Red House* (1947), and *Storm Fear* (1956). To complicate matters further, film noir filmographies by critics almost uniformly include at least a few films in which the crime element is absent, such as *Caught* (1949), *Born to Be Bad* (1950), and *Clash By Night* (1952).

The only factors that unite all of these films under the film noir heading is their hard-bitten, cynical tone and their thematic content. As Gerald Petievich, a for-mer Secret Service agent and contemporary noir screenwriter and novelist (*To Live and Die in L.A.*, 1991; *Boiling Point*, 1993, based on his novel *Money Men*) puts it, "Story and only story defines film noir. Director tastes and techniques have noth-ing to do with the archetype noir tale."

Some modern filmmakers who have indulged in recent years in the genre, and who have to a great extent *defined* the genre, agree. Bob Swaim, who wrote and di-rected *Masquerade* (1988), said in an interview: "What I tried to do with *Masquer-ade* was create a classic film noir without imitating the great films of the genre. I tried replacing the forties' style of long shadows with the wholesome look of a Bruce Weber ad for Ralph Lauren and hired adolescents to play grownups. What I like about film noir is that it's desire rather than action that is the motivation."

At first glance, it might not seem as if film noir had any underlying thematic content. There are films noirs about gangsters (*White Heat*, 1949, and *The Asphalt Jungle*, 1950); private eyes (*The Maltese Falcon*, 1941, and *Murder, My Sweet*,

1944); femme fatales (*The Lady from Shanghai*, 1948, and *Too Late for Tears*, 1949); hostages (*Dial 1119*, 1950, and *The Desperate Hours*, 1955); juvenile delinquents (*City Across the River*, 1949, and *Cry Tough*, 1959); women in jeopardy (*Sleep, My Love*, 1948, and *Sudden Fear*, 1952); psychopathic serial killers (*Follow Me Quietly*, 1949, and *The Sniper*, 1952), sociopaths (*Born to Kill*, 1947, and *Kiss Tomorrow Goodbye*, 1950); doppelgängers (*The Dark Mirror*, 1946, and *The Man with My Face*, 1951); innocent men victimized by fate (*Detour*, 1946, and *D.O.A.*, 1950); and innocent men victimized by the legal system (*Railroaded!* 1947, and *The Wrong Man*, 1956). There are noir semidocumentaries (*The House on 52nd Street*, 1945, and *Call Northside 777*, 1948); police procedurals (*The Naked City*, 1948, and *The Tattooed Stranger*, 1950); prison pictures (*Brute Force*, 1947, and *Caged*, 1950); psychological melodramas (*The Woman in the Window*, 1944, and *The Locket*, 1947); and period pictures (*The Lodger*, 1944, and *Ivy*, 1947) and noirs involving political conspiracies (*The Woman on Pier 13*, 1949, and *The Whip Hand*, 1951) and identity crisis and personality disintegration (*Somewhere in the Night*, 1946, and *Possessed*, 1947). Numerous films noirs have been made depicting the corruption of American social institutions such as the legal profession (*Illegal*, 1955); the police (*Rogue Cop*, 1954); politics (*The Phenix City Story*, 1955); sports (*The Set-Up*, 1949); medicine (*Behind Locked Doors*, 1948); commerce (*Thieves' Highway*, 1949); the press (*The Sweet Smell of Success*, 1957); the family (*Pitfall*, 1948); and even the movie industry itself (*The Big Knife*, 1955).

All these movies are united thematically in that the universe of the protagonist, either internal or external, is out of control. What differentiates *The Asphalt Jungle*, for instance, a film noir about a group of gangsters planning and pulling off a jewelry heist, from earlier gangster movies such as *Little Caesar* (1930) and *The Public Enemy* (1931) is that it is a psychological study showing how flaws of character combined with fate predetermine the failure and ultimately the destruction of the participants in the heist. During the robbery, a series of unforeseen events lead to the deaths of some of the gangsters and the discovery of the identity of the others. The greed of the financier of the operation, a crooked lawyer who plans to double-cross his partners, leads to his own downfall and the death of his confederate. Doc, the mastermind of the heist, might get away at the end of the film, but he is caught because he stops in a bar to ogle a good-looking girl.

Similarly, in the 1956 film noir *The Killing*, about the robbery of a racetrack, a combination of bad luck and personality flaws brings about the destruction of the

gang and foils what would have been the perfect crime. Elisha Cook's doting devotion to his faithless and double-crossing wife leads to the death of everyone but
Sterling Hayden. In the end, Hayden, who now has all the money, plans to leave
the country with his girlfriend. He buys a cheap suitcase at a pawnshop to hold the
money and is about to board a plane to leave the country when a passenger's runaway dog cuts in front of the baggage cart; the suitcase breaks open on the runway,
spilling the stolen millions. As Hayden and his girlfriend try to leave the airport
and the cops are moving in, she urges him to run, but he simply says tiredly,
"What's the use?" Such fatalism contrasts sharply with Edward G. Robinson's last
words in *Little Caesar*. Gunned down and lying in the gutter, he asks with disbelief,
"Is this the end of Rico?" Noir characters know they are one step from their final
one. As Amy LaBowitz, director of production of Fine Line Features, puts it, "I feel
a kind of gallows humor in these movies, and a general sense that life is unforgiving. You can make one mistake—just one—and you're finished."

An unforgiving universe plays a big role in film noir. Edmond O'Brien inno-
cently notarizes a bill of sale and gets poisoned for it in *D.O.A.* Because he resembles an armed robber, Henry Fonda is arrested and his life ruined in *The Wrong
Man* (1956). In *Detour* (1945), Tom Neal, hitchhiking to the West Coast to see his
fiancé, unwittingly accepts a ride from a pill-popping drunk and becomes involved
in two murders. As he is being shoved into the back of a police car at the end of
the film, he tells the audience, "At any time, fate or some mysterious force can put
the finger on you for no good reason at all," a view not far from existentialist Albert Camus's contention that "at any street corner the absurd may strike a man in
the face."

As well as being unforgiving, the universe the noir protagonist dwells in is often
uniformly corrupt, precluding the emergence of a hero as traditionally portrayed in
film or literature. In *The Asphalt Jungle*, the police are almost as corrupt as the
gangsters, a view echoed by Louis Calhern, the crooked lawyer who is financing
the jewelry heist. When his invalid wife asks him how he can associate with the
scummy people he does, Calhern replies calmly, "Crime is simply a left-handed
form of human endeavor." In a world where everything is relative, there is little
room for the absolute hero.

In the noir world, all characters, including cops, are motivated by obsession—by
money or lust—or suffer from alienation and loneliness. Even the private eye, the
protagonist closest to being a noir hero, is not exempt from this fate. His experi-

ence has shown him that everything in the world is corrupt, that nobody is safe; he can trust no one, not even someone he loves. At the end of *The Maltese Falcon* (1941), Sam Spade (Humphrey Bogart) informs his lover-client Brigid O'Shaunessy (Mary Astor) that he is going to turn her in for killing his partner. It doesn't matter that he disliked his partner and was having an adulterous relationship with his wife, or even that he loves Brigid. When a man's partner is killed, "you're supposed to do something about it"; to let her go would be "bad for business . . . bad for detectives everywhere." When she pleads for her freedom, he tells her he "won't play the sap" for her and recites a list of reasons he can't trust her, after which he asks, "What have we got on the other side? All we've got on the other side is that maybe you love me and maybe I love you."

When Brigid retorts that Sam is copping out, that he knows whether he loves her, he replies, "Maybe I do. I'll have some rotten nights after I send you over, but that'll pass. If all I've said doesn't mean anything to you, forget it and we'll make it just this: I won't because all of me wants to regardless of consequences and you've counted on that with me and all the others."

Spade as written by Dashiell Hammett and played by Bogart is the ultimate hunter, a hunter motivated by the same selfishness and greed as his prey. His willingness to turn his back on love and money is rooted in his ultimate goal of self-preservation. He, like other private eyes and cops in films noirs, is "divided away from people," as serial killer Charles Starkweather once described his feelings to a psychiatrist. These hunters are destined to be lonely because of their inability to trust; they have seen too much and dwelled in their dark universe too long.

The themes of alienation, social corruption, obsession, fatalism, and sexual perversity found their way into mainstream cinema in isolated instances before the classic period of film noir, which began in 1939 and was to last twenty years, with films such as *The Underworld* (1927), *Thunderbolt* (1929), *City Streets* (1931), *Payment Deferred* (1932), *Two Seconds* (1932), *I Am a Fugitive from a Chain Gang* (1932), *Blood Money* (1933), *Crime Without Passion* (1934), *The Scoundrel* (1935), *Beast of the City* (1936), *Fury* (1936), and *You Only Live Once* (1937). (Interestingly, one theme that played a major part in film noir after World War II but was absent from the movies in the 1930s was the corruption of the American dream and the bankruptcy of middle-class values. This theme dominated in films such as *Pitfall*, 1948; *All My Sons*, 1948; and *Crime of Passion*, 1957, and in the non-noir *Rebel Without a Cause*, 1955. The reason for this theme's absence during the 1930s is presumably that the American dream did not exist then. When half the country was standing in a bread line, the American dream was a bowl of soup.)

Although Hollywood stuck its toe in the water with some of these darker movies, it quickly withdrew it, returning to the safety and "clean values" of Fred Astaire and Ginger Rogers musicals. It was not until world war was upon us that American filmmakers embraced the "dark side," a side that was in turn embraced by cinemagoers for twenty years. And these themes and iconography were indeed embraced by the American moviegoing public. Otherwise, ten years after Fred MacMurray decided to help Barbara Stanwyck kill her husband in *Double Indemnity*, he would have been able to stop himself from "going to the end of the line" in *Pushover* (1954). In that film, he plays a cop who turns murderer after becoming obsessed with sex and greed in the form of Kim Novak, the subject of his police surveillance and the girlfriend of a gangster who has pulled off a big bank job. MacMurray coldly kills the boyfriend and steals the money to provide a future for himself and Novak, but in film noir, things never work out that neatly. After murdering another cop who witnessed the earlier killing, MacMurray is gunned down trying to get away. As he lies in the street, seriously wounded as a result of turning crooked, he asks Novak the rhetorical question, "We really didn't need the money, did we?"

No noir characters really need the money; they just want it, often for reasons they themselves do not understand. Even if they do understand, their choices are inexorably ruled by their own flaws and compulsions and by events in the world around them, ensuring their own destruction. "Noir has a timeless appeal," says Eugenio Zaretti, art director for the modern film noir *Slamdance* (1987), "because a noir hero has no exit, no options, and is constrained to do what destiny bids. People respond to noir because it is an element of daily life. We are all constrained, because of conditioning, to do things we'd prefer not to do."

2

ROOTS:
THE BOYS IN THE
BACK ROOM

Most accounts by film critics acknowledge the literary origins of film noir as the hard-boiled or tough-guy school of fiction that emerged in the early 1920s with writers such as Ernest Hemingway and John O'Hara but that really reached its zenith in pulp magazines such as *Dime Detective* and *Black Mask.*

The first pulp (so called because of the cheap wood-pulp paper used) was launched by Frank Munsey in 1896 when he turned *Argosy* into a men's adventure magazine. As *Argosy's* circulation exploded, others followed suit, and soon the pulp magazine replaced the dime novel as the most popular form of mass-produced reading material in the U.S. The pulps were usually genre based—westerns and romance, science fiction, and action novels. The first detective pulp was *Detective Story*, which started selling in 1915.

In 1920, professional cynic H. L. Mencken and his partner, George Jean Nathan, founded *Black Mask* to try to pay off the debt they had run up with their intellectual magazine *Smart Set.* The magazine published detective stories along with love stories, westerns, horror stories, and aviation tales. *Black Mask* was an instant success, and six months later Mencken and Nathan sold it at a sizable profit to George Sutton and Harry North. Under North's editorship, the magazine began to lean more toward detective stories, and a new hero—the private eye—debuted in its pages. The year was 1922, and the hero was Race Williams, a character created by Carroll John Daly, who would change the public's image of the detective forever.

Until *Black Mask*, the detective as created by Edgar Allan Poe in "The Purloined Letter" and carried on by writers such as Sir Arthur Conan Doyle, Agatha Christie, A. A. Milne, and Dorothy Sayers was usually an amateur sleuth and master of deduction capable of calmly assembling clues and solving murders by simple ratiocination. Such whodunits were novels of manners in which the universe was an orderly affair and in which an event such as murder was a temporary aberration that could be cleaned up by logic; normalcy was restored in time for afternoon tea.

After World War I, however, many questioned the view of the world as an orderly, rational place. The vision of an irrational world was exacerbated by Prohibition, which led to a rise of gangsterism and violence and turned millions of Americans into lawbreakers every time they entered a speakeasy or took a sip of bootleg gin. Violence, crime, and corruption were no longer viewed as aberrations but as part of the modern world.

The ancestor of this new private eye was not Sherlock Holmes but Wild Bill Hickock. The PI was the western hero reborn in an urban setting, a rugged individualist, a man of action at home in a violent world, a survivalist with his own code of ethics. As Daly would have Williams say in his novel *The Snarl of the Beast*, "Right and wrong are not written on the statutes for me. . . . My ethics are my own." This moral ambiguity, which would be a cornerstone for film noir, was reflected even in Williams's view of crime. Unlike the British amateur detective, Williams was a professional, and as such, a cynical realist. "I'm not a preacher against crime," he says. "I've made too much money out of criminals. They're my bread and butter."

Race Williams instantly increased the sales of *Black Mask* by fifteen percent, demonstrating that readers were ready for a new brand of detective and a new type of detective story, one with a dimension of hard-bitten reality to it. Six months after the publication of the first Race Williams story, *Black Mask* published "Arson Plus," introducing the Continental Op, a short, fat man with no name. (Interestingly, the detective reincarnation of the western hero would later itself be reincarnated in spaghetti westerns with Clint Eastwood's "man with no name.") The Op, so called because he worked for the Continental Detective Agency, was the creation of former Pinkerton detective Dashiell Hammett, and because of his background, Hammett was able to imbue his character with a competent realism Daly could never achieve. Although not above indulging in violence if the situation necessitated it, the Op used real detective methods, going on stakeouts, meticulously sifting through boring details, and poring over statistics to solve a case. In some of his later stories and novels, Hammett made the Op worry that he was getting too attracted to violence. In 1929, in what was to be the first truly hard-boiled novel, *The Red Harvest*, the Op has become completely inured to violence and is at the same time concerned about going "blood simple," like the rest of the town in which he is working.

Raymond Chandler later wrote of the revolutionary character of Hammett's work in his essay "The Simple Art of Murder": "He took murder out of the Venetian vase and dropped it into the alley. . . . Hammett wrote for people [who] were not afraid of the seamy side of life; they lived there. . . . [He] gave murder back to the kind of people who commit it for reasons, not just to provide a corpse."

Although the stories of Hammett and Daly popularized the private eye, his status as the new urban hero did not become fully realized until the editorial helm of *Black Mask* was taken over by Captain Joseph T. Shaw in 1926. Shaw, a saber and fencing champion who had risen to the rank of captain during World War I, was a writer of both fiction and nonfiction and had distinct ideas as to what he wanted to accomplish at *Black Mask*. He envisioned a new type of detective story, one that created the illusion of reality by letting the characters demonstrate their personalities and abilities rather than informing the reader of them by narration. What Shaw wanted from his writers was "simplicity for the sake of clarity, plausibility, and belief." He stressed action, but only when it involved characterization.

Typically clad in trenchcoat and fedora, Shaw's hard-boiled hero was a man of the streets and was usually involved in some aspect of criminal activity as either a private eye, a cop, or a crook. His morality was flexible and utilitarian, and he was not above bending or even breaking the law to achieve his aims. Using Hammett as his paragon, Shaw recruited a cast of writers to create such characters, including Raymond Chandler, Erle Stanley Gardner, Lester Dent, George Harmon Coxe, Raoul Whitfield, Norbert Davis, Roger Torrey, Forrest Rosaire, Frederick Nebel, Paul Cain, William T. Ballard, Horace McCoy, Charles G. Booth, and Cornell Woolrich. This tough-guy school of writing would be adopted by other novelists such as James M. Cain, W. R. Burnett, Jonathon Latimer, Jay Dratler, and Eric Ambler. In spite of the disparaging remarks of influential literary critics such as Edmund Wilson, who referred to these writers as the "boys in the back room," the popularity of their work spoke for itself.

One of the *Black Mask* graduates who did receive grudging praise from "serious" literary critics was Raymond Chandler. Chandler's private eye Philip Marlowe was an exaggeration, but as Chandler called him, "an exaggeration of the possible." Marlowe is an urban hero who wanders through LA's mean streets with nobody to trust but himself. In Marlowe's world, everybody from the gangster to the socially prominent to the cops is corrupt. But unlike the Continental Op, who hunts down criminals because he likes the work, Marlowe is fighting for his ideals. Although he makes cynical observations about the corruption around him, he remains dedicated to the pursuit of justice. He is honest, lonely, and isolated, traits shared by, and indeed central to, many noir heroes to come.

In Paul Cain's novel *Fast One*, published in part in *Black Mask* in 1932, the hard-boiled, antihero type perhaps reached its ultimate realization in the character of Gerard A. Kells. The true existential man, Kells knows his options; he knows the difference between morality and immorality but is simply amoral. His choices are made solely on the basis of self-interest, giving a glimpse of the noir world to come. In the novel, after slaughtering half the gangster population of Los Angeles in an effort to take over the city's underworld, Kells is himself killed. *Fast One* exemplifies the negative attitude brought on by the Depression. The universe had become hostile, capricious, and cold. As one writer put it, "Humanity was still in evidence around the country, but so were rocks."

The novels of another Cain—James M.—were some of the most hard-boiled of the school. His novels of sexual obsession were the first to break with the straight crime novels of the time and were avoided by the studios for that reason. In Cain's novels, the characters were driven totally by desire, and when desire died, the characters almost always did too, either by their own devices or those of society.

The writer who perhaps came closest to the noir mood was Cornell Woolrich. Woolrich's works dealt with amnesiacs (often because of drug or alcohol abuse, with which Woolrich was intimately familiar) trying to determine whether they were guilty or innocent of murder, obsessive love, voyeurism, or greed. His world was one of dark dreams where reality and nightmare became interchangeable. Many of his novels, as visually oriented as they were, seemed made for the screen, perhaps why so many of them were made a decade later into films noirs.

The popularity of these writers with the public was obviously noticed by the studios in the 1930s; the rights to many of their works were purchased for film production during that time. But although some of the work of the tough-guy writers found its way to the screen, particularly in Warner Brothers gangster films such as W. R. Burnett's *Little Caesar* (1931) and *Scarface* (1932), the hard-edged vision of most of these writers would not be transferred onto celluloid until the early 1940s.

The movie private eye of the thirties, for instance, was not the hard-boiled creation of Hammett and Chandler but S. S. Van Dine's urbane, sophisticated, and effete Philo Vance; calm masters of deduction and shallow Oriental philosophy such as Charlie Chan or Mr. Moto; and debonair sleuths such as the Falcon and the Saint. Although Hammett's work was brought to the screen repeatedly during the 1930s, the most successful endeavor was the Thin Man series, based on the one novel of Hammett's that was extremely witty and not hard-boiled. William Powell starred as the once-tough but now socially prominent and alcoholic Nick Charles. Hammett's *The Maltese Falcon* was made twice in the 1930s, once in 1931 starring Ricardo Cortez and a second time in 1936, this time titled *Satan Met a Lady* with Warren William playing the private eye role. In both films, the character of Sam Spade was a watered-down version of the cynical, hard-bitten character that Bogart and John Huston would lift literally from the pages of the novel a few years later. Similarly, the 1935 version of Hammett's *The Glass Key*, starring George Raft, was clearly not noir and lacked the punch of the 1942 Alan Ladd version.

Some hard-boiled novels were purchased by the studios because of their popularity with the book-buying public but were never made. James M. Cain's steamy *The Postman Always Rings Twice* was acquired by MGM in 1934, and his *Double Indemnity* was bought by Paramount in 1936; but neither would make it to the screen until the following decade because of pressure from the Hays Office, which was also largely responsible for the watering down of those hard-boiled texts that did get made in the thirties.

The Hays Office, named after Will Hays, former head of the Republican National Committee and self-appointed arbiter of the national morality, was set up in 1922 to censor what would go into the movies. Sex and lust were out, gangsterism was frowned upon, family values were pushed, and morals clauses in stars' contracts enforced the office's rules in the players' personal lives. In 1933 and 1934, the rules were strengthened when the National Legion of Decency was formed and penned a new set of restrictions called the Code to Govern the Making of Motion and

Talking Pictures. To be exhibited, a film had to pass the code's tests for morality and receive a "purity seal."

So what happened in the early forties that changed things? Critics who point to wartime nihilism as the factor that led to the emergence of the noir style cannot explain why private detectives in the movies began to crack wise, slap women, and mercilessly beat up bad guys after 1941, or why the dark nightmares of Cornell Woolrich and the sexually obsessed, murderous characters from the novels of James M. Cain began to find their way to the screen after 1942, long before any disillusioned veterans were returning home from the war.

Another factor leading to the rise of noir was the writing vacuum left by the war. As many of the studio writers had been drafted or had joined the armed forces, the studios found themselves facing a deficit of material. To fill the void, producers be-gan to look for material that already had the public's stamp of approval—and they found it in the pulps. According to a November 1943 issue of *Variety*, "Shortage of story materials and writers now has film companies seriously ogling the pulp mag scripts and scriptors. It marks the first time that Hollywood has initiated a con-certed drive to replenish its dwindling library supplies and its scripter ranks from the 20 cent-a-word authors of the weird-snappy-breezy-argosy-spy-crime-detective mag school."

In addition to the pulp material bought up by the studios, many of the pulpsters who had created the material were drafted by the studios to fill in their decimated writing ranks. Those pulp writers-turned-screenwriters included Raymond Chan-dler, Charles G. Booth, Frank Gruber, Jonathon Latimer, Jay Dratler, Geoffrey Homes (Daniel Mainwaring), Clarence Mumford, Frederick Nebel, Paul Cain (as R. R. Ruric), Steve Fisher, David Goodis, and W. R. Burnett, and their presence undoubtedly added to the increasingly hard edge of the movies. For example, Jonathon Latimer, author of a series of critically acclaimed hard-boiled detective novels in the late 1930s, wrote the screenplay for the 1942 version of *The Glass Key*; that version was noir, whereas the earlier George Raft version was not.

In spite of the growing influence of the pulp writers in Hollywood and the yearn-ing of certain directors to buck the Production Code, it was not until director Billy Wilder teamed up with a pulp writer, Raymond Chandler, to write *Double Indem-nity* in 1944 that noir production really took off. *Double Indemnity* was an immedi-ate smash hit, and soon the studios were cranking out *Double Indemnitys* by the dozen.

The influence of the tough-guy writers was obvious in the cynicism of the characters on the screen and in their tough, snappy dialogue. Never before in the movies had a man's wife told him, "I go where I want to, with anybody I want. I just happen to be that kind of girl" (Doris Dowling to Alan Ladd in *The Blue Dahlia*, 1946). When Robert Mitchum tells femme fatale Jane Greer in *Out of the Past* (1947), "You're like a leaf blowing from gutter to gutter," she is unperturbed, telling him, "You're no good for anybody else. You're no good and neither am I."

In Billy Wilder's ultracynical *Ace in the Hole* (1951), when Jan Sterling is told by reporter Kirk Douglas to go into a church to pray for her dying husband so that she will look sympathetic to the press, she sneers: "I don't pray. Kneeling bags my nylons."

In this hard-boiled world, love was hard to come by. In *Scene of the Crime* (1950), dying gangster Richard Benedict is asked by the cops if he wants to see his faithful girlfriend, who is going to go to prison for him, one last time. He tells them: "Naw. I hate a tramp. . . . Ya always gotta tell 'em, 'I love you, baby' . . . a waste of time."

Nor could you get more sociopathic than Lawrence Tierney in *Born to Kill* (1947), a film one reviewer called "a little cold around the heart." When Tierney's best and only friend, Elisha Cook, tells Tierney that he just can't "go around killing people whenever the notion hits you. It ain't feasible," Tierney asks: "Why isn't it?" Shortly thereafter, he proves his point by killing Cook.

One seminal event that has been consistently overlooked by film historians but that undoubtedly was responsible for much of the imagery and hard-boiled tone of noir as it would emerge in Hollywood was the invention of the paperback in 1939. Paperbacks were a revolutionary new way of packaging books. They were easily held in the hand, were disposable, portable, and were meant to be read in a short time, for entertainment. Although publishers initially tried to promote more serious literature in paperback form, popular tastes soon caused a turn in the content to whodunits and mysteries and, shortly, to the hard-boiled themes that became closely identified with the form.

After America's entry into World War II, paperback sales picked up dramatically. Portable and escapist, the books could easily be stuffed into a knapsack and as such were perfect GI reading material. In addition, wartime restrictions on paper reduced the number of hardback books, which used high-quality paper, making the paperback a patriotic natural.

After the war, the number of paperback titles in print tripled, but sales dropped as returning vets turned their attention from escapist pursuits to making a living. In an effort to stimulate sales and regain their lost audience, publishers began to get more and more lurid with their book content and cover art. Sensing the ex-GIs had been to hell and back and were ready for stronger stuff, the publishers began to splash their covers with sex and violence to the point that the two often became interchangeable. On these covers, tough guys slugged women; women flaunted their sex openly to manipulate; predatory femme fatales had guns in their hands, and their eyes said they were ready to use them. The titles were *Bodies Are Where You Find Them*, *Sinful Woman*, *Dark Threat*, *Dark Passage*, *Say It With Bullets*, *A Dame Called Murder*, *Dressed To Kill*. Just as film noir would be seen later by critics as an attempt to peel back the false face of society and reveal the corruption beneath, the paperbacks told of a murderous, dark, greed-filled world ruled by sex, money, and violence. As paperback historian Geoffrey O'Brien puts it, "The hard-boiled tradition, and the paperbacks that amplified it and distributed it to a growing audience, seems to have played a subversive role. These novels, and the covers that illustrate them, speak of the ignoble corners of life beyond the glow of Jane Powell, *Father Knows Best*, and the healthy, smiling faces in magazines advertising milk or frozen dinners or trips to California."

In 1952, the paperback industry was denounced as immoral by the House Select Committee on Current Pornographic Materials. Although no official censorship was instituted, local groups put political pressure on publishers, and by 1955, many of those publishers had begun to tone down their cover art as well as their hard-boiled themes. It is perhaps not coincidental that many film critics cite the last gasp of film noir as being that same year, 1955, with the release of Mickey Spillane's *Kiss Me, Deadly*; it featured the brutal violence and sexual sadism characteristic of its hero, private eye Mike Hammer. Regardless, there is little question that the cycles of the hard-boiled paperback and film noir were concurrent and that studio heads were aware of the popularity of the paperback's subject matter and cover art.

Communist William J. Lally shows Hanne Axman it doesn't pay to buck the Party in a publicity shot for *The Red Menace*.

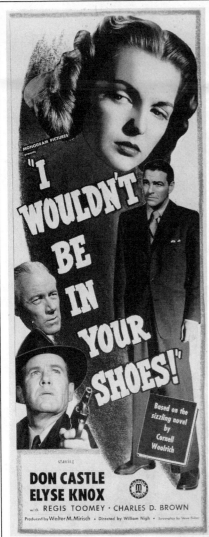

Left. Promotional poster from
I Wouldn't Be in Your Shoes.

Below. Don Castle gets the third degree
in *I Wouldn't Be in Your Shoes.*

Above. Accidents are not all they seem in *Open Secret.*

Below. Dane Clark tries to talk his buddy Paul Carpenter into killing him in *Paid to Kill.*

Above. A couple of the Black Widows get ready for a high voltage confrontation in Roger Corman's *Teenage Doll*.

Below. Mark Rydell and his gang work a man over in *Crime in the Streets*.

Above. The cops and would-be victim Mary Beth Hughes stare at the body of killer Hugh Beaumont in *The Lady Confesses*.

Below. Promotional poster for *The Lady Confesses*.

Above. Turhan Bey prepares to conjure up the spirit of Lynn Bari's dead husband while her little sister Cathy O'Donnell watches in *The Spiritualist*.

Below. Mark Daniels thinks he is watching his wife burn up in *Bury Me Dead*.

Above. "Queen of the B's" Beverly Garland is barely saved by Tom Drake from being strangled in *Sudden Danger*.

Below. Frances Rafferty listens to Hugh Beaumont make ominous plans in *Money Madness*.

Above. Wounded reporter-turned-murderer Hugh Beaumont is about to type his last story in *Apology for Murder.*

Below. Eduardo Cianelli is about to drive to his death in *Fugitive Lady.*

3

ATTACK OF THE KILLER B's

When one mentions the term *B movie*, most people think "B" stands for "bad." Others have the impression that any film cheaply produced or sloppily put together is a B film. Neither view is correct. In fact, although a lot of awful B movies have been made, many of the Bs produced from the 1930s until 1960 were quite good.

B movies were the result of the double feature, which became popularized in the 1930s as an attempt to lure back the 50 million customers who had stayed away from theaters since the advent of the Depression at the beginning of the decade. The double bill originated in New England soon after the advent of talkies and by the beginning of 1932 had become staple fare in 15 percent of the theaters in the U.S. It represented one more attempt by independent theater owners to increase attendance by appearing to give viewers value. Other strategies included changing movie bills three times a week, holding drawings for money or other prizes, and including live acts with the film. At first, movie critics as well as the major studios (which owned 3,000 of the 23,000 theaters in the U.S. but which accounted for 70 percent of the box office receipts) resisted the double bill, but because of the growing popularity of the format with the moviegoing public, most of them began to see the light and convert. By 1935, it was apparent that the double bill was here to stay. RKO and MGM, the last of the majors to hold out, announced they would be showing two features in all but two of their theaters, and one year later, 85 percent of U.S. theaters would be converted to double billing.

Since A movies were rented out to theaters for a percentage of box office receipts, few exhibitors could afford two A movies on a bill. The result was a double bill based on the packaging of one high-budget A film and a low-budget B feature rented out for a flat rate. Hence the label "B" referred not to the movie's quality but to its position on the theater bill. Bs were simply intended to provide the public with three hours of entertainment as economically as possible.

Effects of the double bill were widespread. It put a stake in the heart of whatever was left of vaudeville. It gave theater owners the ability to appeal to a broader audience base by doubling movies of different genres—screwball comedies with westerns, melodramas with musicals, and so on. Perhaps most important, it changed the major studios' production methods and schedules and spurred an increase in the number of independent production companies by increasing the demand for product.

At first, the Bs consisted mostly of a backlog of A features that had been ground out by the major studios (Warner Brothers, MGM, Paramount, Twentieth Century Fox, and RKO) and the three minors (Columbia, Universal, and United Artists) but had never been released or had been unsuccessful during their first runs. As inventories dwindled, those studios that had never made B movies were forced to form B production units to fill the bottom half of theater bills. Because A films usually ran 90 minutes or more and because audiences had only so much time to spend at the movies and theater owners wanted to run their double bills as many times a day as they could to maximize profits, Bs were made to be short, usually 55 to 75 minutes long. Thus B moviemakers were forced to learn to make films economically and fast. The films had to have uncomplicated plots that could be easily understood by viewers in a compressed time frame.

Since the studios' stars were under contract and had to play in whatever productions the studio heads mandated, in the early years of B production, even the bottom half of a double bill might star some of a studio's A talents. In such cases, the studio could capitalize on a star's fame by booking a lower-budget movie at a higher price. Also, many stars at the time ascended so rapidly that by the time a low-budget film was released, a star might have already risen to A status, lending the B more box office power.

Before 1935, there was little differentiation between A and B films, but as stars' salaries and studios' fixed costs escalated, the difference in quality between the two products became more pronounced. All the studios formed specialized B units to grind out low-cost fare in all genres—including the murder mysteries, private eye films, and crime films from which film noir was to spin off as a subgenre. Aside from providing needed product, these units were viewed by the studios as training grounds for their staff production people. Many writers, directors, and cinematographers who would later be important to the development of noir gained valuable experience in these B units.

The Warner B unit, headed by Bryan Foy, one of the Seven Little Foys of vaudeville fame, produced cheap mysteries, comedies, and action flicks. However, the unit had at its disposal the volatile Humphrey Bogart to star in such low-budget crime films as *King of the Underworld* (1939) when Bogie wasn't supporting James Cagney in the A gangster fare that was Warner's specialty. Foy also had tough guy Barton MacLane, who starred in such crime films as *Smart Blonde* (1936) with Glenda Farrell as Torchy Blane, the fast-talking, fast-thinking, crime-busting ace reporter. The Torchy Blane series would last for three years, ending with Jane Wyman in the title role. Warner also bought the Perry Mason series from attorney and *Black Mask* graduate Erle Stanley Gardner, beginning with *The Case of the Lucky Legs* (1935). That crime series starred Warren William, Ricardo Cortez, and Donald Woods before ending in 1937. Foy would later go on to form his own production company, making quite a few films noir released through Eagle Lion and, later, Warners.

Hal Roach, king of the two-reel comedy, worked for MGM, turning out Laurel and Hardy and other slapstick fare, but most of the MGM Bs were produced by former studio writers Samuel Marx, Lucien Hubbard, and Errol Taggart, who had been a producer of short subjects at the studio. Taggart costarred up-and-coming Robert Young and B staple Bruce Cabot in a number of mysteries and crime films and made one superior B, *Man of the People* (1937), starring future noir supporting actor Joseph Calleia in a tale of political corruption, a favorite noir theme. MGM had its own crime series with three Nick Carter entries starting with *Nick Carter, Master Detective* (1939), starring Walter Pidgeon as a modern-day version of the turn-of-the-century private eye. In that same year, Tod Browning, who had achieved fame directing horror flicks for Universal, including *Dracula* (1931), directed his last film for MGM; *Miracles for Sale* featured Robert Young as a magician-turned-detective and was based on the novel *Death from a Top Hat* by mystery writer Clayton Rawson. *They All Came Out* (1939) was originally slated for MGM's *Crime Does Not Pay* series of shorts but was expanded into a feature-length film that was to mark the directorial debut of Jacques Tourneur. He would later work with the Val Lewton unit at RKO and go on to fame as the director of many seminal films noirs.

Two MGM Bs that would preview themes embraced in later films noirs were both released in 1942. In *Fingers at the Window*, Lew Ayres and Laraine Day tried to track down the demented mastermind behind a series of axe murders. This movie presaged later ones that took the serial killer out of the "old dark house" movies of the thirties and put him in the street. Far superior was *Kid Glove Killer*, one of MGM's finest Bs. It starred Van Heflin, who had just won an Academy Award for best supporting actor in MGM's A noir *Johnny Eager*, in which he played a forensic pathologist trying to solve the murder of a reform mayor. Fred Zinneman would later direct Heflin in the minor B noir classic *Act of Violence* (1949) and a few years later would turn out classics such as *High Noon* and *From Here to Eternity*. In *Kid Glove Killer*, he gave audiences a glimpse of things to come when he incorporated elements that would later become staples in films noirs—an innocent man railroaded for the crime through circumstantial evidence; a seemingly upright and respected prosecutor (Lee Bowman) who turns out to be a corrupt, power-crazed killer; and an intrepid sleuth ferreting out the truth. In these films, however, the moral ambiguity that would dominate noir is missing; they are still essentially good-guys-versus-bad-guys flicks.

In 1935, the helm of Twentieth Century Fox was taken over by Joseph M. Schneck with Darryl F. Zanuck put in charge of production. Zanuck kept on Sol Wurtzel from the old Fox studio as the head of the studio's B unit, and Wurtzel immediately began to churn out series films with the accent on crime. The first series, Charlie Chan, began in 1936 and starred Warner Oland. A year later, the Mr. Moto series began with Peter Lorre in the starring role. In 1938, Wurtzel began another crime series, the Roving Reporters murder mysteries, starring Chick Chandler as a crime reporter. In 1940, Fox purchased the rights to the Michael Shayne character created by tough-guy writer Brett Halliday, casting Lloyd Nolan as the hard-nosed private eye. The first entry, *Michael Shayne, Private Detective* (1940), was based on Halliday's novel *Dividend on Death*, but curiously, that was the only one of the seven Shayne movies produced between 1940 and 1942 that would be adapted from a Halliday book. The rest of the entries were based on novels by other hard-boiled writers such as Raymond Chandler, Frederick Nebel, Richard Burke, Borden Chase, and Clayton Rawson. Although Poverty Row studio PRC (Producers Releasing Corporation) picked up the Shayne character in 1946 for five more pictures, the productions lacked the edge of the Nolan films and starred Hugh Beaumont as a soft-boiled version of Shayne.

Universal, which was in financial trouble by 1936 but was temporarily bailed out by the immediate success of its discovery Deanna Durbin, continued to crank out its specialty—horror films. The studio became much more budget conscious, however, with the release of such B entries in the genre as *The Raven* (1935), *Dracula's Daughter* (1936), and *The Invisible Ray* (1936). The success as well as the dark and expressionistic look of many of the Universal horror entries would later be cited by many film critics as a significant contributing factor to the hybridization that went into the creation of film noir.

Universal was also successful with its productions of B comedies and whodunits. Some of the studio's best B fare came from *Irving Starr's Crime Club* series, the insignia of which was taken from the Crime Club imprint of Doubleday Books. Several of the series were adapted from the hard-boiled novels of Jonathon Latimer, featuring alcoholic, wise-cracking private eye Bill Crane and his sidekick Doc Williams, played by Preston Foster and Frank Jenks.

Universal produced one B film noir in 1939, *Rio*, starring Basil Rathbone and directed by German émigré John Brahm (see Filmography), but the studio would continue its horror bent into the early 1940s. It was only after the box office success in 1944 of its own *Phantom Lady*, adapted from a book by Cornell Woolrich, and the smash release of *Double Indemnity* by Paramount that the studio began to increasingly diversify its B product with film noir.

Paramount's B unit, Pine-Thomas, under the control of William C. Pine and William H. Thomas, was an independent unit bankrolled by the studio. Pine-Thomas specialized in low-budget action pictures, often with war themes. Veteran actor Richard Arlen starred in many of the unit's early entries, and the camera work was done John Alton, who went on to superstar status as noir's premier cinematographer. In 1941, the unit turned temporarily away from action to its first crime feature, *No Hands on the Clock*, starring Chester Morris as private eye Humphrey Campbell. The film was based on the novel by hard-boiled writer Geoffrey Homes (Daniel Mainwaring), who would later write the novel and screen-play for the classic noir *Out of the Past* (1947) and whose material would be the ba-sis of other noirs such as *Roadblock* (1951) and *The Hitch-Hiker* (1953). With the advent of World War II, Pine-Thomas would return to its action-war films, but af-ter the war Homes went on to produce several well-recognized noirs, including *Fear in the Night* (1947), *Manhandled* (1949), and *Hell's Island* (1955) as well as the less-well-known and marginal noir *They Made Me a Killer* (1947; see Filmography).

During the 1930s, Paramount found some success in its Bulldog Drummond and Philo Vance crime series. The studio had also built up a roster of B movie players—Anthony Quinn, Lloyd Nolan, Richard Denning, J. Carroll Naish, and Akim Tamiroff. Paramount rotated these actors in various combinations as heroes and villains in a series of crime movies such as *King of the Gamblers* (1937), *Tip-Off Girls* (1938), *Illegal Traffic* (1938), and *King of Alcatraz* (1938). In one such film, *Hunted Men* (1938), Lloyd Nolan plays a gangster on the lam who hides out in the home of an unsuspecting suburbanite family. Nolan is eventually discovered by the cops but sacrifices his own life rather than endanger the family. The Paramount studio heads pushed for a happier ending, as Nolan played a sympathetic charac-ter, but screenwriter Horace McCoy (one of the *Black Mask* boys) stood firm, fore-seeing the effect the hard-boiled writers would have in a few years.

Paramount produced two films noirs in the early 1940s: *Among the Living* (1941), in which Albert Dekker played identical twins, one good and one homicidal, and *Street of Chance* (1942), taken from Cornell Woolrich's novel *The Black Curtain*. The latter starred Burgess Meredith as an amnesiac trying to find out if he was a murderer. Both films were suspenseful and well-done, two of the best Bs of any genre that were produced in those years. But Paramount, perhaps trying to relive its success with *Double Indemnity*, would be the Hollywood studio to produce the fewest B noirs, most of its noir product being higher-budget A films.

Columbia had great success with its B films, probably because studio head Harry Cohn, often said to be the most hated man in Hollywood, was dedicated to the production of what he called "those lousy little B pictures"; he made a lot of them. One of the most successful was the Blondie comedy series starring Penny Single-ton and Arthur Lake, which lasted from 1938 to 1950 and comprised twenty-eight films. Columbia also produced some superior B horror thrillers starring Boris Karloff, among them *The Man They Could Not Hang* (1939) and *The Devil Com-mands* (1941). The latter was directed by Edward Dmytryk, who would a few years later go on to direct *Murder, My Sweet*, one of the noirs that would achieve great box office success and have a major impact in kicking off the noir cycle. Dmytryk directed some of Columbia's B crime films, for which Columbia used such titillating titles as *Parents on Trial* (1939), *Babies for Sale* (1940), and *Under Age* (1941). Columbia also had its own crime-detective series with Chester Morris playing the slick Boston Blackie (1941–1949), Ralph Bellamy playing the comically bumbling Ellery Queen (1935–1942), and a number of different stars, including Melvyn Douglas, Francis Lederer, and Warren William, playing suave jewel thief Michael Lanyard and the Lone Wolf (1935–1949). The screenplay for one Lone Wolf entry, *Lone Wolf Spy Hunt* (1939), was penned by Jonathon Latimer.

Although many critics cite RKO's *Stranger on the Third Floor* (1940) as the first true film noir, 1939 was actually the year that inaugurated the film noir with the release of three prototypical films: *Let Us Live, Rio*, and *Blind Alley* (see Filmography). Of the three, Columbia's *Blind Alley* is by far the best, a little masterpiece about a killer who is afraid he is going insane. The movie was creatively directed by émigré director Charles Vidor and extremely well acted by its cast, which included Chester Morris, Ann Dvorak, and Ralph Bellamy. *Blind Alley* showed audiences how good a B movie could be; movie historian Don Miller cites the film as a primary example of the fact that Bs were starting to achieve respectability by 1939. Columbia released another film noir, *Let Us Live*, in 1939. It starred Henry Fonda and Alan Baxter as two men about to be executed for a murder they didn't commit (see Filmography). Because of its 66-minute length and Fonda's star power, Columbia offered the film to exhibitors as either the top or bottom feature for a double bill. In 1940, Columbia released the last B film noir it would make until after World War II, *Angels Over Broadway*, directed by Ben Hecht. This dark, offbeat tale of a cynical hustler, Douglas Fairbanks, who is talked into trying to convince a desperate businessman not to commit suicide, was breezily written by Hecht. The film was not to everyone's taste, perhaps one reason Columbia waited until 1945 to resume its production of B noirs.

RKO, which in the 1940s would become a film noir factory, was famous in the 1930s for its A musicals starring Fred Astaire and Ginger Rogers and screwball comedies starring Cary Grant. The studio also had plenty of experience producing low-budget movies, however, and thus RKO's transition to the world of Bs was not as strained as it was for many of the other majors. Although the bulk of its Bs were comedies, musicals, and westerns, it did venture into the world of mystery. Two such notable entries in 1936 were hard-boiled detective stories: *Muss 'Em Up*, in which Preston Foster plays a tough private eye who likes to do to crooks what the title says, and *We're Only Human*, in which Foster is a tough cop who isn't above the same behavior. Another interesting entry in the mystery category was *Two in the Dark* (1936), based on the novel by Gelett Burgess. The film is about an amnesiac trying to find out if he is a murderer, a common noir theme. The film was remade in 1946 as the noir *Two o'Clock Courage*, starring Tom Conway.

Like the other studios, RKO tried mystery series and achieved several successes in the genre. In 1938, the studio introduced Louis Hayward as Simon Templar in *The Saint in New York*. George Sanders took over the role after the first picture, and the Saint went through seven more incarnations before dying in 1954.

Sanders quit the Saint series in 1941 to play another series character, the Falcon, a smooth crime-buster introduced in *The Gay Falcon*. The third Falcon entry, *The Falcon Takes Over* (1942), was based on Raymond Chandler's *Farewell, My Lovely*, which RKO had purchased for a paltry $2,000. This hard-boiled novel was not suited, however, to the softer-boiled Falcon series, a fact that must have struck someone at the studio, for it was remade two years later by Edward Dmytryk as the classic *Murder, My Sweet*, with Dick Powell cast against type as a hard-as-nails Philip Marlowe. Dmytryk may well have been the one who noticed, because he directed one of the Falcon series, *The Falcon Strikes Back* (1943). In 1942, after playing in three Falcon films, George Sanders turned the lead role over to his real-life brother, Tom Conway, in *The Falcon's Brother*. Conway went on to star in most of the sixteen Falcons that were made between 1941 and 1949, and the series was one of RKO's most successful B staples. Although most of the series was pretty tame, one film, *The Falcon's Alibi* (1946), showed definite noir influences and featured Elisha Cook Jr. as a murderous disc jockey.

Throughout the thirties RKO was on the verge of bankruptcy. Although it began to add to its B output with series like the Saint and Falcon, it was not until 1942, when the studio's debt ran into the millions, that RKO reorganized and really began to put a heavy emphasis on B production, bringing in Val Lewton to head up the RKO B unit. RKO is usually cited as having produced the first true film noir, *Stranger on the Third Floor* (1940). This is a highly original film starring Peter Lorre as a psychopathic killer and has some amazingly surreal montages by Russian director Boris Ingster.

Val Lewton was given a great deal of autonomy because of the studio's precarious financial situation, and he demonstrated just how good a low-budget movie could be. He produced such early masterpieces as *The Cat People* (1942), *I Walked with a Zombie* (1943), and *The Leopard Man* (1943), films that were billed as horror movies but were thrillers that functioned successfully on more than one level. (*I Walked with a Zombie* was actually loosely based on the classic *Jane Eyre* with the setting transposed from England to Haiti. *The Leopard Man* was in reality a suspenseful little murder mystery based on hard-boiled writer Cornell Woolrich's *Black Alibi*; it comes very close to film noir, especially in a visual sense.)

Lewton used three directors in his unit: Jacques Tourneur, Mark Robson, and Robert Wise, all of whom went on to direct important films noirs throughout the forties and into the fifties. Lewton's pictures undoubtedly had an effect on noirs to come, but it wasn't until the box office success of the higher budget *Murder, My Sweet* that RKO began to really look to hard-boiled crime films to supplement both its A and B product.

Even with the formation of B units, the demand for B product would outstrip the production ability of the Hollywood studios. Independent production companies, "indies" as they were called in the trade, rushed in to fill the void—companies such as Mascot, Majestic, Monogram, Grand National, Academy Pictures, and Republic. As the majors had a chokehold on distribution by virtue of their ownership of a majority of theater outlets, the indies were forced to rely on a complicated system called states' rights to distribute their product. If an indie did not have its own exchange in a given territory, its films would be handled by another distribution company and released under that distribution company's name or the producing company's name, depending on the agreement between the two. The majors would always bill their product as the A part of the bill in those venues they owned, and thus the independent B producers, knowing how their product would be exhibited and that it would be perceived as low budget, deliberately made films of lesser quality.

The situation changed for the indies in 1938, when the Justice Department filed an antitrust suit against Paramount Pictures in the U.S. Supreme Court, citing the major studios' chokehold on distribution outlets by virtue of their practices of block booking and selling. These practices virtually controlled what exhibitors would buy by forcing them to take whatever product was offered or nothing. In

1940, the majors signed a Consent Decree that allowed them to keep their theater chains but prohibited block booking and blind selling and introduced legislation mandating that all films, A or B, should be sold to exhibitors on an individual basis. This ruling greatly opened up the marketplace for the proliferation of independent production companies, which soon numbered over forty; this number would increase greatly over the next ten years.

The Consent Decree was not the only factor leading to the explosion of the indies in the late 1940s. Before World War II, one-quarter of the profits of the majors had come from Europe. With the advent of the war, those profits disappeared. In addition, studio fixed costs began to escalate greatly and only increased with the studio strikes of 1945 through 1947. As films became more costly to make, the majors began to scale back the number of films they produced just at the time the moviegoing public began to return to theaters in droves. In 1939, the eight big studios released 400 films; by 1946, that number was down to 250. This decrease created a gap between big-studio product and demand that the indies were more than willing to fill.

Another trend shaped events in the coming years. An increasing number of the studios' major stars who had been disaffected for some time with the "stable" system (starting with Bette Davis and Humphrey Bogart in the late 30s) openly challenged the studio heads and began to go out on their own, selling their services on a per-picture basis. A new policy thus developed in the industry whereby the large studios increasingly took on the role of financiers and distributors of independent production companies' products.

The final nail was driven into the majors' monopolies in 1948 when the Anti-Trust Commission, not satisfied with the results of the Consent Decree, ordered the five studios that continued to own theatrical venues to divest themselves of their exhibition outlets. Paramount was the first to comply in 1949, followed by RKO a year later, Fox in 1952, and Warner Brothers in 1953. MGM held out stubbornly until 1959 but finally caved in. As the commission's order prohibited fixed rentals to exhibitors, and as low-budget B movies had been created for that purpose, the end of the B was in sight. By the early 1950s, the majors had canceled their B production units, and the double bill was on the wane.

4
THE EMERGENCE OF THE B NOIR

"What becomes apparent in retrospect," writes film historian Don Miller, "is that 1938 was the year in which the low budget or B picture not only came into its own, but attained stature. . . . The B rank seemed to solidify at nearly every major studio. They made films cheaply, but obscuring and overcoming budget deficiencies were tightly-knit stories, often creatively directed."

It is not coincidental that the B movie came into its own in the same period that film noir was born. Aside from literary influences, developments within and outside the movie industry over the next few years would coalesce to ensure that film noir would emerge as a coherent film style.

One commonly noted event was the flood of foreign directors in Hollywood before and during World War II. They brought with them the visual style of German expressionism, which entailed odd camera angles, low-key lighting, the inventive and sometimes surreal use of shadows, and the reflection of light off wet surfaces such as streets. Many of these refugees, for example, Edward Dmytryk, Robert Siodmak, Jacques Tourneur, John Brahm, Boris Ingster, and Charles Vidor (as well as American directors such as Stuart Heisler, Mark Robson, Robert Wise, and Anthony Mann), began their Hollywood careers in B films and would later gain notice and graduate to A films because of their distinctive styles.

The fact that many of the B units and directors were given a large measure of autonomy, such as the Val Lewton unit at RKO, illustrates the fact that the studios were by 1939 viewing the B movie in a different light. The studios and the artists and executives that worked in them were looking for a way to contrast their A and B product and began to look at Bs on their own merits. The creative styles of the refugee directors (as well as American directors and cinematographers) began to be viewed as a way of adding quality to B productions without adding to their cost. This creativity received an effective boost in 1941 when Orson Welles came out with *Citizen Kane*, which employed a whole new grab bag of innovative optics, deep-focus photography, and the fragmentation of time with flashbacks and narrative voice-overs as well as a protagonist who was at worst a bastard and at best morally ambiguous.

This search for differentiation led to an early hybridization in film noir as directors sought to combine the most successful elements of various genres: the Warner Brothers gangster film, the classic whodunit, the woman's melodrama, plots synthesized from the tough-guy pulp writers, and the Universal horror films with their dark cinematography. In fact, two of the earliest films noir, *The Stranger on the Third Floor* (1940) and *Among the Living* (1941), were advertised by the studios as horror films. "In part, of course, this hybrid quality is explicable in terms of studio insecurities about marketing their B products," says Paul Kerr. "Nevertheless, the curiously cross-generic quality of film noir is perhaps a vestige of its origins as a kind of 'oppositional' cinematic mode."

Although only a handful of films noirs were produced during the first years of World War II because Hollywood concentrated on the war effort, producers and directors in the studio's B units continued to refine that "oppositional cinematic mode." Orson Welles has been given much critical credit for helping define the RKO look, but Val Lewton's B unit, given virtual autonomy by the studio, was busy cranking out B gems that, although billed as horror movies, were in many cases fine psychological thrillers. They would have a great effect on film noir to come. Lewton's directors, Mark Robson and Jacques Tourneur, who would go on to direct A noirs, were masters at creating suspense by withholding information from the audience. It wasn't what was in the light that created the suspense but what lurked in the shadows beyond the light. Part of that strategy was dictated by budgetary constraints, of course. In a later interview, Robson recalled that during his work on Lewton's only film noir, *The Seventh Victim* (1943), night shooting was necessitated by the compressed production schedule; it was also an asset, however, as the sets used were the studio lot's streets, and "the less light we put on them the better they looked."

In 1943, the War Production Board cut back the allotment of film allowed the studios by 25 percent and set a limit of $5,000 on the cost of sets for B movies (before the war the limit was $17,500). Props, sets, and costumes were minimized and recycled when possible, an economic trend pioneered by Orson Welles when he used a fake staircase to create the illusion of a cavernous living room in *Citizen Kane*. That same staircase was reused by Welles in *The Magnificent Ambersons* (1942) and borrowed by Val Lewton for his 1942 production of *The Cat People*. Producers and directors were forced to be innovative and disguised this recycling by shooting the sets from different angles and lighting them differently. Stock footage and scenes from previous films were used to create montages with fast-cutting so that the film sequences would not be recognizable. Scenes of fire engines racing to a fire, car chases over mountain roads, police motorcycles pouring out of the underground garage of a police station, sirens blaring, all were commonly recycled without notice by audiences. A bank robbery scene from Fritz Lang's 1937 prenoir film *You Only Live Once* was lifted for Monogram's 1945 production of *Dillinger*.

To accommodate tighter budgets, casts and crews had to be cut back, necessitating smaller story lines. Since 30 percent of the movies in production in 1943 were war related, utilizing larger casts for battle scenes, the studio heads began to look around for new story material. Also, some studio heads anticipated the end of the war and had come to question the long-term economic viability of war movies. Film noir plots filled the bill nicely, as they were character-driven and involved minimal casts. The limit on set costs also played well with the reduced lighting costs inherent to films noirs. The same sets could be given a different look by lighting only portions of them. Studio heads who had been unwilling to buck the Hays Office and the Production Code in the 1930s began to take another look at the material they owned.

In 1943, *Double Indemnity* went into production. It premiered the following year, but not before it was nearly shelved by the combined efforts of the Hays Office, Paramount, and its star, Fred MacMurrray, who had begun to have second thoughts about the film's content. Audiences responded to the film, and the studio's heads, balancing profits against the Production Code, voted for the former, especially after the noirs *Leave Her to Heaven* and *Spellbound* were among the ten biggest grossing pictures of 1945.

Because of its success and the fact that many producers and directors in Hollywood had been chafing for years under the Hays Office restrictions on sex and violence, *Double Indemnity* unleashed a torrent of noir production, A and B. Film noir in general challenged the taboo subjects of the Hays Office—primarily sex and violence—but even the most cynical and perverse A productions, such as *The Postman Always Rings Twice* (1946), *Out of the Past* (1947), and *Criss Cross* (1949), could not beat the B noirs in challenging the Production Code. Some are particularly notable for being anti-Hays Office: Columbia's *Night Editor* (1946), in which Janis Carter watches with sexual excitement as a young girl is beaten to death, then goes into a sexual frenzy as she tries to get a look at the girl's pulverized face; *Blonde Ice* (1948; see Filmography), in which Leslie Brooks plays a socialite who murders her boyfriends because she gets her kicks reading about it in the papers; *Railroaded!* (1947), starring John Ireland, who perfumes his bullets before killing his victims; and *Destination Murder* (1950), in which the possibly homosexual murderer, played by Albert Dekker, refers to himself only by his last name (Armitage) and takes sadistic pleasure in beating people to death to classical music.

The writers, producers, and directors of these B noirs were clearly leading the way by intentionally pushing the morality and filmmaking envelope. Director Martin Scorsese, in a television documentary, referred to the B-movie directors as "film smugglers" who subverted the conventions of filmmaking in both style and content.

Immediately after the war, B noir production increased greatly as independent companies met the demand for B movies and the A production of the major studios was cut back. Camera innovations developed during the war, such as high-speed lenses, more portable equipment, dollies, and generators, as well as the development of more sensitive black-and-white film, allowed B production companies that did not have studio facilities or the money to rent soundstages from the majors to economize on equipment and labor costs by taking to the streets for night-by-night shooting. Location shooting became more and more common, contributing to the new realism of films in the late forties that was so important to the wet-streets-at-night look of film noir.

By the early 1950s, many of the production companies that had specialized in film noir, such as Eagle Lion, were out of business. The photography had gotten flatter, and the tough, hard-boiled dialogue, which had seemed so snappy and new ten years earlier, had started to sound contrived. Certain changes afoot in America and within the movie industry itself would spell the eventual demise of the B movie and the classic period of film noir.

5

POVERTY ROW: THE B FACTORIES

Besides the larger Hollywood studios, which had their own B units, several smaller Hollywood studios in the late 1930s and early 1940s produced almost nothing but B product and were proud of it. These studios—Republic, Monogram, and PRC— were referred to in the business as Poverty Row because of their low budgets and production values. Of the three, Republic produced by far the superior product and was the most respected in the industry.

Republic was founded in 1935 by Herbert J. Yates, owner of Consolidated Film Laboratories, which processed film for several independent production companies. Yates implemented his desire to get into actual film production and distribution by foreclosing on three of his clients—Mascot, Monogram, and Liberty—and merging them into one studio, which he dubbed Republic Pictures.

Taking over the studio facilities of Mascot, Republic focused on westerns, action pictures, and serials. From its inception, its biggest stars were its western heroes, John Wayne and singing cowboy Gene Autry, both of whom reaped great profits for the fledgling studio. Its serials, inherited as a Mascot specialty, also provided a steady stream of income from theater owners looking to ensure reattendance by a youthful audience that would pay to find out how the hero escaped death in the last episode. The studio was so successful financially, in fact, that by 1941 it had ac- complished the impossible for a Poverty Row studio: It managed to produce at least one A feature per year, including *Manhattan Merry-Go-Round* (1937), *Man of Conquest* (1939), and *Hit Parade of 1941*.

After trying to expand its product line into musicals and melodramas with modest results, Republic soon reverted to form, focusing on adventure and action flicks. Its primary bread and butter, westerns, premiered its new smash star, Roy Rogers. The studio did, however, from its inception, produce some whodunits and crime films. Before Ellery Queen moved to Columbia, the detective made his Republic debut in *The Spanish Cape Mystery* (1935). Of higher quality was the *Hollywood Stadium Mystery* (1938), about a prize fighter murdered in front of a boxing audience. *Gangs of New York* (1938), about an undercover cop posing as a lookalike gangster, was so successful it was followed by *Street of Missing Men* (1939), *Gangs of Chicago* (1940), and *Behind the News* (1940). The latter two starred Lloyd Nolan in cynical roles, one as a gangster, the other as a hard-bitten newsman.

Republic dipped its toe into the noir genre early with its superior production of *Whispering Footsteps* (1943; see Filmography). During the 1940s, Republic produced a number of other films noirs, including significant entries such as *The Pretender* (1947) and the artistic *Moonrise* (1948). It continued its noir output until the mid-1950s, producing such superior films as *The House by the River* (1950), *City That Never Sleeps* (1953), *Make Haste to Live* (1954), and *Hell's Half Acre* (1954) as well as less notable movies such as *Hoodlum Empire* (1952) and *The Man Is Armed* (1956).

In 1959, Republic sold out to CBS, and its soundstages became that network's Television City Studio. Although it technically remains in existence as a distributor of videos, it ceased production after being absorbed by the network. Its twenty-five-year legacy remains the shining gem of the Poverty Row studios.

Monogram Pictures started out as Raynart Productions, a small independent company formed in 1924 by W. Ray Johnston. Its output was basically the same as that being cranked out by the other small independents—serials, cheap westerns, and melodramas. After changing names several times, the studio took on the Monogram label in 1931.

In 1935, when Herbert J. Yates rolled Monogram into Republic, he kept on Johnston as an officer of the corporation. Friction soon broke out between the two, and in 1937, Johnston pulled out with his former president, Trem Carr. The two managed to regroup and resume operations under the Monogram name.

Yates and Carr's vision was to provide series pictures to exhibitors. Western stars such as Tom Keene, Johnny Mack Brown, and Tex Ritter, as well as teams of stars such as the Range Busters (Ray "Crash" Corrigan, John "Dusty" King, and Max "Alibi" Terhune), the Rough Riders (Buck Jones, Tim McCoy, and Raymond Hatton), and the Trail Blazers (Ken Maynard, Hoot Gibson, and Bob Steele), played recurring characters to provide viewers with comfort and familiarity. Boris Karloff played detective Mr. Wong in a series of mysteries meant to be Monogram's answer to Fox's Charlie Chan. (Monogram would later pick up the rights to the Charlie Chan character, replacing Warner Oland with Sidney Toler and, later, Roland Winters.) Kane Richmond played masked crime fighter the Shadow, Gilbert Roland was the Cisco Kid, and Bomba the Jungle Boy was Monogram's discounted answer to Tarzan. By far the most successful Monogram series was the Bowery Boys, starring Leo Gorcey and Huntz Hall, who as good-hearted juvenile delinquents butchered the English language from 1941 until the early 1950s. The studio utilized formerly famous stars such as Harry Langdon, Bela Lugosi, and Kay Francis, who were either between parts or whose failed careers at the major studios forced them to take roles in cut-rate productions.

In 1938 and 1939, Monogram turned increasingly to crime-oriented themes in its films with titles such as *Numbered Women*, *Female Fugitive*, *I Am a Criminal*, *Gang Bullets*, and *Convict's Code*, previewing its segue into film noir six years later. In 1944, Monogram produced its first—and one of its best—noirs, *When Strangers Marry*, starring Dean Jagger, Kim Hunter, and a very young Robert Mitchum as a sociopathic killer. The studio must have fallen in love with the work of Cornell Woolrich, because a significant number of its noir productions were based on his novels of drug- or alcohol-induced blackouts, including *Fall Guy* (1947), *The Guilty* (1947), and *I Wouldn't Be in Your Shoes* (1948).

In 1946, Monogram produced its first A noir, *Suspense*. It starred ice-skater Belita, the Poverty Row studio's answer to Sonja Henie, as well as solid actors Barry Sullivan and Albert Dekker. This film gave the industry a glimpse of what would occur later that year when chairman of the board Johnston and his president, Steve Broidy, decided they were ready to produce higher-budget, as well as high-quality, films. To handle that task, they formed Allied Artists Productions, Inc., as a wholly-owned subsidiary of Monogram. The intent was to differentiate their product by label, distributing higher-budget productions under the Allied Artists banner while continuing to release the identifiable low-budget product under the Monogram name. Allied Artists put out several superior noirs in the late 1940s. *The Gangster* (1947) starred Barry Sullivan and was written by proletarian, hard-boiled author Daniel Fuchs, based on his novel *Low Company*. *The Hunted* (1948) starred Preston Foster as a cop who obsesses about his ex-girlfriend, previewing the stalker theme that would become all too familiar in news headlines forty years later.

Although the intention may have been to rehabilitate the Monogram monicker, after a few years the studio heads began to tighten Allied Artists budgets to the point that the product of the two companies began to look more alike than different. In 1953, in a final attempt to shed its Poverty Row image, Monogram changed its name to Allied Artists. Throughout the 1950s, under the leadership of Steve Broidy, it continued to grind out low-budget fare, exploiting fading stars in genre pictures. Although its programmers in the horror, sci-fi, western, and teenage exploitation genres were almost all uniformly bad (some of the studio's movies were so bad, they have become cult classics, for example, *Attack of the 50-Foot Woman*, *From Hell It Came*, and Roger Corman's *Attack of the Crab Monsters*), the studio managed during that period to produce more than a few interesting—and some classic—B noirs, such as *Southside 1-1000* (1950), *The Phenix City Story* (1955), *The Big Combo* (1955), *The Come-On* (1956), and Edgar G. Ulmer's last film, *Murder Is My Beat* (1955).

In the mid-1960s, Allied Artists discontinued film production and shifted its focus to its television subsidiary, Allied Artists Television Corporation. In the 1970s, Allied Artists once again began producing films, including *Cabaret* (1972), *The Man Who Would Be King* (1975), and the studio's all-time biggest grosser, *Papillon* (1973), but the few successes did not make up for the box office failures that continued to plague the company. In 1976, Allied Artists merged with Kalvex, Inc./PSP, Inc. to form Allied Artists Industries, Inc. That move only postponed the inevitable, however, and in 1979, Allied Artists filed for bankruptcy. A year later the studio sold out to Lorimar Productions, thus bringing to an end fifty-five years of filmmaking.

Unquestionably the premier discount production company of the Poverty Row studios was Producers Releasing Corporation, or PRC. Its productions were so cheap and for the most part so bad that at the time, many around Hollywood quipped that the letters stood for Pretty Rotten Crap. Most of its movies, usually westerns and melodramas, were churned out in less than a week by directors such as William Beaudine, Jean Yarbrough, Phil Rosen, Lew Landers, and Sam Newfield. Newfield directed more than 140 films, some of them under pseudonyms to hide the fact that he and his producer brother, Sigmund Neufeld, were behind so much of PRC's product. Although most of Newfield's films were shoddy melodramas such as *I Accuse My Parents* (1949) and *White Pongo* (1945), Newfield did direct several passable noirs for PRC, for example, *The Lady Confesses* (1945) and *Apology for Murder* (1945; see Filmography).

One of the most competent in the studio's roster of directors was German émigré Edgar G. Ulmer, who came to PRC in 1942 and directed three noir films during his tenure there: *Bluebeard* (1944), *Strange Illusion* (1945), and *Detour* (1945). The latter film, about an unlucky, star-crossed piano player who hitchhikes across the country to get to his true love and through little or no fault of his own gets involved in two murders, has gone on to become a cult classic. The last lines of the film, intoned by star Tom Neal as he is being shoved into the back of a police car, have come to symbolize what film noir is all about: "Fate or some mysterious force has put the finger on you or me for no good reason at all." Some of Ulmer's work is remarkable for its quality considering the fact that his unit at PRC was allowed only 15,000 feet of film per picture and most of his films (including *Detour*) were shot in six days.

Most veteran directors worked at studios like PRC because they couldn't get jobs at the majors or because they accepted themselves as hacks and were content to grind out inferior product for the money. But some used studios like Monogram and PRC as places to learn their craft and develop distinctive directorial styles that could overcome shallow script material, low budgets, and tight production schedules. One such director who would go on to fame as an innovative noir stylist and, later, director of A westerns was Anthony Mann. Mann cut his directorial teeth at Columbia, where his *Dr. Broadway* (1942) depicted the dark underbelly of urban life and presaged by a few short years films noirs he would do for Republic, for example, *Strangers in the Night* (1944) and *Strange Impersonation* (1945). But Mann really found himself at PRC with *Railroaded!* (1947), in which his noir style of deep-focus photography and odd-angle camera shots became his trademark.

PRC, founded by Ben Judell in 1939, had started business as Producers Pictures before changing its name to Producers Distributing Corporation, or PDC. Judell had had a vision from the inception of the company of forming his own system of distribution franchises and guaranteeing cheap product to independent theater owners. The company started with a splash by releasing an anti-Nazi movie called *Beast of Berlin*, villifying Hitler and his government. Nazi sympathizers in New York, where the movie was to be premiered, organized protests of the opening of the film, and the New York board of censors bowed to political pressure and banned it. After some censorial cuts, the board allowed the movie to open, and the resultant publicity put PDC on the map.

After a big-bang beginning, however, things did not go so well for Judell's productions. By 1940 the studio was on the verge of bankruptcy, and Sigmund Neufeld, Judell's executive producer, quit PDC to form his own production company. In 1940, after seven pictures, PDC became Producers Releasing Corporation with Harry Rathner as president. The new company limped along for a few months but was absorbed by the Pathe Corporation, although it retained its PRC banner. O. Henry Briggs was made president but was replaced in 1944 by Leon Fromkess, formerly the treasurer for Monogram.

Like Monogram, PRC utilized a lot of between-pictures or once-big-now-nothing stars like Bela Lugosi, Erich von Stroheim, Buster Crabbe, Lee Tracy, Richard Arlen, and Glenda Farrell to fill its bills. This strategy is probably not surprising in that only veteran actors who knew their stuff and wouldn't blow their lines could work on such short shooting schedules.

In 1947, PRC was taken over by Eagle Lion Corporation, owned by British producer J. Arthur Rank, who was looking to expand his releasing market to the U.S. Under the Eagle Lion banner, production values and budgets greatly improved, and over the next few years the studio put out what seemed to be almost exclusively noir product. Many of those films are now considered classics by film buffs. Bryan Foy had by this time broken away from Warner Brothers to form his own production company and produced several superior noirs for Eagle Lion, including *Canon City* (1948), *Hollow Triumph* (1948), *He Walked by Night* (1949), and *Trapped* (1949). Edgar G. Ulmer stayed on to direct *Ruthless* (1948), a bigger-budget, lengthy noir that he considered to be his *Citizen Kane*. Stylistically, Anthony Mann really came into his own at Eagle Lion, directing two noir classics there—*T-Men* and *Raw Deal*—in that same year.

As pressure was put on the double bill and B product was increasingly squeezed out, Eagle Lion found itself in financial trouble. In 1950, having trouble staying on its feet, the company merged with United Artists and ceased to exist.

Two other B studios founded in the 1940s deserve mention because of their production of B noirs. The most significant was Film Classics, founded in 1943 by Irving Shapiro to handle the U.S. release of films by Gaumont British Pictures. A few years later, it handled the distribution of films made by the Selznick Company. Shapiro subsequently started up Film Rights International Ltd. and Other Films Around the World to reissue the product of other foreign studios. In 1947, Film Classics began production of its own films, and although the number it would produce over the remaining three years of its existence was small—no more than fifteen—many of them were films noirs: *Money Madness* (1948), starring Hugh Beaumont as a particularly nasty sociopath; the ahead-of-its-time *Blonde Ice* (1948), about a psychotic female serial killer; and the documentary-style *C-Man* (1949) (see Filmography). The company achieved the most notoriety in 1949, when Ida Lupino produced (and directed a lot of) *Not Wanted*, starring Sally Forrest as an unwed mother who is seduced and abandoned and ends up emotionally unbalanced. The film caused quite a stir at a time when such subject matter was still controversial. The movie is also credited by many to have opened up the male-dominated film industry for other women to work as producers and directors. Ida Lupino went on to form her own production company, Filmakers, which produced several noirs in the 1950s.

In 1950, shortly before its demise, Film Classics released its most well known noir, *Guilty Bystander*, starring Zachary Scott as an alcoholic private eye searching for his kidnapped son. The Film Classics product was low-budget to be sure, but it was certainly superior to that of PRC and occasionally did show some style. Later that year, Film Classics merged with Eagle Lion to become Eagle Lion Classics. Shortly thereafter it disappeared in the Eagle Lion merger with United Artists.

Another company that cropped up in the late 1940s and that was devoted solely to the production of cheap B movies was Screen Guild/Lippert Pictures. In 1945, West Coast theater chain owner Robert I. Lippert formed Action Pictures, Inc., producing three low-budget films that were eventually released through Screen Guild Productions, a Lippert company. For a couple of years, Screen Guild ground out a series of ultracheap westerns and other programmers such as *Scared to Death* (1947), *My Dog Shep* (1947), and *Jungle Goddess* (1948). These films starred many of the old PRC players, for example, Bela Lugosi, Richard Arlen, Tom Neal, Robert Lowery, and Hugh Beaumont. Screen Guild even utilized the old PRC Newfield-Neufeld team to produce and direct. During that period, the studio produced two films noirs, *Shoot to Kill* (1947), which was a cut above the rest of its product, and *Road to the Big House* (1947), which was not (see Filmography).

In 1949, Lippert reorganized the company and began operations under the name of Lippert Pictures, Inc. Lippert continued on in the Screen Guild tradition, cranking out schlock, although it did manage to produce one memorable war movie, *The Steel Helmet* (1951), primarily because it was written, produced, and directed by Samuel Fuller. Although Lippert produced only one true noir, *Loan Shark* (1952) starring George Raft, Lippert had set up his company as a U.S. releasing agent for British-made films that emulated the American noir style.

One of the British companies for which Lippert served as the American releasing agent was Hammer Films, a small company formed in 1932 by Will Hinds (who changed his name to Hammer because of being half of a comedy vaudeville act called Hammer and Smith) and Spaniard Enrique Carreras to provide low-budget product for Carreras's distribution company, Exclusive Films. Hammer produced few films until after World War II, when the company was joined by the pair's sons, Anthony Hinds and Michael Carreras.

In 1950, Exclusive signed a five-year deal with Lippert to release Lippert product in the U.K. At that time, Hammer was producing mostly adaptations of BBC radio programs, but soon moved into the crime-noir field with the release of *Black Widow* (1951), about a murderous wife. Shortly thereafter, Hammer signed a mutual deal with Lippert to release Hammer films in the U.S. and to ensure familiarity with American audiences. Lippert supplied the American actors for the starring roles. Actors such as George Brent, Dane Clark, Scott Brady, John Ireland, Lizabeth Scott, Paul Henreid, Cesar Romero, Lloyd Bridges, and Alex Nicol all starred in early Hammer films. Hammer was heavily into noir in those days, and many of its productions that were not noir had crime themes, such as *Blood Orange* (1953), *White Fire* (1954), *The Black Glove* (1954), *The Unholy Four* (1954), *The Deadly Game* (1954), and *The Glass Tomb* (1955). These films were for the most part the product of producer Anthony Hinds and director Terence Fisher, who seemed to have a penchant for themes of wrongly accused people trying desperately to clear themselves of murder or of femme fatales ensnaring unwitting men and using them for their own evil purposes (see Filmography).

In 1956, Hammer started to change its specialty to science fiction with the release of *The Creeping Unknown* (1956) and its sequels, *Enemy from Space* (1957) and *X the Unknown* (1957). In that year, the company hit the jackpot with *The*

Curse of Frankenstein, a remake of the Mary Shelley classic. The film cost a little over $250,000 to make, raked in millions, and made the company famous. Hammer never looked back, cranking out remakes of all the old Universal horror films, including *The Mummy* and a series of *Dracula* movies, as well as some new original entries of its own. Those films made the careers of Christopher Lee and Peter Cushing, and by that time, Hammer was releasing its product in America through majors like Warner Brothers (Lippert Pictures having gone out of business in 1955).

By the early 1960s, B movie companies like Lippert, PRC, and Republic had become virtually extinct. Some critics cite American-International, which was founded in 1955 by Samuel Z. Arkoff and James H. Nicholson and which lasted well into the 1960s, as the last true B movie studio. There were great similarities between the production methods of the 1940s B studios and those of the 1950s B studios—budgets of $100,000 per picture and one-to-two-week shooting schedules—but American-International billed its B movies together (the B double bill), not as fill-in fodder for major-studio A films. American-International's product— primarily horror, sci-fi, and teenage exploitation movies—was intended to attract younger audiences on its own merits. One sure sign that B film noir had run its cycle was the fact that the exploitation master Arkoff produced only one noir film, *Female Jungle* (1956; see Filmography), resurrecting noir icon Lawrence Tierney to star. The late fifties haunts of the B movie stars were not alleyways and diners but dragstrips and high school gymnasiums, and the villains that haunted them were not gun-wielding gangsters but switchblade-wielding punks with acne.

Today, with the renewal of popularity of film noir, those independent production companies that in the 1940s and 1950s would have been rivals of Poverty Row skip theater exhibition entirely and produce directly for video distribution or for cable networks such as Showtime. In spite of the death of the B, at least in the significant form it assumed in the 1940s, B films and the studios that specialized in making them remain objects of fascination for ardent film buffs and practitioners. This admiration is exemplified by the fact that French director Jean Luc-Goddard dedicated his 1959 film noir classic *Breathless* to Monogram Pictures.

Eric Von Stroheim reveals the murderous face behind the mask in *The Mask of Diijon*.

Left. Heroin kingpin Yul Brynner (with hair) on a poster for *Port of New York*.

Below. Milburn Stone sets up Paul Guilfoyle to kill him in *The Judge*.

Above. The facial bandages are about to come off
in the incomparable Ed Wood's *Jail Bait*.

Below. Mary Anderson does some sleuthing in
The Whispering City.

Above. Don Harvey, a killer, prevents Paul Langton from crying out when police are on their trail in *For You I Die*.

Below. Lee Marvin, head of a commie spy ring, confronts Frank Lovejoy in *Shack Out on 101*.

Above. Gerald Mohr and ex-gangster moll Liz Renay in
A Date with Death.

Below. John Hubbard receives suspicion from the townsfolk
in *Whispering Footsteps.*

Above. Gangsters try to convince Linda Stirling that she has killed a man with her car in *The Mysterious Mr. Valentine*.

Below. John Shelton finds prison is not such an easy gig in *Road to the Big House*.

Above. Phantom pen pals appear to the surprise of Helene Thimig in *Strangers in the Night*.

Below. Bad guy Raymond Burr works out a sleazy deal in *Unmasked*.

Above. Gene Evans is about to get it by Bud Cokes in *Revolt in the Big House.*

Below. Ralph Meeker, coming to make a blackmail payment, checks out the passed-out blackmailer in *A Woman's Devotion.*

6

THE FINAL DECADE: THE DEMISE OF THE B

Film noir output continued to be strong through 1956, but by that time, almost all such films were Bs and very few were being released through the three largest majors, MGM, Paramount, and Twentieth Century Fox. Historically, those three studios had produced the fewest noirs, and the ones they did produce tended to be bigger-budget A productions. Out of the thirty-one films noirs released in 1954, all but one were Bs, and only one of the three films released by a major-major, *Rogue Cop* (MGM), was truly an A feature. The two other major-major releases, *Crime Wave* (Warners) and *The Other Woman* (Fox), were cheaply made Bs. A similar pattern continued for the next few years. The largest majors abandoned noir productions as well as the double bill, and the minors such as Columbia, United Artists, Universal, Republic, and Allied Artists increasingly put out double bills with two low-budget films instead of an A and a B. These double bills were often genre-based—sci-fi, horror, crime, and so on—and were instrumental in redefining the B movie for future generations of moviegoers and critics as low budget rather than the lower half of a high-budget, low-budget double bill. (Actually, this practice began as early as the mid-1940s, promulgated primarily by the Poverty Row studios that catered to discount theaters and "kiddie shows." In 1946, for instance, Republic released in some theaters a double-B bill of *Valley of the Zombies* and *The Catman of Paris*, both hour-long cheapies aimed at the juvenile market.)

By 1958, the number of noir releases had fallen off sharply, to eight films, virtu-ally all of them Bs. This decline was probably in part rooted in social changes, as the Eisenhower years saw large emigrations from the inner city, where most film noir took place, to the suburbs. People became more interested in backyard barbe-quing than crime. More important, technological factors within the entertainment industry had coalesced by the early 1950s and had firmly taken root by the end of the decade to undermine the double bill and film noir production.

Between 1947 and 1954, the number of television sets in the United States in-creased from 14,000 to 32 million. Hoping to cash in on the success of television and foreseeing the eventual death of the double bill, some of the majors and a few of the minor studios that were fighting for their existence began renting their film libraries to television or began forming their own television production units. Co-lumbia formed Screen Gems for that purpose. Warner Brothers and Disney began producing their own weekly shows for the networks. Once more in financial trou-ble, RKO stopped movie production altogether in 1955 and sold its film library to a TV programming syndicate. In 1957, RKO sold the entire studio facilities to De-silu, a TV production company owned by Lucille Ball and Desi Arnaz. As more moviemakers entered the TV arena, the 65-minute B black-and-white movie be-came the one-hour TV drama or melodrama.

China Smith, starring Dan Duryea as a cynical reporter drifting around the Ori-ent, made its TV debut in 1952 and was shot in the noir style. Several episodes were directed by Robert Aldrich, who would go on to direct the famous film noir *Kiss Me, Deadly* (1955) and would also direct the B noir *World for Ransom* (1954), which featured Duryea as a *China Smith*-type character and recycled many *China Smith* sets.

The television show *Dragnet* was allegedly inspired by the classic film noir *He Walked By Night* (1948), though there was little outward cinematic resemblance. By the mid-to-late fifties, many series that had the noir look and feel had come and gone: *Mike Hammer, M Squad, Peter Gunn, Johnny Staccato*. By the time *77 Sunset Strip* came along, the look had changed, and the hard-boiled private eyes were soft-boiled and had sidekicks like Kookie, a parking attendant who constantly combed his hair and talked hip, not tough.

Inspired in part to differentiate the A movie from television fare, filmmakers had also by the early 1950s begun to utilize the Technicolor process on a large scale. The Technicolor process was invented in 1935, and its popularity with movie audiences was clearly seen by the studios in 1939 with the smash successes of *Gone with the Wind* and *The Wizard of Oz*. The process was costly, however, and it was used sparingly in the late 1930s and early 1940s. It was saved for lavish productions with lush sets and lots of action—swashbucklers, musicals, westerns, and epics. Melodramas, horror films, and mysteries were relegated to cheaper black-and-white film. The economic constraints brought on the industry by World War II put color production on a mass scale on hold, but after the war, color production took off, to the point that by 1952 over 75 percent of all features in production were being shot in color.

The wide screen, another development in the early 1950s, also served to differentiate movies from TV and lure patrons back into the theaters. Cinemascope was introduced by Twentieth Century Fox in 1953 with *The Robe*; Paramount followed suit with its VistaVision process; and by 1954, 10,000 movie theaters in the U.S. had converted to the new wide-screen format. Other technical innovations, 3-D and the even wider screen Cinerama, were used to increase box office receipts, but both processes proved too expensive.

TV, color, and the wide screen incited the studios to increase the budgets and spectacle of their productions. By the late 1950s, the blockbuster had taken over the business with all the majors indulging in huge sets, spectacular action, and location shooting. Because these spectaculars were necessarily long and their rental fees were increased to recoup the cost of production, theater owners increasingly went to a single-feature format.

Adding to the squeeze on the double bill was the fact that between 1948 and 1954, 3,000 small theaters in the inner cities that showed B movies or reruns closed down as people emigrated to the suburbs. Temporarily, the slack was more than taken up by the rise of the drive-in, which made its first appearance in 1933. By 1954 there were 4,000 drive-ins around the country. Many charged by the car rather than the person because their sound systems were tinny speakers hooked onto car windows and not made for big-budget sound tracks and because many drive-in owners geared their fare toward younger, car-infatuated audiences to whom the picture on the screen was often less important than the social nature of the venue. It was at the drive-in that the double bill (sometimes the triple bill, with a midnight "spook show" thrown in to increase revenues by encouraging repeated trips to the snack bar) and the cheaper B exploitation films—sci-fi, horror, thrillers, and westerns—gasped their last gasp. (It is undoubtedly that fact that has led many TV cable networks such as American Movie Classics to equate B films with the drive-in by showing them under the "Drive-In Movie" banner). As real estate values increased in the early 1960s and more and more drive-ins were sold to developers or converted to areas for swap meets, the final nail was put into the coffin of the double bill and the B movie.

By 1959, the number of films noirs released was down to eleven, all of them low-budget. The classic period of film noir had ended. The film noir, which evolved in 1939 with the rise of the B movie and worked its way up through the ranks of the A productions, had returned to its roots. The noir themes of crime and police corruption would soon be replaced by themes of corporate conspiracy, political protest, racial injustice, and environmental degradation. Film noir production, although never totally abandoned, would remain relatively dormant for thirty years. It was resurrected in the late 1980s by young filmmakers who would rediscover the artistry and flavor of the films via another technological innovation—the video-tape machine.

7

FILMOGRAPHY

P: Producer
D: Director
Sc: Screenplay
Ph: Cinematographer
Ed: Editor
M: Music
(B&W) Black-and-white
(C) Color
(V) Available on video

Accomplice (1946) PRC. 66m. (B&W) P: John K. Teaford. D: Walter Colmes. SC: Irving Elman, Frank Gruber, based on Gruber's novel, *Simon Lash, Private Detective*. Ph: Jockey Feindel. Ed: Robert Jahns. M: Alexander Laszlo. CAST: Richard Arlen, Veda Ann Borg, Tom Dugan, Michael Branden, Marjorie Manners, Earle Hodgins, Francis Ford, Herbert Rawlinson, Sherry Hall.   Bookish private eye Simon Lash (Arlen) is approached by his ex-fiancée Borg (she left him at the altar). She asks him to find her missing husband, whom she says has been suffering from bouts of amnesia. As the husband is a bank executive, Arlen suspects the man has absconded with bank funds and is using the amnesia as a ploy, but a check at the bank shows no missing funds. It does uncover the fact, however, that another banker has also disappeared. Arlen's trail leads to a secret love nest the banker-husband had set up with another woman. When the banker is found murdered, his head blown off by a shotgun, the police suspect Arlen and Borg. When a witness to the murder is also murdered, as well as the banker's mistress, Arlen ends up at a castle in the New Mexico desert that is run by a crooked marshal as a hideout for criminal fugitives. The banker-husband, very much alive, is one of the house clients, and Arlen finds the entire mess to have been a ruse by his ex-girlfriend and her husband to cover up a bank scam. In a shoot-out, the husband accidentally shoots Borg to death and is dispatched by Arlen.

This film is a typically weak product from PRC. The Arlen character is based on the Simon Lash series by Frank Gruber, a competent writer of hard-boiled private eye novels and short stories as well as westerns, but he drew his gun too fast and shot himself in the foot with this one. The film looks as if it was (and it probably was) shot in four days. Particularly notable in the film is director Colmes's exciting use of endless close-ups of tires during automobile chase scenes.

Accused of Murder (1956) Republic. 74m. (C) P&D: Joe Kane. Sc: Bob Williams, W.R. Burnett, based on the novel *Vanity Row* by Burnett. Ph: Bud Thackery. Ed: Richard L. Van Enger. M: R. Dale Butts. CAST: David Brian, Vera Ralston, Sidney Blackmer, Virginia Grey, Warren Stevens, Lee Van Cleef, Barry Kelley, Richard Karlan, Frank Puglia, Elisha Cook, Greta Thyssen.   Blackmer, a mob attorney, is in his car pitching woo to nightclub singer Ralston, who rejects his proposals of romance. They are being watched by gangster Stevens. When Ralston leaves in her own car, Stevens tails Blackmer as he follows her. Shortly thereafter, Blackmer is shot to death. From the window of a nearby dance hall, Grey, a dime-a-dance girl, sees Stevens flee the scene. Police lieutenant Brian and his partner, Van Cleef, are called into the case. Stevens meets with the crooked owner of the dance hall and is paid off for killing Blackmer, who was the dance hall owner's partner in a uranium mine. Grey tries to shake down Stevens and gets slapped around for her trouble. Cook, in the meantime, has identified the murder gun as his own and tells the cops he sold it to Ralston. Van Cleef is convinced of Ralston's guilt so is at odds with Brian, who has started to fall for the singer. Grey tries to shake down Stevens again, and this time he beats her so badly she winds up in the hospital. She tells Brian about seeing Stevens at the scene, and Brian arrests

Stevens, who denies the murder. Things seem satisfactorily wound up until Ralston, guilty about an innocent man going to the gas chamber and confronted by Brian, admits that Blackmer committed suicide and that Stevens was only a witness. She turns herself in and is exonerated. The dance hall owner and Stevens are indicted for conspiracy, and Brian and Ralston resume their romance.

This is a very soft entry by the usually hard-boiled Burnett (*The Asphalt Jungle* and *Little Caesar*). Ralston (formerly Vera Hruba Ralston) was a former ice-skater who became a regular leading lady for Republic because she was married to a studio head. In this film she is her usual awful self. The most distinguishing feature of *Accused of Murder* is that it was one of the few color noirs of the forties and fifties. It is also one of the few movies of Van Cleef's early career in which he did not play a bad guy. (V)

Apology for Murder (1945) PRC. 67m. (B&W) P: Sigmund Neufeld. D: Sam Newfield. Sc: Frank Minton. Ph: Jack Greenhalgh. Ed: Holbrook N. Todd. CAST: Ann Savage, Hugh Beaumont, Charles D. Brown, Russell Hicks, Bud Buster, Pierre Watkin, Norman Willis, Eva Novak, Archie Hall, Elizabeth Valentine, Henry Hall. Savage, the sultry wife of a wealthy newpaper owner, seduces reporter Beaumont into helping her kill her husband. After the deed is done, she throws Beaumont over for the attorney who is going to help her get her dead husband's money. Beaumont, in the meantime, is put on the story to investigate the murder he and Savage committed. When he finds out he has been a stooge, there is a falling-out resulting in Savage's death and his being mortally wounded. As he dies, Beaumont types out his confession to the crime.

Some contend that this rip-off of *Double Indemnity* was not a rip-off but based on the same true case on which James M. Cain based his novel, the 1927 New York murder of Albert Snyder by his wife, Ruth, and Judd Gray for $100,000 in insurance money. Not that it really matters; either way, this is no *Double Indemnity*, although Savage paints as powerful a picture of sinister feminity as she did of a nasty virago in the noir cult classic *Detour*.

Backlash (1947) Twentieth Century Fox. 66m. (B&W) P: Sol M. Wurtzel. D: Eugene Forde. Sc: Irving Elman. Ph: Benjamin Kline. Ed: William Claxton. M: Darrell Calker. CAST: Jean Rogers, Richard Travis, Larry Blake, John Eldredge, Leonard Strong, Robert Shayne, Louise Currie, Douglas Fowley, Richard Benedict,

Sara Berner. While driving down the highway, attorney Eldredge stops to offer a lift to Fowley, who is really a bank robber. When the car is found crashed and burned, the body in it is identified as Eldredge's. The police investigation focuses on four suspects—Eldredge's partner; his wife, Rogers; Travis, who, it turns out, is in love with Rogers; and Fowley. When Eldredge turns up very much alive, it is revealed that he planned the whole thing to get even with all the people he hated. The burned body was that of his caretaker, whom Eldredge killed and put in the car. As Eldredge returns to kill his wife, his plot is foiled by the police.

Told in a series of complicated flashbacks, this is not a bad little flick. It is one of the small handful of noirs produced at Fox by the Sol Wurtzel B unit (which one of the Ritz Brothers comedy team once referred to as "going from bad to Wurtzel").

Bad Blonde (1953) Hammer/Lippert. (Brit.) 80m. (B&W) AKA: *The Flanagan Boy*. P: Anthony Hinds. D: Reginald Le Borg. Sc: Guy Elmes, Richard Landau, based on the novel by Max Catto. Ph: Walter Harvey. Ed: James Needs. M: Ivor Slaney. CAST: Barbara Payton, Frederick Valk, John Slater, Sidney James, Tony Wright, Marie Burke, Selma Vaz Diaz, Enzo Coticchia, Betting Dickson, Joe Quigley. Wright is a boxer who falls under the sexual spell of femme fatale Payton, who also happens to be the wife of his manager, Valk. When Payton announces she is pregnant, both men think they are the father. Payton manipulates Wright into drowning her husband. Valk's mother arrives from Italy and suspects Payton faked the pregnancy; Payton admits she is right. When Wright gets a fit of conscience and is about to turn himself in, Payton poisons him, making it look like suicide. Wright's trainer doesn't believe he killed himself, however, and turns in Payton to the police.

Again, pieces of the Albert Snyder case were used in the story line. This was one of a number of fifties noir films produced by British Hammer Films and released in the U.S. by Lippert.

NOTE: Payton, once a promising Hollywood glamor queen (she costarred with James Cagney in the noir *Kiss Tomorrow Goodbye*), ended up in this picture because her film career began to seriously slide in 1951 after she was the sexual object of a fistfight on her front lawn between actors Franchot Tone and Tom Neal (whose modern claim to fame is having starred in the cheapie noir classic *Detour*). Tone, who wound up in the hospital as a result of the altercation, later married Payton. He divorced her seven weeks later, accusing her of adultery with Neal.

The scandal virtually ended Payton's career, as well as Neal's. Neal worked as a gardener in Palm Springs and eventually went to prison for shooting his wife to death during a jealous rage. Payton ended up as a call girl and was arrested for prostitution, drunkenness, and passing bad checks. As a last grasp for fame, she laid out her fall from Hollywood grace and into the gutter in a lurid autobiography titled *I Am Not Ashamed.* Ironically, Payton and Neal starred together at the tail ends of their careers in the 1953 Lippert production *The Great Jesse James Raid.* Robert I. Lippert, who supplied Payton for this film, was more than willing to exploit her bad-girl image in his U.S. advertising for the movie. The American poster showed a skimpily dressed Payton lying on a bed with a quote beneath: "They called me BAD . . . spelled M-E-N!" Before she took to hooking, one of Payton's last films was the noir *Murder Is My Beat* (1955).

Bait (1954) Columbia. 79m. (B&W) P&D: Hugo Haas. Sc: Samuel W. Taylor. Ph: Edward Fitzgerald. Ed: Robert S. Eisen. M: Vaclav Divina. CAST: Cleo Moore, John Agar, Hugo Haas, Emmett Lynn, Bruno VeSota, Jan Englund, George Keymas. Prologue by Sir Cedric Hardwicke.   Haas and Agar are partners who find a lost gold mine. Haas tries to get all the gold by using his wife as sexual bait for Agar, catching the couple in the act, then killing Agar and claiming it the act of an outraged husband. Of course, the plot backfires, and Haas gets it.

Haas, a Czech-born actor who decided to start a film career at the age of fifty, went on to become one of the world's worst writers-directors-actors and seemed intent on dedicating his entire film career to remaking bad copies of *The Postman Always Rings Twice.* In this one, he wedded the plot to *Treasure of the Sierra Madre* with the usual awful results. The only reason to watch the film is the precredit prologue by Sir Cedric Hardwicke as Satan.

Behind the High Wall (1956) Universal. 85m. (B&W) P: Stanley Rubin. D: Abner Biberman. Sc: Harold Jack Bloom, based on a story by Wallace Sullivan and Richard Polimer. Ph: Maury Gertsman. Ed: Ted J. Kent. M: Ted Gershenson. CAST: Tom Tully, Sylvia Sidney, Betty Lynn, John Gavin, Don Beddoe, John Larch, Barney Phillips, Ed Kemmer, John Baradino.   Tully, a prison warden with a crippled wife, is kidnapped by convicts during a jailbreak in which a guard is killed and convict Gavin is forced to go along. When the entire crew except Tully and Gavin are killed in a car wreck, Tully steals $100,000 of the gang's money and puts the blame on Gavin for the guard's death. Gavin is sentenced to be executed but escapes again. The cops nab him, but Tully is mortally wounded trying to retrieve the money and confesses that Gavin had been dragged into the whole mess.

NOTE: Gavin, whose most well remembered role is probably the hero in Alfred Hitchcock's *Psycho*, later became ambassador to Mexico under the Reagan administration.

Big Frame, The (1953) RKO. (Brit.) 67 min. (B&W) P: Robert S. Baker and Monty Berman. D: David Macdonald. Sc: Steve Fisher and John Gillig. Ph: Monty Berman. Ed: Reginald Beck. M: William Hill-Rowan. CAST: Mark Stevens, Jean Kent, Garry Marsh, John Bentley, Dianne Foster, Jack Lambert, Leslie Perrins, Brian Coleman.   An American pilot in Britain, during a reunion of his old RAF unit, gets into a bar brawl with an old buddy who's drunk. The next morning the pilot, Stevens, wakes up in a strange hotel room with blood on his suit, not remembering how he got there. He finds out that the man he'd fought with was murdered the night before and he is a suspect. Stevens is convinced he was drugged, and he and his girlfriend, Kent, start retracing his steps. Kent enlists the aid of Marsh, another buddy of Stevens's who was at the bar on the fatal evening. When Stevens goes to the apartment of the bartender who was serving at the pub on the night of the murder, he finds the man dead and himself now blamed for two killings. The trail leads Stevens to the first dead man's partner, who relates that the man had been utilizing their company in an illegal smuggling operation. During the conversation, the partner is shot dead by an unknown assailant. Stevens is caught by the police, and Kent and Marsh are left to clear his name. During their pursuit of the truth, Kent becomes suspicious of Marsh and leaves a note for the police in a garage bathroom. Marsh, realizing Kent suspects the truth, pulls a gun on her and reveals he was in the smuggling business with the dead man (as well as having an affair with his wife) and killed him because he was being double-crossed. The drugged drink was meant for the dead man, but Stevens got it by mistake and was then framed for the killing. The cops, alerted by Kent's note, arrest the widow and take off after Marsh, who with Kent as a hostage tries to escape by a private airplane. His attempt to escape is thwarted by Stevens, who blocks his takeoff in a car, and Marsh is arrested by the cops.

Weak in almost all departments, this is one of the many noirs produced in England with American stars.

Blackmail (1947) Republic. 67m. (B&W) D: Lesley Selander. Sc: Royal K. Cole; story by Robert Leslie Bellem based on his character Dan Turner, Hollywood detective; additional dialogue by Albert DeMond. Ph: Reggie Lanning. Ed: Tony Martelli. M: Mort Glickman. CAST: William Marshall, Adele Mara, Ricardo Cortez, Grant Withers, Stephanie Bachelor, Richard Fraser, Roy Bancroft, George J. Lewis, Tristram Coffin, Gregory Gay.   Private eye Dan Turner (Marshall) is hired by Cortez, an entertainment tycoon, to put a stop to a blackmail plot against him. It seems that a few nights before, at a gambling club called the Silver Swan, Cortez ran into the club singer, an old flame who expressed some animosity about being dumped for a new singer and proceeded to drug Cortez's drink. When he awakened, Cortez found himself alone in the singer's apartment. After incriminating photos arrived, the singer made contact and demanded $50,000 for the negatives but was soon after murdered. While Marshall is contemplating whether to take the case, the singer's gigolo boyfriend, who also worked at the Silver Swan, shows up at Cortez's house and demands $100,000 for the same incriminating pictures, the extra money being compensation for his girlfriend's murder. He and Marshall get into a fistfight, and during the scuffle, the gigolo is shot and falls into the swimming pool. Mara, Cortez's new girlfriend and protégée singer, shows up to witness the event, but when the cops show up, the body is missing and she denies she ever saw a body. Marshall's investigation eventually leads to Cortez's chauffeur and Mara, who are lovers and in cahoots to shake down Cortez. In a showdown, Mara accidentally shoots her boyfriend to death and is taken away by the cops.

This film is in the running for the worst tough-guy private eye movie ever made. Republic cast William Marshall, who had been a singer with the Fred Waring band in the 1930s, presumably trying to repeat the coup staged by RKO in casting crooner Dick Powell against type as hard-boiled Philip Marlowe in *Murder, My Sweet*. Marshall only manages to come off as a buffoon, delivering in a wooden manner classic lines such as "I suppose this gun just sprouted in your duke like a daffodil," "Don't move, sweetheart. This thing doesn't shoot marshmallows," and "Hey, you . . . you with the muff on your mitt" (a chauffeur polishing a car with a buffing glove). Although his patter is tough, Marshall is about the only hard-boiled private eye I can recall who gets knocked cold by being pushed into a swimming pool!

This film is really more of a film noir wannabee than a true noir but is included here because of the attempt. Another reason for its inclusion is that it brought to the screen Dan Turner, the longest running of all the private eye characters from the pulps. Humorist S. J. Perlman once called Turner "the apotheosis of all private investigators out of Ma Barker by Sam Spade." Robert Leslie Bellem, Turner's creator, was the ultimate pulpster, publishing over 3,000 stories in his lifetime under various pen names and in various genres. Dan Turner debuted in 1934 in *Spicy Detective* and by 1942 was so popular that he began to appear in his own magazine, *Dan Turner, Hollywood Detective*, which remained in print until 1950. One can only assume that the screenwriter (with additional dialogue by Albert DeMond) was trying to capture Bellem's prose, which was almost a parody of hard-boiled writers like Chandler; but he managed to achieve only low comedy.

Blackout (1954) Hammer/Lippert. (Brit.) 87 min. (B&W) AKA: *Murder by Proxy*. P: Michael Carreras. D: Terence Fisher. Sc: Richard Laundau, based on the novel by Helen Nielsen. Ph: Jimmy Harvey. Ed: Maurice Roots. M: Ivor Slaney. CAST: Dane Clark, Belinda Lee, Betty Ann Davies, Eleanor Summerfield, Andrew Osborn, Harold Lang, Jill Melford, Albis Maben.   Clark, drunk and down on his luck, runs into a beautiful, rich woman in a bar who offers him 500 pounds to marry her. She gives no reason for the offer, and he accepts it without asking for one. Later he wakes up from an alcoholic stupor with blood on his coat in the studio of a female artist who has the money and a portrait she has painted of his missing wife. Clark leaves and finds that the mystery woman is a missing heiress and that her father was a rich man who was murdered the night before. The heiress turns up again, claiming she and Clark are indeed married and that he was present when she found her father bludgeoned to death but that he hadn't done the crime. Together, they set out to find the killer, whom she suspects is her fiancé, an obsessive she had been trying to get away from and her reason for marrying Clark. She now says she loves Clark but then turns up at her mother's home in the company of her fiancé; Clark gives her the kiss-off. After the fiancé is shot to death, the killer is revealed to be the evil mother, who killed her husband and intended to do away with her daughter. The daughter either loves Clark at the end or doesn't. I don't think either they or the audience knows or cares.

This is yet one more I-can't-remember-what-I-did-last-night-and-why-is-there-blood-on-my-clothes? movie except that the plot of this one is so muddled, it is extremely hard to follow.

Blind Alley (1939) Columbia. 71m. (B&W) P: Fred Kohlmar. D: Charles Vidor. Sc: Philip MacDonald, Michael Blankfort, and Albert Duffy, based on the play by James Warwick. Ph: Lucien Ballard. Ed: Otto Meyer. M: Morris Stoloff. CAST: Chester Morris, Ralph Bellamy, Ann Dvorak, Joan Perry, Rose Stradner, Melville Cooper, John Eldredge, Ann Doran, Marc Lawrence, Milburn Stone.   Morris is a cold-blooded killer who breaks out of prison and, with several gangster accomplices and his girlfriend, takes psychiatrist Bellamy and his family hostage. Bellamy discovers Morris is afraid of becoming insane and convinces him to undergo hypnotic therapy to uncover the reason for his behavior. Morris finds he has covered up the abuse he underwent at the hands of his gangster father and the fact that he turned the man in to the police, resulting in his death. When the police arrive, Morris finds that facing the truth has rendered him incapable of pulling the trigger, and he is shot down by the cops.

This film is a superior B noir all the way with a good script, direction, and performances and moody cinematography by Ballard, who would go on to carve out a niche for himself in the rest of the noir cycle. Ten years later, the movie would be remade as *The Dark Past* with William Holden playing the Morris role.

Blind Spot (1947) Columbia. 73m. (B&W) AKA: *Trapped.* D: Robert Gordon. Sc: Martin Goldsmith, from a story by Barry Perowne. Ph: George B. Meehan. Ed: Henry Batista. M: Paul Sawtell. CAST: Chester Morris, Constance Dowling, Steven Geray, Sid Tomack, James Bell, Paul E. Burns, William Forrest.   Morris is a novelist who makes little money writing books, partly because of the type of books he writes and partly because his publisher (Forrest) holds him under a contract that squeezes him. He bursts into his publisher's office and makes a row while Forrest is talking to one of his best-selling mystery writers, Geray. Morris proclaims anyone can write a mystery and on the spot makes up a murder plot about a dead man found in a locked room. Morris goes to a bar and gets drunk and Dowling, Forrest's secretary, comes in, her dress torn, and says the publisher made a pass at her. The two get chummy; Morris gets drunker and returns to the publisher's office, which he rifles, destroying his contract in the process. The next day, Forrest is found dead in his office, and the scene is exactly that earlier described by Morris. Morris is the police's prime suspect but can't remember a thing because of being drunk. He tracks down the bartender who'd waited on him the night before but finds him murdered with one of Dowling's earrings near his body. The elevator man, thinking Morris killed the man, shoots him in the arm. When Morris finds a $500 check in his pocket, he remembers telling the story to Forrest and that Geray overheard it. Geray also had access to Dowling's earrings, having been there when her tussle with Forrest had taken place. The bartender, who knew Geray was the killer, had tried to blackmail him and was bumped off for his trouble. In the end, Geray confesses all to the police.

Another "blind" noir starring Morris, this one is a sleeper and very well written and acted. Dowling plays a good part and Morris, who was a B staple at Columbia, starring in fourteen *Boston Blackie* movies between 1941 and 1949, pulls off a convincing performance.

Blonde Ice (1948) Film Classics. 78m. (B&W) D: Jack Bernhard. Sc: Kenneth Gamet, based on a story by Whitney Chambers. CAST: Leslie Brooks, Robert Paige, Walter Sande, John Holland, James Griffith, Russ Vincent, Michael Whalen, Mildred Coles, Emory Parnell, Rory Mallinson, Julie Gibson, David Leonard.   Brooks is a beautiful, cold-hearted columnist nicknamed Blonde Ice who is going with sportswriter Paige when she suddenly dumps him to marry a very rich man. She can't get Paige out of her system, however, and when her new husband finds her writing him a love letter, he tells her he's going to divorce her. Before he can, she murders him and inherits his money. She fixes herself up with a clever alibi, but a blackmailer shows up, threatening to upset her plans. She kills him, too. All the while, she gets unwholesome kicks by reading about her misdeeds in the newspapers. She sets her sights on a wealthy attorney with a political background, but he suspects pathology and intends to dump her. When she murders him, some of her cronies at the newspaper start to get suspicious, as does criminal psychologist Leonard. Paige is the cop's main suspect, but Leonard traps Brooks into confessing her deeds, and she is killed in a struggle for her gun.

A truly odd and cold-hearted film for the femme fatale forties, *Blonde Ice* is seemingly a precursor to the fifties psycho-killer noir cycle and, later, films like the neonoir *Black Widow* (1987), starring Theresa Russell as the woman who mates and kills. Brooks is appropriately icy as the murderess, and the camera work was nicely done by George Robinson, a veteran cinematographer from the Universal B horror films of the 1930s. Edgar G. Ulmer, also a graduate of Universal horror films such as *The Black Cat* (1935) and later director of Poverty Row noir cult classics such as *Detour* (1945) and *Ruthless* (1948), claimed to have written the original story for *Blonde Ice* but is uncredited. Robert Paige, a leading man in the early 1940s, was on his way down the Hollywood chute when he made this film; a few years later he was reduced to doing Schlitz commercials for TV.

Blonde Sinner (1956). Allied Artists. (Brit.) 73m. (B&W) AKA: *Yield to the Night.* P: Kenneth Harper. D: J. Lee Thompson. Sc: John Cresswell, based on the novel *Yield to the Night* by Joan Henry. Ph: Gilbert Taylor. M: Ray Martin. CAST: Diana Dors, Yvonne Mitchell, Michael Craig, Geoffrey Keen, Olga Lindo, Mary Mackenzie, Joan Miller, Marie Ney, Liam Richmond.   Sexpot Dors, on death row, recalls in flashback the events that got her there, namely, murdering the rich mistress of her pianist lover. She recounts in maudlin detail her broken marriage, her alliance with a smooth playboy type who ran out on her, and eventually her affair with the musician who cheated on her.

This film is extremely downbeat and slow moving.

Burglar, The (1957) Columbia. 90m. (B&W) P: Louis W. Kellman. D: Paul Wendkos. Sc: David Goodis, from his novel. Ph: Don Malkames. Ed: Wendkos. M: Sol Kaplan. CAST: Dan Duryea, Jayne Mansfield, Martha Vickers, Peter Capell, Mickey Shaugnessey, Wendell Phillips, Phoebe Mackay, Stewart Bradley, Frank Orlsson, Ned Barey.   After casing the mansion of a rich old woman, Mansfield reports back to her burglary ring, headed by Duryea. While the burglars are robbing the old woman's safe, a police patrol car stops by the burglars' car, forcing Duryea to make an appearance in order to convince the cops that he has car trouble. They go on their way and Duryea consummates the robbery, getting away with a very valuable necklace. In the meantime, a composite sketch of Duryea is circulated, and the gang lays low, waiting for things to cool down. Friction breaks out among the group, primarily because of Shaughnessy's lusting after Mansfield. Duryea sends Mansfield to Atlantic City on a vacation to eliminate the problem. In a flashback, Duryea explains that as a child he had run away from an orphanage and been picked up and cared for by Mansfield's father, a burglar who taught him the trade. Duryea had made a promise to her father that if anything ever happened to him, Duryea would take care of Mansfield. When the father was shot to death during a burglary, Duryea split with Mansfield and has been taking care of her since. While Mansfield is in Atlantic City, she meets a mystery man who has been following the gang since the burglary, and she begins to date him. Duryea is picked up in a bar by Vickers and, after a brief tryst, overhears her making plans with the mystery man to glom the necklace. The gang is pulled over by the cops, and trigger-happy Shaugnessy shoots a policeman and is himself killed. Duryea and his remaining partner go to Atlantic City to warn Mansfield, and Duryea discovers that her new boyfriend is the cop who originally stopped him outside the old lady's mansion. Duryea tries to explain to Mansfield, but she refuses to believe him, telling him she's always had a thing for him but he would never give her a tumble. Duryea leaves the necklace with Mansfield, then returns to his hideout, where he finds Vickers and the crooked cop who has killed his partner. Warned by Duryea, Mansfield escapes and is chased into an amusement park by the cop. Mansfield turns the necklace over to the crooked cop to keep him from shooting Duryea, but he shoots him to death anyway. Vickers turns on her cop-boyfriend and turns him over to the police.

This film is a strange, tautly done noir with Duryea turning in his usual good performance and Mansfield proving she could indeed act. The writer, David Goodis, is an example of a hard-boiled writer of paperback originals who has not been given his due even though scholarly studies have been done on his work and several of his novels have been made into well-known films noirs, including *Dark Passage* (1947), *Nightfall* (1957), and François Truffaut's *Shoot the Piano Player* (1960). It is perhaps fitting that Goodis, like Horace McCoy, achieved his greatest literary popularity in France, the country that gave film noir its name. It is also perhaps fitting that a French production company remade *The Burglar* as *The Burglars* in 1972, starring Jean-Paul Belmondo and Dyan Cannon in the Duryea and Mansfield roles. The French remake suffers in comparison in large part because it was shot against a lavish Greek backdrop, losing in the process a lot of the quirkiness and claustrophobic sleaziness of the original.

Bury Me Dead (1947) PRC. 71m. (B&W) P: Charles Riesner. D: Bernard Vorhaus. Sc: Karen DeWolf and Dwight W. Babcock, from a radio story by Irene Winston. Ph: John Alton. Ed: W. Donn Hayes. M: Emil Cadkin. CAST: Cathy O'Donnell, June Lockhart, Hugh Beaumont, Mark Daniels, Greg McClure, Milton Parsons, Virginia Farmer, Sonia Darrin, Cliff Clark.   Lockhart, allegedly killed in a fire, returns home to attend her own funeral. The real dead woman turns out to have been a homewrecker who had been having an affair with Lockhart's philandering husband, among others, making the husband a prime suspect for the murder. Lockhart's little sister, O'Donnell, also has designs on Lockhart's hubby, not ruling her out as the culprit. The murderer, however, turns out to be the family lawyer, Beaumont, who controls Lockhart's money and wants her out of the way to take over her sizable estate. The husband and police come to Lockhart's aid just as Beaumont is about to complete his plan and kill her, after which Lockhart and her husband reconcile.

The interesting opening premise (we've all fantasized about being at our own funeral to see who was really broken up by our passing) doesn't live up to its potential, although it's not a bad little flick. This was one of the first films of Hungarian-born John Alton, who is considered by many to have been one of the best, and certainly one of the most prolific, noir cinematographers of all time. NOTE: O'Donnell, who plays Lockhart's oversexed little sister who has designs on Lockhart's hubby, was loaned by RKO to PRC–Eagle Lion for this and another B noir, *The Spiritualist*, after making a hit in the Academy Award-winning *The Best Years of Our Lives*.

C-Man (1949) Film Classics. 75m. (B&W) P: Rex Carlton. D: Joseph Lerner. Sc: Berne Giler. Ph: Gerald Hirschfeld. Ed: Geraldine Lerner. M: Gail Kubik. CAST: Dean Jagger, John Carradine, Lottie Elwen, Harry Landers, Renee Paul, Walter Vaughan, Adelaide Klein, Edith Atwater, Walter Brooke.   Treasury agent Jagger, upon returning from vacation, learns his best friend and fellow agent has been murdered. The dead agent was trying to track down a valuable necklace stolen in Paris from rich socialite Atwater. The primary suspect is slick, dangerous Paul, who, authorities suspect, is going to try to smuggle the necklace into the U.S. Jagger, posing as a private detective, goes to Paris and takes the same plane as Paul in an attempt to catch him in the act. On the plane, he meets Elwen, a Dutch national who is going to New York to marry her American fiancé. During the flight, Elwen is knocked out and tended to by Carradine, an alcoholic doctor who is really part of Paul's plot. Carradine plants the necklace in unconscious Elwen's head bandage. The plane is met by Landers, a thug working for Paul, and a female accomplice. Posing as Elwen's fiancé, whom Landers murdered earlier, the pair accompany Elwen to the hospital and try to recover the necklace, but she comes to. In the ensuing struggle, the ambulance crashes and Elwen gets away with the necklace. Elwen goes to her fiancé's apartment, finds her fiancé dead and Jagger waiting for her. Thinking she is just a patsy, Jagger sends her to a safe place. In the meantime, Landers and his moll show up. Jagger pretends he wants a cut of the necklace and is beaten to a pulp by the thug. Jagger hunts down the drunken Carradine to try to pull the case together but is interrupted by Landers, who beats him up again and kills Carradine. Jagger wakes up to find himself in the bedroom of Atwater, who says she wants to pay him to get the necklace back. In reality, Atwater and Paul are lovers and in cahoots to keep the necklace and collect the $350,000 insurance money. Jagger finds Landers and leads him to believe Paul has double-crossed him. Jagger returns to his place and finds his landlady beaten up and the necklace gone. Landers goes to Paul's apartment, pulls a gun, and tries to take all the money but is knifed by Paul. Jagger arrives and in a scuffle with Paul, Atwater accidentally shoots Paul. Atwater is arrested, and Elwen is allowed to stay in the country in Jagger's custody.

   C-Man is a low-budget example of the semidocumentary style pioneered by producer Louis de Rochemont, who cranked out the March of Time newsreel as a part of theater bills during the 1930s and 1940s. The style stressed realism through the use of location shooting as well as frequently overlaying narration of the story line in a newslike way. Although much inferior to some other noir documentary-style productions such as House on 92nd Street (1945), Walk a Crooked Mile (1948), and Walk East on Beacon (1952), C-Man captures some of the grit of New York streets and accomplishes some tense moments in spite of the fact that the story line is needlessly overcomplicated and has some significant holes. An odd but interesting musical score adds to the atmosphere. (V)

Calling Homicide (1956) Allied Artists. 61m. (B&W) P: Ben Schwalb. D: Edward Bernds. Sc: Bernds. Ph: Harry Neumann. Ed: William Austin. M: Marlin Skiles. CAST: Bill Elliott, Don Haggerty, Kathleen Case, Myron Healey, Jeanne Cooper, Thomas B. Henry, Lyle Talbot, Almira Sessions, James Best, John Dennis, Mel Wells, Jack Mulhall.   Lt. Doyle and Sgt. Duncan, two LA sheriff's detectives, investigate the bombing murder of a policeman. The trail leads to a modeling agency whose female owner is found strangled to death. While investigating, the detectives discover that the dead woman had been running a black market baby racket in conjunction with the agency. Suspicion points to Healey, who owns a construction company and used to date the dead woman when they both were in the movies. During the investigation, all the records of the baby racket are destroyed in an explosion, and Talbot, an executive at the agency, is murdered as he is about to identify the killer. The hunt narrows to Dennis, a handyman at the agency. As he tries to get away, he is shot by Elliott. Before he dies, he admits that he was hired by the agency owner to kill the policeman because the cop was getting too close to the truth and that he strangled her when she taunted him.

This movie is number two in a series of four Allied Artists films beginning with *Sudden Danger* in 1955 and featuring Bill Elliott as Lt. Doyle and Don Haggerty as Sgt. Duncan and produced by Ben Schwalb, who also produced many of the Bowery Boys films for Allied Artists during the 1950s. Before becoming a hard-hitting LA cop, "Wild" Bill Elliott was the hero of such memorable Monogram westerns as *Waco* and *Fargo* (no semblance to the Coen brothers modern noir classic). He played both a cop and a cowboy with the same monotonic, sleepwalking verve.

Cast a Dark Shadow (1955) Distributors Corporation of America. (Brit.) 84m. (B&W) P: Herbert Mason. D: Lewis Gilbert. Sc: John Cresswell, based on the play *Murder Mistaken* by Janet Green. Ph: Jack Asher. Ed: Gordon Pilkington. M: Anthony Hopkins. CAST: Dirk Bogarde, Margaret Lockwood, Kathleen Harrison, Kay Walsh, Robert Fleming, Lita Roza.   Bogarde is a scheming bluebeard who marries and kills his much older wife for her money. Although foul play is suspected by the deceased woman's attorney, the death is ruled accidental. But Bogarde has killed her too soon, and most of the inheritance goes to a younger sister. He meets another wealthy widow and marries her, thinking he'll bilk her for her dough, but finds she is a tough, street-smart woman and is not about to let her money go. She has married Bogarde, thinking he himself has money, when in reality all he has is the house he is living in. When another seemingly wealthy lady comes along, Bogarde strikes up a relationship with her and plans to dump his wife. When he finds that the woman is his dead wife's sister, who has shown up to prove him a murderer, Bogarde fixes the brakes on her car and confesses to his wife he's a killer. The sister is stopped by the attorney before she can hurt herself, and in an attempt to escape, Bogarde mistakenly takes the car with no brakes and winds up killing himself when the car goes over a cliff.

In this nicely put together little film, Bogarde turns in a fine performance as a sociopathic killer. (V)

Chain of Evidence (1957) Allied Artists. 62m. (B&W) P: Ben Schwalb. D: Paul Landres. Sc: Elwood Ullman. Ph: Harry Neumann. Ed: Neil Brunnenkent. M: Marlin Skiles. CAST: Bill Elliott, James Lydon, Don Haggerty, Claudia Barrett, Tina Carver, Ross Elliot, Meg Randall, Timothy Carey, John Bleifer, Dabbs Greer, Hugh Sanders.   Lydon is paroled from the honor farm and suffers a beating by old enemy Carey, resulting in amnesia. He makes friends with Sanders, who is later murdered by his wealthy, adulteress wife. The wife uses Lydon's amnesia to frame him for the murder, but the young man is cleared through the efforts of Lt. Doyle and Sgt. Duncan.

This film is another inconsequential entry in the Doyle-Duncan series.

Chicago Confidential (1957) United Artists. 75m. P: Robert E. Kent. D: Sidney Salkow. Sc: Raymond T. Marcus, based on the book by Jack Lait and Lee Mortimer. Ph: Kenneth Peach. Ed: Grant Whytock. M: Emil Newman. CAST: Brian Keith, Beverly Garland, Dick Foran, Douglas Kennedy, Beverly Tyler, Elisha Cook Jr., Paul Langton, Tony George, Gavin Gordon, Jack Lambert, John Morley, Benny Burt.   On his way to turn over evidence to state's attorney Keith that the Workers National Brotherhood union is being taken over by mobsters, the treasurer of the union is murdered by thugs working for the crooked union vice president, Kennedy. When drunken bum Cook finds the murder weapon and is coached by the bad guys to say he witnessed the honest president of the union, Foran, commit the murder, Foran is indicted. In court, a phony tape recording and perjury by an intimidated B-girl witness seal Foran's fate, and he is sentenced to die. At the constant nagging of Foran's fiancée, Garland, Keith begins to believe he prosecuted the wrong man. He and Garland try to unravel the puzzle, but all of the crucial witnesses, including Cook and the voice impersonator who made the phony tape, are murdered before they can get to them. As a final desperate effort to get rid of the two last remaining witnesses—the B-girl and Garland—Kennedy's men beat up Keith and take the two women to an airport, intending to drop them out of a plane. Keith and the cops arrive in time to stop them, and after a car chase, Kennedy and his hired killers are killed. The union is cleaned up, Foran is freed and reelected its president, and Keith goes on to national notoriety.

Based on the tabloid "confidential" true-crime book series popularized by Lait and Mortimer in the 1950s, *Chicago Confidential* manages to sustain a level of suspense and grittiness, mostly as a result of competent performances by all of its cast.

Come-On, The (1956) Allied Artists. 83m. (B&W) P: Lindsley Parsons. D: Russell Birdwell. Sc: Warren Douglas and Whitman Chambers, from the novel by Chambers. Ph: Ernest Haller. Ed: Maurice Wright. M: Paul Dunlap. CAST: Ann Baxter, Sterling Hayden, John Hoyt, Jesse White, Walter Cassell, Alex Gerry, Paul Picerni, Theodore Newton.   Baxter meets fisherman Hayden on a Mexican beach, and they are immediately drawn to each other. That night, she visits him on his boat and they arrange to meet the next night. In a nightclub later that evening, Baxter meets her drunk and abusive "husband," Hoyt, who is in the company of a rich American businessman. Hoyt slaps Baxter and is himself punched out by Hayden, who witnesses the event. The businessman, Baxter, and Hoyt return to Hoyt's yacht, where Hoyt pretends to pass out and Baxter accepts $2,000 from the businessman, agreeing to leave Hoyt and meet him in LA. Baxter meets Hayden and tells him that she's not really married but partners with Hoyt to run a blackmail operation; she baits the suckers, and Hoyt, playing the outraged husband, shakes them down. She tells Hayden she wants to quit the racket and go away with him, but Hoyt won't let her have her share of the money. Later, Baxter tells Hoyt, who has taken the businessman for $25,000, that she wants out and she wants her money, but he refuses in order to keep her under his control. Hoyt forces her to leave for California with him. Hayden sells his fishing boat and follows. Baxter and Hayden meet up again, and she talks him into helping her kill Hoyt by blowing up his yacht, knowing she is the beneficiary in Hoyt's will. Hoyt knows she has been seeing Hayden, and jealousy drives him to hire private investigator White to follow her. Hoyt tries to buy off Hayden with $10,000, but Hayden slaps him around and takes the money. White takes pictures of Baxter buying dynamite for the murder scheme, but Hayden changes his mind and tells Baxter they can be happy without the money. She apparently agrees, but the couple are questioned by the police when Hoyt's yacht is mysteriously blown to bits. White contacts them and shows them the incriminating pictures, for which he wants the $10,000 Sterling lifted from Hoyt. White tells them that he knows they didn't kill Hoyt, that Hoyt had accidentally killed himself in a scheme to make it appear that he had been murdered and frame Baxter and Hayden for the crime. Hayden gives White the money and they leave, but greedy Baxter returns and pulls a gun on White, demanding the $10,000. She shoots and kills White, but not before he manages to mail a letter incriminating her to the police. Baxter and Hayden flee the country and return to Mexico, where they met. Hoyt, who faked his own death, shows up and tells Baxter he will never let her go. She shoots him, mortally wounding him. Baxter and Hayden return to the beach where they met, and Hoyt finds them, killing Baxter before dying himself.

This well-done film has enough plot twists to keep viewers interested as well as good performances by all involved, particularly White as the smarmy PI Lindsley Parsons. Parsons had his own production company, producing low-budget films for Monogram and later Allied Artists, including the noirs *Fear* (1946), *Loophole* (1954), and *Cry Vengeance* (1954).

Crime Against Joe (1956). United Artists. 69m. (B&W) P. Howard W. Koch. D: Lee Sholem. Sc: Robert C. Dennis. Ph: William Margulies. Ed: Mike Pozen. M: Paul Dunlap. CAST: John Bromfield, Julie London, Henry Calvin, Patricia Blake, Joel Ashley, Robert Keyes, Alika Louis, John Pickard, Frances Morris, Rhodes Reason, Mauritz Hugo, Joyce Jameson.   Jameson, wild-eyed and hysterical, enters a police station and relates that a man just tried to kill her. Across town, Bromfield, an artist depressed about how his career is going, slashes the picture he is working on and goes out to get drunk. At a nightclub, he meets London and her boyfriend, Calvin. London is sympathetic to Bromfield's mood and takes a liking to him in spite of the fact that she is with Calvin. The singer at the nightclub also takes a shine to Bromfield, which is not appreciated by her boyfriend, the club bartender; he beats up Bromfield. When the singer is later found murdered, Bromfield finds himself arrested for the murder. The main clue is the 1945 high school graduation class pin (Bromfield's class) clutched in the dead woman's hand. After determining that several other people have lied about Bromfield to the cops, London gets him released by providing him with a phony alibi, and the two of them set out to find the killer. They go to a dance at Bromfield's old high school and find a yearbook revealing that Calvin was also a member of the class of '45 but was expelled because of an incident with a girl. Calvin, stalking the couple, finds out about their discovery and sets out to eliminate them, but Bromfield manages to lead Calvin away from London and into the arms of the police, who determine that Calvin not only killed the nightclub singer but also assaulted Jameson in the beginning of the movie.

This is a run-of-the-mill, innocent-man-tracking-down-the-actual-killer film.

Crime in the Streets (1956) Allied Artists. 91m. (B&W) P: Vincent M. Fennelly. D: Don Siegel. Sc: Reginald Rose, based on the television play by Rose. Ph: Sam

Levitt. Ed: Richard C. Meyer. M: Franz Waxman. CAST: James Whitmore, John Cassavetes, Sal Mineo, Mark Rydell, Denise Alexander, Malcolm Atterbury, Peter Votrian, Virginia Gregg, Ray Stricklyn, Daniel Terranova, Will Kuluva. Cassavetes's gang takes a prisoner from a rival gang after a rumble. They beat up and threaten to kill the hostage with a zip gun. Citizen Atterbury witnesses the crime and turns them in to the police. Whitmore is a social worker who won't give up on the "rotten apples." Cassavetes, who lives with his poor widowed mother and younger brother, who idolizes him as a tough guy, decides to kill Atterbury, but most of the gang draws the line at murder and backs out. Only psychotic Rydell and weak-sister Mineo go along with the scheme. They do a dry run on a bum but let him go. The trio finally corner Atterbury in an alley, and Cassavetes, egged on by psycho Rydell, beats him up. Cassavetes is unable to knife him to death, however, when he realizes his kid brother is going to witness the crime. In the end, he is taken by Whitmore to the cops to turn himself in.

This was Siegel's first outing after his smash sci-fi classic *Invasion of the Body Snatchers*. Cassavetes, Mineo, and Rydell (who later directed *On Golden Pond*) played their original parts from the television play that aired on the *Elgin Playhouse*; this was Cassavetes's first film role.

Criminal Court (1946) RKO. 63m. (B&W) P: Martin Mooney. D: Robert Wise. Sc: Lawrence Kimble, based on a story by Earl Felton. Ph: Frank Redman. Ed: Robert Swink. M: Paul Sawtell. CAST: Tom Conway, Martha O'Driscoll, June Clayworth, Robert Armstrong, Addison Richards, Pat Gleason, Steve Brodie, Robert Warwick.   A slick criminal attorney (Conway) who has political aspirations of being DA accidentally kills gangster-owner Armstrong, in whose nightclub Conway's fiancée is a singer. Conway has covered his tracks so that he has an airtight alibi for the time of the killing, but his unfortunate girlfriend finds the body and is arrested for the murder. Ironically, in defending the woman in court, Conway has to try to prove his own guilt and her innocence. Fortunately, an unknown witness to the crime—Conway's secretary, who was Armstrong's spy—breaks down on the witness stand and both Conway and his girl go free.

This film is a nifty little package, probably due in part to the fact that the producer, Mooney, was a former crime reporter. NOTE: Tom Conway, who is best remembered for taking over his brother George Sanders's role as the Falcon and who made more than $1 million in his film career, was discovered in 1965 living in a

$2-a-day Santa Monica flophouse. He died two years later of a liver ailment at the age of 63. (V)

Dangerous Intruder (1945) PRC. 65m. (B&W) P: Martin Mooney. D: Vernon Keays. Sc: Martin M. Goldsmith, based on a story by Philip MacDonald and F. Ruth Howard. Ph: James Brown. Ed: Carl Pierson. M. Karl Hajos. CAST: Charles Arnt, Veda Ann Borg, Richard Powers, Fay Helm, John Rogers, JoAnn Marlowe, Helena P. Evans, Roberta Smith.   While hitchhiking across the country, an unemployed actress (Borg) is hit by a car driven by Arnt. Arnt, a wealthy art dealer, takes her to his nearby estate to recuperate. When Arnt's wife is poisoned, Borg discovers that Arnt is a paranoiac and has also murdered his wealthy mother-in-law. When Arnt's assistant, Rogers, tells Borg about his own suspicions and that Arnt is planning to also kill his stepdaughter, Arnt overhears and kills him, too. Borg tries to get away, and the homicidal maniac is killed in a car wreck while trying to run her down.

Although an average story, the film manages to work up moments of mild suspense. Ironically, model and bit player Borg was in real life involved in a bad auto accident in 1939 and had to go through extensive plastic surgery to reconstruct her face. She resumed her career in the early forties and went on to play many more roles.

Date with Death (1959) Pacific International. 81m. (B&W) P: William S. Edwards. D: Harold Daniels. Sc: Robert C. Dennis. CAST: Gerald Mohr, Liz Renay, Harry Lauter, Robert Clarke, Stephanie Farnay, Ed Erwin, Red Morgan, Lew Markman, Tony Redman.   Mohr plays a hobo who falls off a train and stumbles upon the body of a dead New York city cop. He assumes the dead man's identity but soon finds by doing so he has also assumed the dead man's job, which is to rid a small desert community of a local crime ring headed by Clarke. He succeeds after a lot of death and destruction.

This movie was shot in "psychorama" (it should have been called "stinkorama"), a "revolutionary new process" through which "images are subliminally impressed on the brain." In the film's trailers, Mohr admits that the process is "controversial" and was "banned on television for being too powerful." Renay, whose movie career went belly up when her romantic relationship with LA gangster Mickey Cohen was publicized, fittingly plays a gangster's moll in the film. One of the all-time worst. (V)

Deadliest Sin, The (1956) Allied Artists. (Brit.) 77m. (B&W) P: Alec Snowden. D: Ken Hughes. Sc: Hughes, based on a play by Don Martin. Ph: Philip Grindrod. Ed: Geoffrey Muller. M: Richard Taylor. CAST: Sydney Chaplin, Audrey Dalton, John Bentley, Peter Hammond, John Welsh, Jefferson Clifford, Patrick Allen, Pat McGrath.   Chaplin is a thief who double-crosses his partner by stealing the proceeds of their holdup. The partner hunts him down but is killed by Hammond, Chaplin's future brother-in-law, to save Chaplin's life. Feeling guilty, Hammond goes to a priest to confess and is murdered by the ungrateful Chaplin, who then plans to kill the priest, thinking the cleric knows too much. The cops arrive in the knick of time and the sociopath meets his end in the church.

Decoy (1947) Monogram. 76m. (B&W) P: Jack Bernhard and Bernard Brandt. D: Jack Bernhard. Sc: Ned Young, from an unpublished story by Stanley Rubin. Ph: L. W. Connell. Ed: Jason Bernie. M: Edward J. Kay. CAST: Jean Gillie, Edward Norris, Herbert Rudley, Robert Armstrong, Sheldon Leonard, Marjorie Woodworth, Philip Van Zandt, John Shay.   Investigating reports of gunfire, police detective Leonard goes to the apartment of Gillie to find that Rudley, a doctor who worked for the prison system, is dead and Gillie is dying. Gillie, knowing she is a goner, relates her sordid past to Leonard, admitting she had been a partner of gangster Armstrong, who had pulled off a $400,000 robbery before being sentenced to the gas chamber for a cop killing. Since Armstrong was going to go to his death without telling the gang the whereabouts of the money, Gillie hatched a plan to snatch Armstrong's body immediately after his execution and revive him with the cooperation of Rudley. Armstrong is brought back to life and draws a map of the location of the money; he gives half to Gillie. When he goes to kiss his former sweetheart, however, Norris, the third member of the gang, shoots him and takes the other half of the map. The two gangsters kidnap Rudley in their search for the loot. On the way, Gillie fakes a flat tire; when Norris gets out to fix it, she runs him over repeatedly. Finding the burial spot, Gillie forces Rudley to dig up the money, but when she sees the treasure, she begins to laugh hysterically and shoots the doctor. Rudley has enough strength to make it back to Gillie's apartment, where he shoots her before dying himself. Gillie laughs in Leonard's face before dying and Leonard opens the treasure box to find a one-dollar bill and a note from Armstrong saying he left the dollar to his betrayers and the rest to the worms.

An unregenerate film noir, this Monogram cheapie contains a knockout, cold-hearted performance by British actress Gillie. The ultimate sadistic femme fatale, she seduces everybody in the film (including Leonard, after suckering him into listening to her tale, then laughing in his face at the end) and fully demonstrates her absence of humanity when she runs her car back and forth over her partner, Norris. Although *Decoy* is listed in many filmographies of film noir, I have included it here because it has been a "missing" film for many years, not even appearing in Leonard Maltin's comprehensive *Movie and Video Guide*. Fortunately, a restored 35-mm print was shown in March 2000 at the Second Annual Festival of Film Noir at the famous Egyptian Theatre in Los Angeles.

Destiny (1944) Universal. 65m. (B&W) P: Howard Benedict and Roy William Neill. D: Reginald Le Borg and Julian Duvivier. Sc: Roy Chanslor and Ernest Pascal. Ph: George Robinson and Paul Ivano. Ed: Paul Landres. M: Frank Skinner. CAST: Gloria Jean, Alan Curtis, Frank Craven, Grace McDonald, Vivian Austin, Frank Fenton, Minna Gombell, Selmer Jackson, Lew Wood.   On the lam and framed for a crime he didn't commit, Curtis takes refuge at an isolated farmhouse inhabited by Craven and Jean, his blind daughter. Intending at first to rob the pair, Curtis is instead reformed by Jean. In the end, Curtis is arrested and found innocent and returns to Jean at the farm.

The abundance of dual credits for producer, director, and screenplay is because this film was originally an episode of Duvivier's *Flesh and Fantasy* (1943), a prestige film of the supernatural comprising three distinct stories. The original opening story of the film was felt to be too downbeat and was cut and put on the shelf. Universal, not wanting to waste the footage, assigned Neill to create a new film by padding it with an extra 35 minutes of new celluloid. In the original sequence, Curtis was killed by the police, his body floating in a river, and the story was told in flashback. Although *Destiny* in spots attains a mystical, dreamlike quality, it is choppy and its hybridization is obvious. Its saving grace is the performance by teenager Jean, who was looked upon by Universal as a new threat to the studio reign of songstress Deanna Durbin; Jean's career never took off, however.

Escape (1948) Twentieth Century Fox. 79m. (B&W) P: William Perlberg. D: Joseph L. Mankiewicz. Sc: Philip Dunne, based on the novel by John Galsworthy. Ph: Frederick A. Young. Ed: Alan L. Jaggs. M: William Alwyn. CAST: Rex Harrison, Peggy Cummins, William Hartnell, Betty Ann Davies, Norman Wooland, Jill Esmond, Frederick Piper, Cyril Cusack, Marjorie Rhodes, John Slater.   Shot in Britain, Harrison is a former World War II fighter pilot who strikes up a conversation with a prostitute in Hyde Park. When a policeman shows up and starts treating the girl harshly, Harrison reacts and a scuffle ensues. The cop falls and is killed when he hits his head. Harrison is sent to prison for three years but escapes. He is taken in by Cummins, who tries to convince him to turn himself in, but he vows he'll never go back to jail again. Pursued, he takes refuge in a church but, knowing the pastor will have to lie to protect him, gives himself up to the cops. Cummins vows she will be waiting for him.

This is the only film noir, let alone B noir, that megastar of stage and screen Harrison ever made. This quite good film is an example of studios' occasional willingness to throw top-notch talent—in this case producer Perlberg, director Mankiewicz, and writer Dunne—at a B production when they had to fill the bottom half of a bill. This is a remake of a 1930 film adapted from the Galsworthy novel.

Escape in the Fog (1945) Columbia. 65m. (B&W) P: Wallace MacDonald. D: Oscar Boetticher, Jr. Sc: Aubrey Wisberg. Ph: George Meehan. Ed: Jerome Thoms. CAST: Nina Foch, William Wright, Otto Kruger, Konstantin Shayne, Ivan Triesault, Ernie Adams, Mary Newton, Ralph Dunn, John Tyrell, Charles Jordan. Navy nurse Foch is recuperating from shaken nerves at a San Francisco inn. One night, she dreams she is walking across a bridge and sees a car in which two men are trying to kill a third. She is awakened by her own screams. When she meets Wright, an officer in psychological warfare, she recognizes him as the would-be victim in her dream. She tries to warn him of his impending peril, but he is unconvinced and, in spite of her obsession, falls in love with her. In the meantime, he is given an assignment to carry a top secret message to American agents in the Philippines. One night, Foch is walking home and, crossing a bridge, witnesses the scene in her dream. Her screams save Wright's life, and remembering her dream, he throws the message off the bridge into the water. Foch and Wright are captured by the German agents who were trying to murder him and are put into a gas chamber, but before they can be killed, Wright smashes the glass in the chamber and the couple are rescued.

This minor programmer is notable only because of the fact that the director later changed his name to Budd Boetticher and went on to direct two other B noirs, *Behind Locked Doors* (1948) and *The Killer Is Loose* (1956), as well as a number of well-received 1950s westerns starring Randolph Scott.

Female Jungle (1956) American International. 73m. (B&W) P: Burt Kaiser. D: Bruno Ve Sota. Sc: Kaiser and Ve Sota, based on a story by Kaiser. Ph: Elwood Bredell. Ed: Carl Pingitore. M: Nicholas Carras. CAST: Kathleen Crowley, Lawrence Tierney, John Carradine, Jayne Mansfield, James Kodl, Rex Thorsen, Jack Hill, Bruce Carlisle, Connie Cezon, Jean Lewis, Robert Davis, Gordon Urquhart. Tierney is a police detective who suffers an alcoholic blackout while drinking in a bar outside which a well-known actress is murdered. In hot water with his superiors and not knowing if he himself is guilty, he sets out to solve the crime. Crowley is a waitress married to a depressive, alcoholic artist who does caricature sketches in the bar. John Carradine, a famous gossip columnist, shows up at Crowley's apartment late the night of the murder, allegedly to get his caricature done by her husband. While there, Crowley and her husband get into a beef, and he leaves. She, in turn, leaves with Carradine. During his investigation, Tierney finds that Carradine was with the actress earlier in the evening and that they fought: Carradine had been in love with the woman and had made her career, but she'd dumped him. Tierney also finds out he himself was with Mansfield earlier in the evening. Mansfield, it turns out, is a regular slut and is carrying on a torrid affair with Crowley's husband. Mansfield tries to get him to divorce Crowley, but the artist, who is the real killer, goes crazy and kills her. The police shoot the artist down as he tries to escape, and Carradine reveals that the dead actress had been in love with the artist and that the artist had been blackmailing her. Why the artist killed the actress, and why a big-time actress would fall for such a loser, are left unexplained.

This film, although shoddily written, produced, and directed, is significant for several reasons. It was American International's only foray into film noir, although aside from its staples of sci-fi, horror, and teenage exploitation movies, the low-budget studio did produce such gangster period pieces as *Machine Gun Kelly* (1958). The film also marked a return to the screen of noir icon Lawrence Tierney, whose off-screen bar brawls and numerous arrests during the 1940s had made him persona non grata in Hollywood. In the early days of American International, studio head Sam Arkoff cast many once-famous actors, including Tom Conway, Chester Morris, and Kent Taylor, in an effort to milk them for whatever discount star power they still had. Their comebacks were usually short-lived, as was Tierney's, at least for some years. After *Female Jungle*, the actor couldn't buy a role, and he wound up driving a hansom cab in Central Park in New York. He was cast in some minor roles in low-budget films in the 1970s, then was hired by John Huston to play a crooked cop in *Prizzi's Honor* in 1986. His return to noir occurred a year later when Norman Mailer cast him in a meaty part in his *Tough Guys Don't Dance*. Tierney's growling, tough-guy persona was subsequently reresurrected by neonoir producer-director-writer Quentin Tarantino in *Reservoir Dogs* (1992). As well as marking a temporary return to the screen for Tierney, *Female Jungle* introduced a new actress to moviegoing audiences, blond bombshell Jayne Mansfield, who would go on to sex goddess status before her career went on the wane; her life ended tragically in an automobile accident in 1967. (V)

Finger Man (1955) Allied Artists. 81m. (B&W) P: Lindsley Parsons. D: Harold Schuster. Sc: Warren Douglas, based on a story by Morris Lipsius and John Lardner. Ph: William Sickner. Ed: Maurice Wright. M: Paul Dunlap. CAST: Frank Lovejoy, Forrest Tucker, Peggie Castle, Timothy Carey, John Cliff, William Leicester, Glenn Gordon, John Close, Hugh Sanders, Evelynne Eaton.   Ex-convict Lovejoy is caught by the feds heisting a truck shipment; to keep from going back to the slams, he works undercover to nail syndicate head Tucker. Lovejoy's ex-girlfriend and gangster's moll Castle throws in with Lovejoy and gets murdered by Tucker's henchman, Carey. In the end, after nearly being killed himself, Lovejoy brings down Tucker's gang and is allowed to go on his way.

Lovejoy, who played in other noir films such as *Try and Get Me*, *The Hitch-Hiker*, and *I Was a Communist for the F.B.I.* turns in his usual steady, low-key performance. Carey, playing—as usual—a psychotic killer, is as convincingly weird in this film as he was in every other film he ever played, leading one to wonder what he was like in real life. (V)

Footsteps in the Night (1957) Allied Artists. 62m. (B&W) P: Ben Schwalb. D: Jean Yarbrough. Sc: Albert Band and Elwood Ullman, based on a story by Band.

Ph: Harry Neumann. Ed: Neil Brunnenkant. M: Marlin Skiles. CAST: Bill Elliott, Don Haggerty, Eleanore Tanin, Douglas Dick, James Flavin, Gregg Palmer, Robert Shayne, Harry Tyler.   During an argumentative poker game, the winning player steps into the kitchen of his apartment to get a drink and returns to find the loser strangled to death. He is arrested for the crime, but once again, the team of "Wild" Bill Elliott and Don Haggerty (Lt. Doyle and Sgt. Duncan) uncover the real culprit, gas station attendant Palmer, who intended to rob and kill another man but got the wrong apartment.

Most of this entry in the Lt. Doyle-Sgt. Duncan series was shot in producer Schwalb's studio bungalow to save money, and it shows. (V)

For You I Die (1947) Film Classics. 76m. (B&W) P: Robert Presnell and John Reinhardt. D: Reinhardt. Sc: Presnell. Ph: William Clothier. Ed: Jason Bernie. M: Paul Sawtell. CAST: Cathy Downs, Paul Langton, Mischa Auer, Roman Bohnen, Jane Weeks, Marion Kirby, Manella Callejo, Don Harvey, Charles Waldron Jr. Convict Harvey forces inmate Langton, who is trying to go straight, into a prison break. After they escape, the two separate and Langton hides out in a roadside café, where Harvey's girlfriend, Downs, works as a waitress. The two fall in love, and when Harvey shows up, there is a showdown during which the cook, Bohner, gets killed and Langton gets beaten up. Harvey flees, but the cops catch up with him. Langton turns himself in to finish out his time and Downs tells him she will wait for him.

This film with soap opera elements inserted into a noir setting is a combination of low-key, straight performances by Langton and Downs and over-the-top portrayals by Bohnen and Auer, who was apparently inserted for comic relief.

Four Boys and a Gun (1957) United Artists. 74m. (B&W) P&D: William Berke. Sc: Philip Yordan and Leo Townsend, based on a novel by Willard Wiener. Ph: J. Burgi Contner. Ed: Everett Sutherland, Marie Montagne. M: Stanley Rubin. CAST: Frank Sutton, Larry Green, William Hinant, James Franciscus, Otto Hullett, Robert Dryden, J. Pat O'Malley, Diana Herbert, Patricia Sloan.   During an attempted holdup of the box office of a boxing arena, a cop is shot to death. The investigation leads to the arrest of four youths, who are told that the one who did the shooting will probably get the chair and the rest will get lighter sentences, so they'd better turn over the one who pulled the trigger. Flashbacks by all the boys show how they got sucked into the mess and reveal that Sutton did the shooting. They decide to draw straws to see who will take the rap, and one of the accessories comes up unlucky. In the end, they decide they are all equally guilty and tell the cops they all did it, leaving the possibility they'll all be executed.

This depressing story is competently written by noir veteran Yordan (*The Big Combo*, *The Harder They Fall*, *Detective Story*, and many more).

Fugitive Lady (1951) Republic. 78m. (B&W) P: M. J. Frankovich. D: Sidney Salkow. Sc: John O'Dea, based on the novel by Doris Miles Disney. Ph: Tonino Delli Colli. Ed: Nino Baragli. M: Willy Ferrero. CAST: Janis Paige, Binnie Barnes, Massimo Serato, Eduardo Ciannelli, Tony Centa, Alba Arnova, Dino Galvani. Filmed in Italy, this told-through-flashbacks film has an insurance investigator looking into the death of Ciannelli, who drove his car off a cliff. Those with motives for murder are Paige, Ciannelli's greedy and adulterous widow, and Barnes, Ciannelli's stepsister, who loved Ciannelli and was resentful of the marriage. The truth comes out: Paige got Ciannelli drunk, sent him out for more liquor, and changed the roadsigns so he would drive off the cliff. As a final twist, Paige, in running from the police, drives off the same cliff and dies.

Gambler and the Lady, The (1952) Hammer/Lippert. (Brit.) 71m. (B&W) P: Anthony Hinds. D: Pat Jenkins. Ph: Walter Harvey. Ed: Maurice Roots. M: Ivor Slaney. CAST: Dane Clark, Kathleen Byron, Naomi Chance, Meredith Edwards, Anthony Forwood, Eric Pohlmann, Enzo Coticchia, Julian Somers, Anthony Ireland, Thomas Gallagher. Clark, a recovering alcoholic and compulsive gambler, arrives in London after his release from an American prison for manslaughter. Through his gambling, he finds himself the owner of a nightclub and a racehorse and starts to date a dancer at the club. He soon gets social-climbing ambitions and dumps the dancer for the daughter of an English Lord. Clark's social climbing also alienates his relationship with his club manager, Edwards. Clark's good luck turns bad when gangsters move in on his club operation and he is swindled in a stock deal by the "respectable" English lord. When the gangsters murder his former friend Edwards, Clark vows revenge. In a shootout, he is wounded and, staggering into the street, is run down by a car driven by his jilted dancer-lover.

This was the first of three noirs Hammer produced starring Clark. The film was originally slated for American Poverty Row director Sam Newfield, but Newfield had just completed *Lady in the Fog* for Hammer, and his employment would have violated British labor quotas on the number of foreign directors allowed to direct British films in any one year.

Gangbusters (1955) Visual Drama. 75m. (B&W) P: William J. Faris and William Clothier. D: Bill Karn. Sc: Phillips H. Lord. Ph: Clothier. Ed: Faris. M: Richard Aurandt. CAST: Myron Healey, Don C. Harvey, Sam Edwards, Frank Gerstle, Frank Richards, Kate MacKenna.   The film follows the repeated prison escapes of master criminal Healey and his destructive effects on the criminals who surround him. During one particularly nasty sequence, a wounded Healey has his criminal cohort bury him alive to keep from getting caught by the cops. Healey manages to dig his way out and survive, however. The cold-blooded Healey is so admired by one young con that the kid ends up murdering a helpless old man just to impress his idol. Healey, of course, could care less, and when the kid is executed at the end of the film, all Healey has to say is, "Some punks never learn."

This ultracheapie, adapted from the radio show of the same name, was filmed documentary-style with a lot of voice-overs, probably to avoid the expense of sound equipment. According to *Johnny Legend's Untamed Videos*, this film had a major impact on Martin Scorsese and inspired some key scenes in *Taxi Driver*. I can't think of any scenes in that or any Scorsese film that remotely resemble this low-budget zero. (V)

Girl on the Bridge (1951) Twentieth Century Fox. 76m. (B&W) P&D: Hugo Haas. Sc: Haas and Arnold Phillips. Ph: Paul Ivano. Ed: Merrill White and Albert Shaff. M: Harold Byrns. CAST: Hugo Haas, Beverly Michaels, Robert Dane, Tony Jochim, Johnny Close, Darr Smith, Judy Clark, Maria Bibikoff, Al Hill, Richard Pinner.   Kindly watchmaker Haas, whose family was killed by the Nazis, saves unwed mother Michaels from committing suicide by throwing herself off a bridge. He convinces the sexy bombshell to marry him, but things go awry when Michaels's ex-lover's cousin shows up and threatens to expose Michaels's misdeeds unless Haas pays him off. Haas kills the man and puts the blame on the ex-lover but, in a fit of remorse, kills himself by throwing himself off the same bridge. His suicide belatedly puts the audience out of its misery.

Glass Alibi, The (1946) Republic. 68m. (B&W) P&D: W. Lee Wilder. Sc: Mindret Lord. Ph: Henry Sharp. Ed: John F. Link. M: Alexander Laszlo. CAST: Paul

Kelly, Douglas Fowley, Anne Gwynne, Maris Wrixon, Jack Conrad, Selmer Jackson, Cy Kendall, Cyril Thornton, Walter Sonderling.   Fowley, a scheming reporter, marries rich socialite Wrixon, who he believes is dying of a heart condition. When she not only doesn't die but gets better, Fowley and his girlfriend, Gwynne, plot Wrixon's demise by other means. Fowley shoots Wrixon, not knowing she has already died of a heart attack. Kelly nails him for the crime even though he knows the true nature of Wrixon's death, and Fowley is convicted.

B movie producer-director W. Lee Wilder was the elder brother of Billy Wilder and was forced to use the first initial and middle name to prevent confusion. Wilder remade *The Glass Alibi* in 1955 as *The Big Bluff*. He did it much better the first time, with a better cast and better direction.

Great Flamarion, The (1945) Republic. 78m. (B&W) P: William Wilder. D: Anthony Mann. Sc: Anne Wighton, Heinz Harold, Ricard Weill, from the story "Big Shot" by Vicki Baum. Ph: James Brown. Ed: John F. Link. M: Alexander Laszlo. CAST: Erich von Stroheim, Mary Beth Hughes, Dan Duryea, Stephen Barclay, Lester Allen, Esther Howard, Michael Mark, Joseph Granby.   Von Stroheim is a misogynistic vaudeville sharpshooter who falls under the romantic spell of his assistant, Hughes. She is married to Duryea, a drunk who also works for the sharpshooter. Hughes is carrying on an affair with another vaudevillian who has a bicycle act and talks Von Stroheim into shooting the drunken Duryea during his act so that she and Von Stroheim can be together. When the death is ruled accidental, Von Stroheim finds that he has been ditched by Hughes. His life spirals downward and he eventually finds that Hughes and the bicyclist now have an act together. Von Stroheim confronts her, and she tells him she's always hated him and merely used him to get rid of Duryea. She mortally shoots Von Stroheim, but not before he strangles her to death.

Von Stroheim, who achieved fame in the 1920s as the director of such classics as *Greed* and *The Merry Widow*, also achieved infamy for being difficult to work with, a sexual decadent, and, more important to the studios, extravagant with his productions. After he had overshot miles of film and wasted millions of dollars at MGM, Universal, and Paramount, word got around town that his name was really spelled $troheim. Also, the Hays Office was not too pleased with the rumors of massive twenty-hour orgies on some of his "closed set" shoots. After finding himself blacklisted as a director, he returned to Europe, proclaiming, "Hollywood killed me." When he returned to the States in the 1940s, he found he could get parts only with Poverty Row studios, which were willing to cash in on his name and screen presence. Von Stroheim manages to resist overacting in this nicely done melodrama. Ironically, his most triumphant role was a caricature of himself, a once-great silent-movie director reduced to working as a servant and chauffeur for a whacko reclusive silent-movie star (Gloria Swanson) in the 1950 noir classic *Sunset Boulevard*. (V)

Heat Wave (1954) Hammer/Lippert. (Brit.) 69m. (B&W) AKA: *The House Across the Lake*. P: Anthony Hinds. D: Ken Hughes. Sc: Hughes, based on his novel *High Wray*. Ph: Jimmy Harvey. M: Ivor Slaney. CAST: Alex Nicol, Hillary Brooke, Paul Carpenter, Sidney James, Susan Stephen, Paul Carpenter, Alan Wheatley, Cleo Rose, Peter Illing.   Nicol, an American writer living in England, is seduced by femme fatale Brooke, who manages to get him enmeshed in a plot to murder her rich husband and make it look like an accidental drowning. After the couple are cleared by an inquest, they part for appearance's sake. When Nicol doesn't hear from Brooke for some time, he goes to visit her and finds she has moved. He eventually hunts her down and discovers she has remarried. When Brooke coldly informs him she has always loved her current husband and used Nicol to do her bidding, he tells her he is going to the cops to confess, leaving her screaming.

This not-very-original film is nevertheless well done; Brooke puts in a convincing performance as the cold-hearted bitch. Writer-director Ken Hughes said in a later interview that when he wrote his novel *High Wray*, he tried to emulate the style of his favorite author, Raymond Chandler. (V)

Hell Bound (1957) United Artists. 69m. (B&W) P: Howard W. Koch. D: William J. Hole Jr. Sc: Richard Landau, based on a story by Landau and Arthur Orloff. Ph: Carl E. Guthrie. Ed: John A. Bushelman. M: Les Baxter. CAST: John Russell, June Blair, Stuart Whitman, Margo Woode, George Mather, Stanley Adams, Frank Fenton, Gene O'Donnell, Virginia De Lee, Dehl Berti.   Russell is a criminal mastermind who cooks up a plot to steal a $2 million shipment of surplus war narcotics from a ship in LA harbor. After securing underworld financing, he recruits inside men to help with the job, including the ship's health officer and the purser. Russell's girlfriend, Blair, poses as a nurse and is to arrange for the ambulance in which she is riding to take the stuff away; after she's on the job, however, she goes soft and falls for Whitman, the unsuspecting intern who drives the ambulance. When she tells Russell she wants out, he stabs her and leaves her for dead. The robbery goes awry, and Russell, fleeing the police, gets killed when he hides in a railroad car and a ton of scrap metal falls on him. Blair recovers from her stab wounds and is reunited with Whitman.

Either the writer or the director went out of his way to fill this movie with bizarre characters, such as a blind man who likes to "watch" strip shows and a ship's health officer who has diabetes. Cheap production and flat direction make this a very weak caper flick.

High Tide (1947) Monogram. 70m. (B&W) P: Jack Wrather. D: John Reinhardt. Sc: Richard Presnell and Peter Milne, based on the story "Inside Job" by Raoul Whitfield. Ph: Henry Sharp. Ed: Stewart S. Frye and William Ziegler. M: Rudy Schrager. CAST: Lee Tracy, Don Castle, Julie Bishop, Anabel Shaw, Regis Toomey, Douglas Walton, Francis Ford, Anthony Warde.   A car careens around a corner in Malibu and goes off an embankment, trapping the two occupants, newspaper editor Tracy and reporter-turned-PI Castle. Knowing he is dying, Tracy divulges in flashback to Castle how his former boss at the paper, Walton, was murdered. At the time, it was believed the man had been bumped off by gangster Warde, whom Tracy had been trashing in the paper. Tracy hires Castle as a bodyguard to protect him from Warde, allegedly having received some death threats from the gangster. Things become complicated when Walton's alcoholic widow, who used to be Castle's girlfriend, tries to renew the relationship. Suspects abound as cop Toomey tries to sort out the clues, but Castle's suspicions settle on Tracy, who admits that he killed Walton to get control of the paper and hired Castle as a ruse. Castle manages to free himself from entanglements as the incoming tide washes over Tracy.

Raoul Whitfield, who wrote the story on which the screenplay was based, was one of the original pantheon of writers who regularly contributed to *Black Mask*. This Monogram entry is not bad. The professional Tracy breezes through his role.

Highway Dragnet (1954) Allied Artists. 71m. (B&W) P: Jack Jungmeyer Jr. D: Nathan Juran. Sc: Herb Meadow and Jerome Odlum, from a story by U.S. Anderson and Roger Corman. Ph: John Martin. Ed: Ace Herman. M: Edward J. Kay. CAST: Richard Conte, Joan Bennett, Wanda Hendrix, Reed Hadley, Mary Beth Hughes, Iris Adrian, Harry Harvey, Tom Hubbard, Frank Jenks, Murray Alper, Zon

Murray.   Conte, a Marine just discharged from a stint in Korea, is in Vegas, where
he picks up a drunken blond in a bar. The next day while hitchhiking, he is arrested by the police for the woman's murder. He escapes from custody and ends up
getting a ride from professional photographer Bennett and her model, Hendrix.
When Bennett and Hendrix hear some motorcycle cops talking about the fugitive
"strap killer" (the victim was strangled with a strap), they get nervous and try un-
successfully to ditch Conte. Hendrix wants to notify the police, but she is stopped
by Bennett, who reminds her that the dead woman was having an affair with Bennett's husband, who later killed himself. Bennett is afraid she herself will be a police suspect. Conte, pursued by the police, steals another car. With the two women
hostage, he makes his way across the desert in a desperate attempt to rendezvous
with a Marine buddy who can provide him with an alibi for the night of the
killing. They end up at the Salton Sea only to find that Conte's friend left the day
before. Cop Hadley catches up to Conte, and Hendrix is about to reveal the truth
of Bennett's husband when Bennett grabs Conte's service automatic and shoots
Hadley. She tries to get away, but when she gets stuck in quicksand, she confesses
to having killed the blond with a dog leash. The police, overhearing the confession, let Conte and Hendrix go.

   Photographed in bright desert daylight, *Highway Dragnet* is a good example of
the flat, fifties style of noir that relied less on visual tone and more on story line to
get its message across. The Salton Sea is a good choice for the ending sequence.
With its deserted, flooded-out houses, it provides a particularly bleak, surreal setting that rivals for stark emptiness the dark, shadowy urban settings of earlier films
noirs.

Hit and Run (1957) United Artists. 85m. (B&W) P,D,&Sc: Hugo Haas, based on
a story by Herbert Q. Phillips. Ph: Walter Strenge. Ed: Stefan Arnsten. M: Frank
Steininger. CAST: Cleo Moore, Hugo Haas, Vince Edwards, Dolores Reed, Mari
Lea, Pat Goldin, Carl Militaire, Robert Cassidy, John Zaremba.   Haas delivers yet
another stinko performance. This time, he's a rich old man who owns a gas station–wrecking yard and marries the young and voluptuous Moore. (Moore was
Haas's favorite star, probably because her acting talents equaled his own; they
made seven movies together.) Moore falls for Haas's younger and more virile employee, Edwards, and together they hatch a scheme to kill the old man in a hit-
and-run accident. The estate ends up going to Haas's twin brother, an ex-con, and

in an ending from O. Henry, it is revealed that the murdered man was really the ex-con and the surviving twin is Moore's real husband. Haas, of course, had to play the parts of both twins, doubling the pain for the audience.

Hollywood Story (1951) Universal. 76m. (B&W) P: Leonard Guthrie. D: William Castle. Sc: Frederick Kohner and Fred Brady. Ph: Carl Guthrie. Ed: Virgil Vogel. M: Joseph Gershenson. CAST: Richard Conte, Julia Adams, Richard Egan, Henry Hull, Fred Clark, Jim Backus, Houseley Stevenson, Paul Cavanagh, Katherin Meskill, Louis Lettieri, Francis X. Bushman, Helen Gibson, Joel McCrea.   Conte is a stage director who comes to Hollywood to try his hand at pictures. Backus, his agent, has rented a studio for him and Conte becomes obsessed with a bungalow on the lot where the unsolved murder of a silent movie director took place twenty years earlier. He decides to write a screenplay about it and begins interviewing the dead director's contemporaries, many of whom try to discourage him from delving into the matter. A series of events force Conte to try to solve the murder and find the killer. Prime suspects are bit player Cavanagh, the director's partner, Clark, and Hull, the director's screenwriter. In the end, the culprit turns out to be Hull, who was in reality the brother of the dead man. He had been jealous of his brother's fame and resentful of the fact that the director had stolen Hull's work and put his own name on it.

 Hollywood Story was an apparent attempt by Universal to cash in on the success of Paramount's *Sunset Boulevard*, released a year before. Loosely based on the un-solved murder of silent movie director William Desmond Taylor, the film would have been more interesting if it had stuck to the facts of the real case.

 On February 2, 1922, Taylor, chief director of Paramount subsidiary Famous Players–Lasky, was shot to death in his bungalow court apartment in LA's Westlake district. A witness saw a man, or a woman dressed in man's clothes, leaving the scene. The fifty-year-old Taylor, besides being quite a lothario, had liberally used cocaine and alcohol (in 1922 Prohibition was in effect), and when police arrived at his apartment the next morning after being notified of the murder by Taylor's manservant, they found Paramount head Adolph Zukor burning in the fireplace the love letters to Taylor from Paramount stars. Other studio execs had rushed to the site and cleaned up evidence of Taylor's substance abuse. The Paramount brass did not have time to get rid of all the evidence, however, and it soon came out that Taylor had been carrying on sexual affairs with Paramount superstar Mabel Normand; Paramount's answer to Mary Pickford, twenty-year-old Mary Miles Minter; and Minter's mother, Charlotte Selby. Both Minter and Normand had visited Taylor on the night of the murder. To compound the scandal and mystery, it was discovered that Taylor was really William Deane-Tanner, who had changed his identity and left a wife and child in New York in 1908; also, Taylor's butler (who disappeared and was never seen again) was in reality Deane-Tanner's younger brother. As details of the case came out, Hollywood was rocked to its moral foundations. The screen virgin Minter's career was ruined, and she spent the rest of her life as an eccentric recluse. Normand, who, it was discovered, had a big cocaine habit, also retired from the screen. The self-righteous clamor from church and antivice groups following the revelations was a primary force leading to the formation of the Hays Office and the implementation of the Production Code.

Upon the release of *Hollywood Story*, Universal promoted the appearance of several formerly famous silent screen stars in the film. Francis X. Bushman and Helen Gibson, who had speaking parts, received $55 a day for their roles in the film. Others, such as Elmo Lincoln, the first screen Tarzan, were used as extras and did not talk. At the time, Lincoln complained bitterly to the press about being exploited, saying that the studio paid him $15 for one day's work and got $15,000 worth of free publicity out of it. Said Lincoln: "Every time they want to spoloit something like *Hollywood Story* they call on us. . . . The motion picture business is the most unappreciative, selfish business in America today."

Hoodlum, The (1951) United Artists. 61m. (B&W) P: Maurice Kosloff. D: Max Nosseck. Sc: Sam Neuman and Nat Tanchuck. Ph: Clark Ramsey. Ed: Jack Killifer. M: Darrell Calker. CAST: Lawrence Tierney, Allene Roberts, Marjorie Riordan, Lisa Golm, Edward Tierney, Stuart Randall, Ann Zika, John De Simone, Tom Hubbard.   Hard-case Tierney, in jail for an armed robbery, is paroled into his mother's custody. He starts to work at his brother's gas station (Tierney's real-life younger brother) but immediately gathers a gang together and plans an armored car robbery. To get information from the bank, he starts to date a secretary who works there. At the same time he seduces Roberts, his brother's longtime fiancée. When Roberts tells Tierney she wants to break up with his brother and marry him, he rebuffs her and she commits suicide by throwing herself off the roof. When an autopsy reveals the girl had been pregnant, Tierney's mother realizes who did the deed. Tierney's brother catches on to the armored car robbery scheme and tries to stop Tierney, who knocks him out. During the robbery, two guards are killed, and the gang gets away with the money. Tierney is double-crossed by the rest of the gang, who KO him and abscond with the loot. Desperate and hiding from the cops, Tierney goes to the bank secretary and threatens to tell the cops she was in on it unless she hides him out, but she refuses. He goes to his mother, who also turns him away, telling him he's rotten before she dies. Tierney's brother, knowing the truth about his fiancée, enters the house and at gunpoint takes Tierney to the dump, where he intends to kill him. He can't bring himself to do it, but the cops show up and take care of the job, shooting Tierney down on the heap of garbage he always complained about the smell of.

The Hoodlum is considered by some to be not noir but simply a gangster film. Some elements do, however, clearly put it in the noir category—Tierney's sociopathy, his isolation resulting from his willingness to betray everyone, including his own brother, and the underlying tone of sexual perversity. The difference between the old-style Cagney-Bogart-Robinson gangster films and the noir gangster film is pivotally summed up in the beginning of *The Hoodlum* when one of the parole board, vehemently protesting Tierney's release, intones that Tierney's type is "not like the old style gangsters anymore. These people are committing crimes against *people.*" Cheaply made in the extreme, *The Hoodlum* suffers from poor production values. Tierney's role was probably the only kind he could get at the time, as his career was in serious decline. His performance, however, was appropriately menacing, and he apparently still had enough clout to manage the introduction of his brother as an actor, whose career for all intents and purposes began and ended with this film. (V)

Houston Story, The (1956) Columbia. 79m. (B&W) P: Sam Katzman. D: William Castle. Sc: James B. Gordon, based on a story by him. Ph: Henry Freulich. Ed: Edwin Bryant. M: Mischa Bakaleinikoff. CAST: Gene Barry, Barbara Hale, Edward Arnold, Paul Richards, Jeanne Cooper, Frank Jenks, John Zaremba, Chris Alcaide, Jack V. Littlefield, Paul Levitt.   Barry is an oil driller who has come up with a scheme for stealing millions of dollars worth of oil from the oil fields. Hale is a nightclub singer whose husband, a friend of Barry's, was recently killed in an accident. Barry knows that the nightclub where she works is owned by the mob and that her connections will enable him to get to the local syndicate boss, Arnold, to acquire financing for his scheme. Barry sets up a dummy corporation as a front and puts his unwitting longtime friend, Jenks, in charge. In the meantime, Barry has thrown over his loving waitress girlfriend for the treacherous but sexy Hale. As Barry moves up in the organization, he kills one of his rivals in the gang and sets up the nightclub owner and Arnold so that they are killed by the police. Zaremba, the head of the syndicate, thinking Barry is getting too ambitious, sends two gunmen to kill him. Barry learns about it and goes back to his old waitress flame and talks her into going to his apartment to get his clothes so he can go on the lam. In an effort to find Barry, the two thugs beat up Jenks, then pick up Hale. After she tells them Barry is waiting for her at a café, they kill her. The waitress calls the cops, who arrive at the café, but not before a shootout during which the two thugs are killed and Barry is wounded. At the urging of his old flame and Jenks, Barry gives himself up.

Similar to Katzman's *Miami Expose* (1956) and *The Miami Story* (1954), *The Houston Story* is the only film of the three that qualifies as a true noir. Barry is believable as an amoral climber, and although there are some holes in the script, the film is not a bad little programmer. Producer Katzman first carved out a niche in the early forties at Monogram, where he had under contract Bela Lugosi and the East Side Kids (later the Bowery Boys). He later moved to Columbia, where in the 1950s he produced a lot of low-budget fare including the *Jungle Jim* series. Probably his finest works were two science-fiction–horror films, *The Werewolf* and *Earth vs. the Flying Saucers* (1956). The latter was the inspiration for director Tim Burton's 1996 satire of fifties sci-fi flicks *Mars Attacks!* (1996). (V)

Hunted, The (1948) Allied Artists. 88m. (B&W) P: Scott R. Dunlap. D: Jack Bernhard. Sc: Steve Fisher. Ph: Harry Neumann. Ed: Richard Heermance. M: Edward J. Kay. CAST: Preston Foster, Belita, Pierre Watkin, Edna Holland, Russell Hicks, Frank Ferguson, Joseph Crehan, Larry Blake, Cathy Carter, Charles McGraw, Tristram Coffin, Paul Guilfoyle.   Belita gets out of prison on parole, having been sent up by her police detective boyfriend, Foster, for a jewel robbery. She claimed she had been framed, but the evidence was too overwhelming for Foster to ignore. She returns to Foster after her release and toys with his emotions. He is torn, not knowing whether to believe in her innocence, and his emotions are complicated by the fact that she threatened to kill him. In the end, he can't keep away and forces himself to believe her even though her own attorney, Watkin, claims she was guilty. Foster wangles her a job in an ice-skating show, and she is a sensation. When Watkin is murdered, the finger of guilt once more points at Belita, and she bolts. Foster catches up with her and is about to arrest her, but she shoots him. In the hospital, Foster decides in spite of it all to help her and resigns from the force. At the same time, thief Guilfoyle is arrested for killing a stoolie and confesses to the murder of Watkin, who had been the brain behind the gang of jewel thieves and who had framed Belita. Guilfoyle had murdered the man after being double-crossed. In the end, Foster and Belita finally get their honeymoon.

This was the second noir released under the Allied Artists banner to differentiate Monogram's cheap from upscale product, the first being *The Gangster* (1947), a far superior picture. Belita, an ice-skater Monogram hoped would be its answer to Sonja Henie, accomplished stardom only in a handful of Monogram films. Hardboiled writer Steve Fisher was responsible for the screenplay for *The Hunted*, surprising considering the implausibility of the story and everybody's sappy willingness to forgive and forget.

I Love Trouble (1947) Columbia. 93m. (B&W) P&D: Sylvan Simon. Sc: Roy Huggins, based on his novel *The Double Take*. Ph: Charles Lawton Jr. Ed: Al Clark. CAST: Franchot Tone, Janet Blair, Janis Carter, Adele Jergens, Glenda Farrell, Steven Geray, Tom Powers, Lynn Merrick, John Ireland, Donald Curtis, Eduardo Ciannelli, Raymond Burr, Eddie Marr, Arthur Space.   Private detective Tone is hired by politician Powers to check into the background of his wife, who is missing. In his search, Tone finds out that the wife's background is not as savory as portrayed by her husband. It seems she used to be a honkytonk dancer in a nightclub, and when Tone tries to dig deeper, the nightclub owner has him worked over. The missing woman turns up murdered, and Tone is framed for the crime but manages to escape the clutches of the police. He eventually discovers that Powers's wife is still alive and has assumed the identity of an old friend (the murdered woman) in an effort to disappear. Tone proves that Powers's wife, before changing identities the first time, stole $40,000 from the nightclub owner at the behest of Powers. Tone takes some vicious beatings before catching up with her.

Sort of a mixture of *Farewell, My Lovely* and *The Lady in the Lake,* the overly convoluted plot is handled adeptly and creates a lot of suspense.

I Wouldn't Be in Your Shoes (1948) Monogram. 70m (B&W) P: Walter Mirisch. D: William Nigh. Sc: Steve Fisher, from the novel by Cornell Woolrich. Ph: Mack

Stengler. Ed: Roy Livingston. M: Edward J. Kay. CAST: Don Castle, Elyse Knox, Regis Toomey, Charles D. Brown, Rory Mallinson, Robert Lowell, Bill Kennedy. Castle and Knox are a husband-and-wife dance team hard up for work. Unexpectedly, they inherit some money, and Castle throws away his dance shoes in light of the windfall. The shoes, which are custom-made, turn up as clues in a murder, and Castle is tried and convicted for the crime. Knox hires detective Toomey to help her clear Castle. After the pair uncover a series of clues and in an O. Henry twist, Toomey turns out to be the killer.

  I Wouldn't Be in Your Shoes is typical Monogram product, saved in great part by the low-key performance of seasoned veteran Toomey. It is notable for several reasons, however. Like *Decoy*, it has been totally lost to the general public, presumably (one hopes) remaining stored away in the studio vaults. The screenplay was by hard-boiled writer Steve Fisher, from a novel by Monogram favorite and "King of Noir" Cornell Woolrich. Finally, it was the only noir produced by Walter Mirisch, who went on to produce higher-budget westerns in the fifties.

Impulse (1955) Tempean. (Brit.) 80 min. (B&W) P: Robert S. Baker. D: Charles de la Tour. Sc: Lawrence Huntingdon and Jonathon Roach, based on an original story by Carl Nystrom and Robert S. Baker. Ph: Jonah Jones. Ed: Jack Slade. M: Stanley Black. CAST: Arthur Kennedy, Constance Smith, Joy Shelton, Jack Allen, James Carney, Cyril Chamberlain, Cameron Hall, Jean St. Clair, Bruce Beeby.   Kennedy is an American real estate agent living in England. Allegedly happily married, he feels his personal and professional lives are in a rut. When his wife goes to visit her mother for a few days, he gives a lift to nightclub singer Smith when he finds her stranded on the road. He is strongly attracted to her but soon finds he has fallen for trouble. Smith reveals to Kennedy that the police are after her brother for a jewel robbery and that she needs to locate him. She convinces him that she wants to help her brother when in reality she's after the jewels for herself. Kennedy locates the "brother," who pulls a gun and tells Kennedy he is not a brother at all and that Kennedy's been played for a chump. Kennedy KOs the brother and leaves. He returns to his dull life and picks up with his wife but soon receives a phone call from Smith, who tells him that the brother is dead, killed by Kennedy's blow. Kennedy goes to meet her to find out more and is tailed by the police, who break in and begin searching her room for the diamonds, which she now has. Kennedy gets suspicious, and his suspicions are confirmed when the owner of the nightclub where Smith sings shows up and it is revealed that the cops are really mobsters who were part of the jewelry heist. The nightclub owner is about to slice up Smith with a knife when Kennedy manages to get a gun away from one of the gangsters and shoot him. Kennedy and Smith escape and hide out. Kennedy is now a wanted man, hunted by both the cops and the mob. Smith and Kennedy plan to escape the country by ship. In the meantime, he makes her hand the diamonds over to him. Kennedy bribes the crooked captain of a ship to take them out of the country, but when Smith reveals her true greedy self, Kennedy gets disgusted. He decides to stay and face the consequences and turns himself in. Smith returns to clear Kennedy of the crime, saying that she saw the "brother" alive after Kennedy hit him; she wanted Kennedy to think he was a murderer so he wouldn't leave her. The true killers are the nightclub owner and his gang, all of whom are in police custody for both the robbery and the murder. Smith goes to jail as a participant in the robbery, and Kennedy returns to his wife, who forgives him.

Taking place in England, *Impulse*, like the far superior American *Pitfall*, deals with the themes of middle-class dissatisfaction and the fall of the weak husband from respectability, demonstrating that feelings of middle-class malaise were not restricted to the United States in the 1950s. Although it is a thriller with only modest thrills, the film manages to hold viewer interest, primarily through plot twists and the management of a fair level of suspense.

Incident (1948) Monogram. 66m. (B&W) P: Harry Lewis and Hall Shelton. D: William Beaudine. Sc: Fred Niblo Jr. and Samuel Roeca, based on a story by Harry Lewis. Ed: Ace Herman. M: Edward J. Kay. CAST: Warren Douglas, Jane Frazee, Robert Osterloh, Joyce Compton, Anthony Caruso, Harry Lauter, Eddie Dunn, Meyer Grace, Harry Cheshire, Lynn Millan, Robert Emmett Keane.   Douglas is a stock salesman who misses his bus one night and gets seriously beaten up by Grace, a thug who mistook him for another thug, Osterloh, whom he strongly resembles. Arrested as a drunk, Douglas is bailed out by his buddies Lauter and Compton. Not willing to let the incident go, Douglas goes looking for Grace and meets Frazee, who is also interested in the thug for reasons of her own. While driving her home, Douglas sees Grace go into a house and follows him inside, where he has been knifed to death. He and Frazee are taken in by the cops, resulting in Douglas losing his job. Frazee, who is an insurance investigator working on a hijacking case, moves into the murder house. Douglas is picked up and interrogated by crime boss

Caruso, who wants to know about Osterloh. Caruso had ordered Grace to beat up Osterloh for double-crossing him. Frazee becomes friendly with Osterloh and gets into a confrontation with the gangster's jealous girlfriend, who sees Frazee's identification. She tips Caruso about Frazee's identity, and he orders Osterloh to take the investigator to a warehouse and kill her. Douglas tails them and tips the cops, allowing them to get there in time to save Frazee and break up the hijack gang.

When *Incident* was released, Monogram tried the gimmick of allowing exhibitors to pay the studio whatever they wanted if audiences didn't like it. The studio was taking a big chance, as the film was directed by William "One Shot" Beaudine, who earned his nickname by filming virtually every scene in his more than 150 films in one take. It didn't matter if the corpse moved or somebody answered a phone that didn't ring; One Shot would print the scene anyway. The director of such epics as *Get Off My Foot, Mr. Cohen Takes a Walk, Bela Lugosi Meets a Brooklyn Gorilla, Billy the Kid Versus Dracula,* and *Jesse James Meets Frankenstein,* Beaudine is probably most famous for the remark he made while working on a Bowery Boys movie at Monogram: "You'd think someone out there was really waiting to see this." Fortunately for Monogram, this was one of Beaudine's better efforts.

Inner Sanctum (1948) Film Classics. 62m. (B&W) P: Samuel Rheineer and Walter Shenson. D: Lew Landers. Sc: Jerome Todd Gollard. Ph: Al Zeigler. M: Emil Newman. CAST: Charles Russell, Mary Beth Hughes, Lee Patrick, Nana Bryant, Billy House, Dale Belding, Roscoe Ates, Eve Miller, Fritz Lieber, Eddie Parks. Russell kills his wife at a train station and finds out later that the crime was witnessed by a young boy (the ugliest kid actor ever cast in a film). Because a storm has washed out all the roads, the killer can't get out of the area and ends up staying at a boarding house owned by the boy's mother. Although the kid thought that the dead body he saw Russell throwing on the train was just a heavy package, he begins to suspect the stranger when news of the murder comes out. Hughes, a boarder at the house who admits she always falls for the wrong kind of guy, falls for Russell and is willing to go away with him even though she knows he killed his wife. When she finds out that Russell plans to kill the kid, however, she draws the line, telling him, "You're pretty awful. You're even too bad for me." The kid manages to escape, and Russell ends up waiting on a porch swing with Hughes for the cops. In an ending with a twist, the audience learns that the entire story is being told by an old man who had been with the murdered woman on the train. He had warned her not to get off the train, but she had spotted her husband on the platform and rushed out to meet her fate.

Although the makers of the film exploited the name of the popular *Inner Sanctum* radio show, this not-bad little noir had no connection. Neither did it have any connection to the Inner Sanctum series of mysteries Universal put out in the early 1940s starring Lon Chaney Jr. (V)

Inside Job (1946) Universal. 65m. (B&W) P: Ben Pivar and Jean Yarbrough. D: Yarbrough. Sc: George Bricker and Jerry Warner, based on a story by Tod Browning and Garrett Ford. Ph: Maury Gertsman. Ed: Otto Ludwig. M: Frank Skinner. CAST: Preston Foster, Alan Curtis, Ann Rutherford, Joe Sawyer, Joan Fulton, Milburn Stone, Jimmie Moss, Samuel S. Hinds, Howard Freeman, John Berkes. Husband and wife Curtis and Rutherford are former criminals who work at a department store and are trying to straighten out their lives. Gangster Foster, who knows about their pasts, blackmails them into arranging a burglary of the store. They unwillingly agree but arrange things so that Foster gets gunned down by the cops, after which they turn themselves in for the burglary.

Generally weak, this film is notable only in that the story was written by Tod Browning, who directed the horror classics *Dracula* (1931) and *Freaks* (1932).

Invisible Wall, The (1947) Twentieth Century Fox. 72m. (B&W) P: Sol Wurtzel. D: Eugene Forde. Sc: Arnold Belgard, based on a story by Howard J. Green and Paul Frank. Ph: Benjamin Kline. Ed: William Claxton. M: Morton Scott. CAST: Don Castle, Virginia Christine, Richard Gaines, Arthur Space, Edward Keane, Jeff Chandler, Harry Cheshire, Mary Gordon, Harry Shannon.   Picked up for the murder of Space, Castle recounts to the DA events leading up to the killing: Returning from the war, Castle takes up his old job as assistant to big-time bookie Keane. His first job is to deliver $20,000 to a woman in Vegas. While waiting for the woman to show up, Castle gives in to his gambling habit and loses $5,000 of the money. Gaines, a con man posing as a mining engineer, cons Castle out of another $10,000. Castle catches up with the con man, and during a scuffle, Gaines is accidentally killed. Castle finds out Gaines sent the money to Denver, so he goes there, posing as Gaines. Christine, unhappily married to Gaines, shows up and finds Castle posing as her ex. Castle scrams and is pursued by Christine. Gaines's crooked partner, Space, enters the picture, threatens blackmail, and in a turn of events is killed by the cops. Castle is released and he and Christine, who have fallen for each other, go off into the sunset.

Well-paced with adept acting by all, this is another competent entry by the Wurtzel unit.

Jail Bait (1954) Howco. 70m. (B&W) AKA: *Hidden Face*. P&D: Edward D. Wood Jr. Sc: Wood and Alex Gordon. Ph: Bill Thompson. Ed: Charles Clement and Igor Kantor. M: Hoyt Xurtin. CAST: Lyle Talbot, Dolores Fuller, Steve Reeves, Theodora Thurman, Herbert Rawlinson, John Martin, Clancy Malone, Timothy Farrell, Scott McCloud, Bud Osborne, Mona McKinnon.   "Jail bait" in this film refers not to fodder for a statutory rape charge but to the punk son of dottering plastic surgeon Rawlinson. The son and his partner, Farrell, plan to rob a theater for its huge payroll. (The theater show that's racking in the dough features a live vaudeville act done in blackface.) During the robbery, the punk son kills a night watchman and Farrell shoots a woman in the back. The woman lives, however, and identifies the pair to police detectives Talbot and Reeves. The son wants to turn himself in, but before he can do so he is murdered by Farrell. Farrell goes to Rawlinson and tells him to change his face or he will never see his son alive again. Rawlinson agrees, but before the surgery he finds his son is already dead when the kid's body falls out of a closet. Rawlinson goes ahead with the operation, and when the bandages are removed, Farrell discovers to his dismay that the doctor made him into the spitting image of his son. The police, mistaking Farrell for Rawlinson's cop-killer son, kill Farrell as he is trying to escape.

Legendary filmmaker Ed Wood, winner of the coveted Golden Turkey Award for Worst Director of All Time and whose monumental works such as *Glen or Glenda*, *Bride of the Monster*, and *Plan 9 from Outer Space* were so bad that they inspired a biographical movie about his life, lives up to his reputation in his sole (and largely neglected) attempt at noir. The film is filled with brilliant bits of dialogue such as Rawlinson saying to his daughter: "Plastic surgery seems to be at times to me very, very, complicated." The following snappy exchange occurs between Rawlinson's daughter and detective Talbot:

Talbot: "Carrying a gun can be a dangerous business."

Daughter: "So can building a skyscraper."

This was Steve Reeves's first speaking role and reveals why the Italians dubbed over his voice in his later Hercules roles. McKinnon was so impressive, she went on to star in Wood's masterpiece *Plan 9 from Outer Space*, as did Talbot. Considering the mortality rate of Wood's leading men, you would think actors would have avoided his productions like the plague. Bela Lugosi died during the first days of filming *Plan 9* and had to be replaced by Wood's chiropractor; Rawlinson died the day after completing *Jail Bait*. Economical and original to the end, Wood lifted the oddball musical score (a constantly strumming flamenco guitar interspersed with a dissonant pounding piano) for *Jail Bait* from *Mesa of Lost Women*, a film he probably admired, as it ranks up there with his own work as one of the worst horror films of all time. (Imagine Jackie Coogan as a mad scientist!) (V)

Jealousy (1945) Republic. 71m. (B&W) P&D: Gustav Machaty. Sc: Arnold Phillips and Machaty, based on a story by Dalton Trumbo. Ph: Henry Sharp. Ed: John Link. M: Hanns Eisler. CAST: John Loder, Jane Randolph, Nils Asther, Karen Morley, Hugo Haas, Holmes Herbert, Michael Mark, Mauritz Hugo. Asther plays a famous alcoholic novelist who is experiencing a bad case of writer's block and would rather drink than write. His wife tries to augment the couple's income by becoming a taxi driver, and when she picks up Loder, the two become friends. Asther becomes jealous, and when he is murdered, Loder and Randolph become the prime suspects. Randolph is arrested by the cops, and Loder sets out to prove her innocence. The day before she is to be tried for murder, Loder marries her in jail and proves that Asther's assistant, Morley, committed the murder and spread around evidence to throw the blame on Randolph.

Moody direction and good work by the cast make this an entertaining entry.

Judge, The (1949) Film Classics. 69m. (B&W) P: Anson Bond. D: Elmer Clifton. Sc: Samuel Newman, Elmer Anson Bond, based on the story by Bond and Jullius Long. Ph: Ben Kline. Ed: Fred Maguire. M: Gene Lanham. CAST: Milburn Stone, Katherine deMille, Paul Guilfoyle, Stanley Waxman, Norman Budd, Jonathon Hale, John Hamilton, Joe Forte, Jesse Kirkpatrick.   Stone is a cynical defense attorney soured on his life, his profession, and his adulterous wife. After he gets a guilty Guilfoyle off on a murder charge on a technicality, he decides to end it all by tricking Guilfoyle into killing him, setting it up so that his widow and her lover take the rap. The attorney kills himself, and the widow is left penniless. In the end, Guilfoyle confesses, so that everybody in the film ends up badly.

This film was presumably set up to be a series, as it begins with a preface wherein the judge, Jonathon Hale, pulls this case out of his filing cabinet and comments on it to the audience. The implication is that he has a whole drawerful of cases, but the drawer stayed closed after this one. Although this film was shot in a flat, shadowless style, the plot is about as noir as it gets. (V)

Key Witness (1947) Columbia. 67m. (B&W) P: Rudolph C. Flothow. D: Ross Lederman. Sc: Edward Bock and Raymond L. Shrock, from a story by J. Donald Wilson. Ph: Philip Tannura. Ed: Dwight Caldwell. M: Mischa Bakaleinikoff. CAST: John Beal, Trudy Marshall, Jimmy Lloyd, Helen Mowery, Wilton Graff, Barbara Reed, Charles Trowbridge, Douglas Fowley, Harry Hayden, William Newell, Selmer Jackson.   Beal is an architect who invents gadgets he can't sell. His wife, Reed, pressures him to stop tinkering and make some money. One week when she is out of town, he goes to the racetrack with a friend and, through a mistaken bet, wins a small fortune. To celebrate, he throws a party with his buddy and two women. He gets drunk and passes out, and Lloyd leaves with his date. Fowley, Beal's girl's estranged husband, shows up and, during an argument, shoots her. Beal wakes up to find the dead woman and takes it on the lam, the cops on his tail. He becomes a hobo and goes to Arizona, where he finds the body of a dead man on the railroad tracks. He takes the dead man's ID and assumes his name, Arnold Ballin. Ballin is buried as Beal, but after Beal gets hit by an automobile and an article on the accident appears in the paper, he is contacted by Trowbridge, a millionaire who thinks Beal is his long lost son. Trowbridge takes in Beal and finances his inventions, which take off. In the meantime, Beal's wife has remarried and, while on a shopping spree, spots one of Beal's inventions. Thinking the idea was stolen and that she can collect money for the patent, she uncovers Beal's identity and he is arrested by the police for the girl's murder. When Fowley confesses, it looks as if Beal is out of the soup, but then he is arrested for Ballin's murder. He is finally cleared when a hobo friend comes forth and corroborates his story of finding the body.

There are way too many coincidences and far too many plot complications for a 67-minute film. Dumbly overwritten and only marginally acted, this forgettable programmer has appropriately pretty much been forgotten.

Kill Her Gently (1958) Columbia. (Brit.) 75m. (B&W) P: Guido Coen. D: Charles Saunders. Sc: Paul Erickson. Ph: Walter J. Harvey. Ed: Margery Saunders. M: Edwin Astley. CAST: Marc Lawrence, George Mikell, Griffith Jones, John Gayford, Roger Avon, Maureen Connell, Shay Gorman, Marianne Brauns, Frank Hawkins. Convicts Lawrence and Mikell escape from prison and are picked up on the road by Jones, who recognizes them but says nothing. After helping them get through a roadblock, he proposes to give them $1,000 and help them get out of the country if they will kill his wife. Jones has just been released from a mental institution and blames his wife for his commitment. He takes them to his home, where the only other person besides his wife, Connell, is the maid, Brauns. It is revealed that Jones was just released from a mental institution. Mikell is sympathetic to Connell and is reluctant to go ahead with the plan, but Lawrence wants the money. Lawrence tells Jones he won't do the deed until he has the money in his hand, so they have to wait for the next day until Jones can get the money from the bank. The next day, Jones goes to the bank but does not have enough money in his account to cover the contract, so he borrows on his car. When he gets back to his house, Jones finds that Lawrence has killed the maid after she recognized him from the papers. Jones goes into a rage and is overheard by his wife, who now knows the awful truth about her husband. In a panic, she phones the family doctor, who comes over to help her. The police, in the meantime, have identified the car that picked up the convicts. Mikell tries to stall Connell's killing and is calmly shot to death by Jones. The doctor arrives. Lawrence is about to kill him and Connell when he hears police sirens. Jones takes off in a jeep, leaving Lawrence, and as the car crashes through the front gate, Lawrence, miffed at being double-crossed, shoots Jones to death. Lawrence is arrested and carted off to jail.

In this rather brutal film, Marc Lawrence, a staple from thirties and forties gangster and noir films, competently plays his familiar, ominous killer-for-hire role.

Lady Confesses, The (1945) PRC. 64m. (B&W) P: Alfred Stern. D: Sam Newfield. Sc: Helen Martin, based on a story by Irwin R. Franklin. Ph: Jack Greenhalgh. Ed: Holbrook Todd. M: Lee Zahler. CAST: Mary Beth Hughes, Hugh Beaumont, Edmund MacDonald, Claudia Drake, Emmett Vogan, Barbara Slater, Edward Howard, Dewey Robinson, Carol Andrews. Hughes gets a visit from her fiancé Beaumont's wife, who has been missing for seven years and is supposed to be dead. The nasty woman tells Hughes that she won't let anyone marry Beaumont even though she is not interested in him. Hughes immediately tries to get hold of Beaumont, who is drunk in a nightclub. Beaumont talks to MacDonald, the nightclub owner, and then goes to sleep in the dressing room of the club singer. Hughes finally locates Beaumont, and when he is awakened, he sees Mac-Donald sneaking in the back door of the club. When Beaumont and Hughes go to his wife's place to straighten things out, they find the cops and his wife dead, strangled with a wire. Trying to convince the cops of his innocence, Beaumont takes them to the club, where everyone but MacDonald admits to having seen him. Under questioning by the cops, MacDonald says he knew the dead woman and that years ago she had loaned him $10,000 to start up the club and had returned to claim an interest. To determine MacDonald's motive for lying, Hughes gets a job at the club in order to do some spying. She finds out that MacDonald and the singer had something going at one time and that MacDonald had been at the dead woman's house the night of the murder. In a jealous rage at having been dumped by MacDonald, the singer tries and fails to shoot the club owner. She then writes a note to the homicide squad and goes home. In her apartment, the singer is confronted by Beaumont, who insists that she tell him what she told Hughes. She insists she said nothing about her giving Hughes an alibi, but he strangles her with a wire to make sure. Hughes finds the note the singer wrote and takes it to Beaumont without reading it. He reveals to her that he killed both women and is about to kill her when the cops bust in and shoot him.

This film is extremely low budget but not bad. (V)

Lady in the Death House (1944) PRC. 56m. (B&W) P: Jack Schwarz. D: Steve Sekely. Sc: Harry Hoyt, based on a story by Fred C. Davis. Ph: Gus Peterson. Ed: Richard O. Crandall. CAST: Jean Parker, Lionel Atwill, Douglas Fowley, Marcia Mae Jones, Robert Middlemass, Cy Kendall, John Maxwell.   Parker is on death row, ready to be executed for killing a man who used her family's criminal past to blackmail her. The big twist is that Parker's fiancé, Fowley, a doctor who doubles as the state executioner because of his experiments in reviving the dead, is going to have to pull the switch on the electric chair. (Although he is eaten up by guilt, Parker tells him, "I'm glad it's going to be you.") Noted criminologist Atwill, convinced of Parker's innocence, relates the story of her arrest and trial in flashback to a group of reporters and also races to save her. In the end, he proves the killer to have been Parker's sister's boyfriend, who murdered the blackmailer for his money.

One wonders what kind of an attorney Parker had in that the testimony that convicted her was an identification by two passers-by of Parker's silhouette on a pulled shade. This pretty bad and very cheap movie was filmed almost entirely on two sets.

NOTE: By the time this film was made, Atwill, a noted actor who had worked in some of the most prestigious films in the thirties as well as many memorable Universal horror films, had been blacklisted by the major studios because of a 1942 perjury conviction resulting from a well-attended orgy he'd held at his Pacific Palisades home. (Atwill was heavily into kinky sex, particularly S&M.) After his scrape with the law, Atwill was reduced to a PRC regular, where features were shot in five days. Not long after the completion of this forgettable movie, he died of pneumonia while working on the serial *Lost City of the Jungle*. (V)

Let Us Live (1939) Columbia. 66m. (B&W) P: William Perlberg. D: John Brahm. Sc: Anthony Veiller and Allen Rivkin, based on a story by Joseph F. Dineen. Ph: Lucien Ballard. Ed: Al Clark. M: Karol Rathaus. CAST: Maureen O'Sullivan, Henry Fonda, Ralph Bellamy, Alan Baxter, Stanley Ridges, Henry Kolker, Peter Lynn, George Douglas, Philip Trent, Martin Spellman.   Fonda and Baxter are two innocent men convicted for robbery and murder and sentenced to death. Fonda's fiancée, O'Sullivan, believes in Fonda's innocence and enlists the aid of police detective Bellamy to try to clear him before the impending execution date. The pair manage to find the real culprits just in time to save the two innocent men.

This small film came on the heels of Fonda's starring in a similar role in Fritz Lang's *You Only Live Once* (1937) but is definitely a B version of the "wrong man" theme. At the time the film was released, a real case of two cab drivers accused of murder was pending in the Commonwealth of Massachusetts. That state warned the studio not to make the movie too similar to that case. The cab drivers were eventually cleared.

Louisiana Hussey, The (1959) Bon Aire/Howco. 66m. (B&W) P: Charles M. Casinelli. D: Lee Sholem. Sc: Charles Lang. Ph: Ted and Vincent Saizis. Ed: John Bushelman. M: Walter Greene. CAST: Nan Peterson, Peter Coe, Robert Richards,

Betty Lynn, Harry Lauter, Howard Wright, Rosalie Calvert.   Two Cajun brothers in the Louisiana bayou stumble on injured sexpot Peterson, who has been thrown from a horse. There is already trouble between the brothers because the younger one is marrying a young lady the older one loves. The older one takes in the injured girl, who immediately sets the two against each other. When the younger brother sees a newspaper report on the suicide of a wealthy woman in a nearby town with the same name as the vamp, he and his wife investigate. They find a grieving and drunken Lauter, who reveals the imposter to be a companion he hired to take care of his ill wife. Peterson had done her thing on Lauter's household, too, causing a bout of lust in him and his wife to put a bullet in her head. Peterson had fallen off the horse when trying to get away from Lauter, who was going to shoot her. Lauter tries to hunt her down to complete the job but is stopped by the younger brother. In the end, Peterson, faking a stalled car and evil to the end, flags down another unsuspecting sucker.

For my money, this is the front-runner for the worst femme fatale movie ever made. Besides this picture, Peterson's main claim to fame was as Robert Clarke's singer-girlfriend in *The Hideous Sun Demon*. Howco (which probably stood for How come?) was the North Carolina studio that gave the world such epics as *The Brain from Planet Arous* and *Teenage Monster*. (V)

Man Bait (1952) Hammer/Lippert. (Brit.) 78m. (B&W) AKA: *The Last Page*. P: Anthony Hinds. D: Terence Fisher. Sc: Frederick Knott, based on a story by James Hadley Chase. Ph: Walter Harvey. Ed: Maurice Rootes. CAST: George Brent, Marguerite Chapman, Raymond Huntley, Diana Dors, Peter Reynolds, Eleanor Summerfield, Meredith Edwards.   Brent is the manager of a bookstore where clerk Dors catches small-time crook Reynolds trying to steal a rare book. Instead of turning him in, she starts dating him. When Brent later makes a pass at Dors, she tells Reynolds, who suggests blackmail. Brent refuses to pay, and Reynolds writes a note to Brent's sick wife about the affair, causing her death from a heart attack. A guilty Brent pays up, and Dors tries to hit him up again. Reynolds discovers Dors is stashing part of the payoff money and kills her, stuffing her body in a packing case. Brent discovers the body and, thinking he will be accused, flees. He enlists the aid of his secretary, Chapman, who helps him hunt for clues. She stumbles on Reynolds alone and is nearly killed by him, but Brent arrives to save her as the police arrive to arrest Reynolds.

This was a landmark in that it was the first film in the Hammer-Lippert association and resulted in seventeen Lippert releases of Hammer product in the U.S. between 1952 and 1955. As with most Hammer films starring American actors, Brent was supplied by Lippert; Dors was borrowed from British Rank Productions. After this film, Dors signed a long-term contract with Lippert, launching her American career. After she had established her U.S. reputation as a sexpot, *Man Bait* was rereleased as part of a "Double Blonde Dynamite" double bill with *Bad Blonde*.

Man in the Dark (1953) Columbia. 70m. (B&W) P: Wallace MacDonald D: Lew Landers. Sc: George Bricker and Jack Leonard, adapted by William Sackheim from a story by Tom Van Dycke and Henry Altimus. Ph: Floyd Crosby. Ed: Viola Lawrence. M: Russ di Maggio. CAST: Edmond O'Brien, Audrey Totter, Ruth Warren, Ted de Corsia, Horace McMahon, Nick Dennis, Dayton Lummis, Jan Riss. O'Brien is a convicted bank robber who submits to a brain operation to correct his criminal tendencies in exchange for his release from prison. The operation is successful but erases his memory as well as his antisocial behavior. He is abducted by his old gang members, who want to know the whereabouts of the $130,000 O'Brien stole. They beat him half to death, but O'Brien can't remember where he stashed the loot. With the help of his old girlfriend, Totter, he interprets a recurring dream and finds the money at an amusement park. Realizing that O'Brien has regressed to his old greedy self, Totter leaves him. Chasing him on a roller-coaster ride, bad guy de Corsia is killed. Although he has a chance to get away, O'Brien turns himself and the money in and wins back Totter.

A remake of the 1936 film *The Man Who Lived Twice* with Ralph Bellamy, *Man in the Dark*, although not bad, is an unremarkable film noir. It is primarily notable because it was directed by king of the Poverty Row cheapies Lew Landers; starred noir icons O'Brien, hard-boiled femme fatale Totter, and bad guy de Corsia; was shot in part at the no longer existent LA fun park Pacific Ocean Park (the West Coast's onetime cheap imitation of Coney Island); and was one of the two films noirs to be filmed in 3-D (the other being the terrible adaptation of Mickey Spillane's *I, the Jury*)—an expensive process for such a low-budget production.

Man in the Vault (1956) RKO. 73m. (B&W) P: Robert E. Morrison. D: Andrew V. McLaglen. Sc: Burt Kennedy, based on the novel *The Lock and the Key* by Frank

Gruber. Ph: William H. Clothier. Ed: Everett Sutherland. M: Henry Vars. CAST: William Campbell, Karen Sharpe, Anita Ekberg, Berry Kroeger, Paul Fix, James Seay, Robert Keys, Mike Mazurki, Nancy Duke.   Campbell, an innocent locksmith, gets tied up with cheap hood Kroeger, who intends to rob the safe deposit box of crime boss Seay. Kroeger offers Campbell $5,000 to make the keys to open the box, which contains $200,000. Campbell rejects the proposal until he falls for Sharpe, a wild and crazy rich girl. Knowing Sharpe's expensive habits are beyond his locksmith's salary, Campbell agrees to go along with the scheme. After pulling off the job, Campbell is chased by the crooks, barely managing to escape with his life before getting to the cops.

This entire film is so dark, it appears to have been shot at night. Anita Ekberg manages to generate some interest as the buxom gangster's moll, but the only exciting scenes are when Campbell is inside the vault, frantically trying to make keys to open the safe deposit box, and when he is in a dark bowling alley, trying to dodge bowling balls and bullets. John Wayne's production company, Batjac, made the film with Wayne's cronies—Kennedy and Wayne's old buddy Victor McLaglen's son Andrew—in on the deal. Based on hard-boiled writer Gruber's work once again.

Man Who Died Twice, The (1958) Republic. 70m. (B&W) P: Rudy Ralston: D: Joseph Kane. Sc: Richard C. Sarafian. Ph: Jack Marta. Ed: Fred Knudtson. M: Gerald Roberts. CAST: Rod Cameron, Vera Ralston, Mike Mazurki, Gerald Milton, Richard Karlan, Louis Jean Heydt, Don Megowan, John Maxwell, Robert Anderson, Paul Picerni, Don Haggerty, Luana Anders.   After her husband, Megowan, is burned to death in an automobile accident, nightclub singer Ralston witnesses the murder of two undercover narcotics agents and suffers a nervous breakdown. The police suspect that Megowan was part of a heroin ring and that Ralston was also in on the racket. In her apartment they find a large heroin stash hidden inside a statuette. They replace the dope with milk sugar and bug her apartment, hoping to solve the murders of their colleagues and break the ring. Cameron, Megowan's brother, is also suspicious of Ralston, thinking she was behind his death. To everyone's surprise, Megowan shows up very much alive and admits to Ralston that he faked his own death and killed the two agents to secure the heroin. When he goes for the statuette, she grabs it and tries to throw it out the window. He stops her and tries to kill her but is interrupted by the eavesdropping cops and is gunned down after a chase across the rooftops.

The script is not bad but is trashed by the performances of Cameron, who in every role brought to the screen the emotion of a tree stump, and former ice-skater Ralston. Rounding out the masterful acting troupe is Cameron lookalike and act-alike Megowan, whose most animated performance was as Gillman in Universal's *The Creature Walks Among Us* (1956), the third and last in the *Creature from the Black Lagoon* series. Thankfully, this was Ralston's final, painful film appearance. This movie was also the last movie Joseph Kane, one of Republic's most prolific directors since the 1930s, directed for the studio, which by 1958 was in its death throes. Filmed in *Naturama*, whatever that was.

Marilyn (1953) Astor. (Brit.) 70m. (B&W) AKA: *Roadhouse Girl*. P: Ernest G. Roy. D/Sc: Wolf Rella, based on the play *Marian* by Peter Jones. Ph: Geoffrey Faithfull. CAST: Maxwell Reed, Sandra Dorne, Leslie Dwyer, Vida Hope, Ferdy Mayne, Hugh Pryse, Kenneth Connor. This film is yet another discount *Postman* rip-off with randy mechanic Reed lusting after his older boss's seductive wife, Dorne. Tension builds between the two men and eventually leads to a fight and the husband's death. Dorne helps Reed cover up the crime, and together they open a roadhouse. A rich man, Mayne, also attracted to Dorne, lends her some money, and seeing the chance to move up in life, she gives Reed the cold shoulder, using him basically as an employee. Mayne shies away when he learns what really happened to Dorne's husband, and she tries to convince Reed he is the man she really loves. Reed isn't buying it, and neither are the police, who come to pick up the murderers. (V)

Mark of the Whistler (1944) Columbia. 60m. (B&W) P: Rudolph C. Flothow. D: William Castle. Sc: George Bricker, based on the story "Dormant Account" by Cornell Woolrich. Ph: George Meehan. Ed: Reg Brown. M: Wilbur Hatch. CAST: Richard Dix, Janis Carter, Porter Hall, Paul Guilfoyle, John Calvert, Matt McHugh, Matt Willis, Howard Freeman. In this second in the series of *Whistler* movies based on the successful radio program (see *The Whistler*), a drifter, Dix, claims an old bank account and finds himself targeted by two men whose father went to jail because of a conflict with Dix over the money. Dix finally extricates himself from the mess and later befriends a crippled peddler who turns out to be the real owner of the money.

William Castle, who directed quite a few of the seven *Whistler* films as well as several other B noirs, went on in the fifties to specialize in low-budget horror films. He became famous for the gimmicks he used to promote his films, such as having "nurses" hand out $1,000 life insurance policies in lobbies of theaters showing *Macabre* just in case patrons died of fright; installing electric buzzers (for an effect dubbed "Percepto") under selected seats in the theater to shock patrons at certain points in *The Tingler*; and providing "ghost viewers" (the effect was called "Illusion-O") so they could see the ghosts in *Thirteen Ghosts*. Castle, who always appeared at the beginning of his gimmicky films to set up the audience, was beautifully caricatured in the entertaining 1993 film *Matinee* by John Goodman.

Mask of Diijon, The (1946) PRC. 73m. (B&W) P: Max Alexander and Alfred Stern. D: Lew Landers. Sc: Arthur St. Claire and Griffin Jay, from a story by St. Claire. Ph: Jack Greenhalgh. Ed: Roy Livingston. M: Karl Hajos. CAST: Erich Von Stroheim, Jeanne Bates, William Wright, Edward Van Sloan, Mauritz Hugo, Denise Vernac, Robert Malcolm, Hope Landin, Shimen Ruskin.   Von Stroheim is an emotionally unbalanced magician who is living with his wife and assistant, Bates, in a seedy boarding house that caters to down-on-their-luck acts. He is insanely jealous of piano player Wright and is convinced he and his wife are having an affair, and he hatches a plan to do away with his rival by using hypnosis. He practices on Hugo, a dancer who as a result of hypnotic suggestion does himself in. After Bates gets a job singing at a nightclub where Wright works, Von Stroheim hypnotizes her and tries to influence her to shoot Wright during one of her numbers. She tries but takes the wrong gun, which is loaded with blanks. Von Stroheim, on the run from the cops, tries to hide out in Van Sloan's magic store by acting as a dummy under a guillotine, but his head gets chopped off when a house cat, playing with the string holding up the blade, trips the mechanism.

Another Lew Landers cheapie, this one is notable only as another reminder of Von Stroheim's fall from grace. Of some interest is the fact that Denise Vernac and Von Stroheim were living together when this film was made. Von Stroheim reportedly used whatever influence he had left to get her in the movie, maybe thinking it would help with household expenses. Van Sloan is best remembered as Dr. Van Helsing, vampire-killer, in the original Bela Lugosi version of *Dracula*. (V)

Money Madness (1948) Film Classics. 73m. (B&W) P: Sigmund Neufeld. D: Peter Stewart. Sc: Al Martin. Ph: Jack Greenhalgh. Ed: Holbrook N. Todd. M: Leo Erdody. CAST: Hugh Beaumont, Frances Rafferty, Harlan Warde, Cecil Weston, Ida Moore, Danny Morton, Lane Chandler.   The film begins with Rafferty being sentenced to ten years in prison for being an accomplice to murder. Flashback is used to reveal the story to that point. Beaumont, a killer and bank robber on the lam, decides to hide out in the small town Rafferty lives in with her invalid aunt, whom she cares for. Beaumont gets a job as a cab driver and ingratiates himself with Rafferty by saving her from a man making an unwanted pass at her. Beaumont turns on the charm, and soon Rafferty finds herself falling for him. She and Beaumont get married, and Beaumont convinces her to keep the marriage a secret, as the aunt wouldn't approve. Beaumont begins to poison the aunt, and when Rafferty finds out, he stops her from telling the cops by reminding her that she herself administered the poison, although unknowingly. He tells her he has $200,000 in cash from a bank robbery but can't spend it, so they will stash it in the house and pretend to discover it in the aunt's trunk. Rafferty will then inherit the money, and she and Beaumont will live happily ever after. Rafferty begins to crack under the strain and tries to split, but she is stopped by Beaumont. In the meantime, Beaumont's partner from the robbery shows up, demanding his share of the money; Beaumont coldly guns him down in Rafferty's living room and forces Rafferty to help him dump the body. When the body is found, Beaumont's picture as the robbery-murder suspect and former mental patient appears in the paper and is recognized by the family lawyer, who has started to fall for Rafferty. The lawyer searches Beaumont's room and finds the marriage certificate. He goes to Rafferty's house and is about to be murdered by Beaumont, but Beaumont is killed by some passing police who have stopped because of the blaring radio Beaumont has turned up to cover the sound of the gunshot.

One of the better "lost" noirs, this grim film has its moments, and it is fun to watch Ward Cleaver as a cunning but whacko killer. (V)

Murder Without Tears (1953) Allied Artists. 64m. (B&W) P: William F. Broidy. D: William Beaudine. Sc: Jo Pagano and Bill Raynor, based on the story "Double Jeopardy" by Pagano. Ph: Virgil Miller. Ed: Ace Herman. M: Edward J. Kay. CAST: Craig Stevens, Joyce Holden, Richard Benedict, Eddie Norris, Clair Regis, Tom Hubbard, Murray Alper, Bob Carson.   Norris has his wife murdered and makes it look like he did the killing during an alcoholic blackout so that the DA will indict him for the crime. When bank clerk Holden provides his alibi for the time of the murder, he is acquitted. Detective Stevens is still not convinced and finds out that Norris hired Benedict to kill his wife. Knowing Norris can't be tried again for the same crime, Stevens sets up a situation in which Benedict kills Norris. Stevens ends up killing Benedict and going off with Holden.

Since virtually every scene of this film was shot in shadowless broad daylight, some critics might argue this film is not noir; the story line more than qualifies, however. Extremely talky and made for seventy-five cents, *Murder Without Tears* is another entry in the immortal pantheon of films directed by William "One Shot" Beaudine (the film was probably filmed in daylight to save on lighting costs). Stevens, who played supporting roles in Poverty Row films throughout the forties, would "break out" five years later on TV, when he starred as a detached private eye in the noir series *Peter Gunn*.

My Gun Is Quick (1957) United Artists. 88m. (B&W) P&D: George White, Phil Victor. Sc: Richard Collins and Richard Powell, from the novel by Mickey Spillane. Ph: Harry Neumann. Ed: Frank Sullivan. M: Marlin Skiles. CAST: Robert Bray, Whitney Blake, Pat Donahue, Donald Randolph, Pamela Duncan, Booth Coleman, Jan Chaney, Hina Core, Richard Garland, Charles Boaz.   Mike Hammer comes to the aid of a hooker being assaulted in a diner and notices she is wearing a distinctive ring. When the hooker turns up dead minus the ring and the ring turns out to be part of a shipment of Nazi jewelry that had been smuggled out of France by an American army colonel named Holloway during World War II, the detective takes an interest. The trail leads him to the dead hooker's stripper girl-friend (who later is murdered), a French mute (who is later murdered), the butler of a rich Newport Beach heiress (who is later murdered), the sexy heiress herself, and eventually to Colonel Holloway, who hires Hammer to help him find the jew-els. The problem is that a French gang (led by a villain with a hook on his hand) also wants the jewels. Before the jewels are recovered, everybody dies except Ham-mer and the heiress, who turns out to be a murderess, too.

Although Biff "Mumbles" Elliott has to take first prize for the worst Mike Ham-mer of all time in *I, the Jury*, Bray comes in a close second. Clichéd from start to finish (replete with the bad-guy gang leader dying by falling on his own hook and the obligatory the-gun-is-out-of-ammo-so-I'll-throw-it-at-you ploy), the film even has some shameless rip-offs of *The Maltese Falcon*. Donald Randolph as Colonel Holloway plays his character as a combination of Sydney Greenstreet and Peter Lorre, and in the end, Bray does Bogie by telling the villainous heiress, "The cops will be after us soon. Talk." After she confesses the whole thing and he tells her he's going to turn her in, she does her disbelieving Mary Astor, saying, "We belong together." I take it back: Everybody dies in this one.

Mysterious Intruder (1946) Columbia. 61m. (B&W) P: Rudolph C. Fothow. D: William Castle. Sc: Eric Taylor, based on a story by Taylor from *The Whistler* radio program. Ph: Philip Tannura. Ed: Dwight Caldwell. M: Mischa Bakaleinikoff. CAST: Richard Dix, Barton MacLane, Nina Vale, Regis Toomey, Helen Mowery, Mike Mazurki, Pamela Blake, Charles Lane, Paul Burns, Arthur Space.   In this fifth of the Whistler films, Dix is an unscrupulous private eye who is hired by the Swedish owner of a music store to find Alora Lund, a girl who grew up next door. To find out why the old man is willing to pay to find the girl, Dix sends a ringer to the music store. Believing the ringer to be the grown-up girl, the old man reveals that the girl's mother left with him her belongings, among which are two very valuable old Jenny Lind records for which a millionaire is willing to pay $200,000. Before the old man can hand over the records, however, he is stabbed to death by Mazurki. Mazurki is later killed by the cops, and Dix, confronting the ringer, finds out about the records. The cops locate the real Alora Lund in a sanitorium, where she is recuperating from a car accident; they talk her into going to Dix to find out what he knows. Dix tells her about the records and cuts himself in for 25 percent of the proceeds. When the ringer is found strangled in her apartment, Dix is suspected by the cops as the killer. Dix goes to the record store and finds another body; the ringer's landlord, Toomey, and a partner are searching the place. They find the records, but Dix gets the drop on them and, after a gun battle, comes out on top. Dix calls the cops, intending to clear himself, but when he hears the cops coming up from the store basement, he mistakes them for one of the killers and fires blindly down the stairs. The cops kill him, breaking the records in the process.

It all sounds pretty silly, but all in all, this film is nicely handled and a solid entry in the series.

Mysterious Mr. Valentine, The (1946) Republic. 56m. (B&W) P: Donald H. Brown. D: Philip Ford. Sc: Milton Raison. Ph: Alfred Keller. Ed: Richard L. Van

Enger. M: Mort Glickman. CAST: William Henry, Linda Stirling, Virginia Christine, Thomas Jackson, Barbara Woodell, Kenne Duncan, Virginia Brissac, Lyle Latell, Ernie Adams, Tristram Coffin, Arthur Space, Robert Bice.   Innocent Stirling gets a flat tire and ends up having her car stolen. When the car is involved in another accident resulting in a man's death, the body is planted in her car to make it look as if Stirling was driving. Things get further muddled for her when the gang (headed by Coffin) responsible for the deed tries to blackmail her for $25,000. When she can't come up with the money, the gangsters up the ante and try to get her involved in their illegal activities. Luckily for Stirling, Henry, a smart-cracking private eye who is always on the outs with the law, is called in by the insurance company and clears her while rounding up the gang.

Although there is undoubtedly too much plot in this movie for 56 minutes, it is still not a bad little item; Christine is especially effective as a femme fatale. NOTE: This film was a new kind of role for Linda Stirling, who up to this time had spent most of her time at Republic dressed in a leopard cat suit and beating up bad guys in *The Tiger Woman* serials. Tristram Coffin, in contrast, was right at home, having been a staple minor villain in many a Republic feature. In 1951, he finally got a taste of what it was to play a good guy when he starred as Commando Cody in *Lost Planet Airmen*, Republic's feature release of its serial King of the Rocketmen.

No Escape (1953) United Artists. 76m. (B&W) P: Matt Freed, Hugh MacKenzie. D&Sc: Charles Bennett. Ph: Benjamin Kline. Ed: Roy V. Livingston. M: Bert Shefter. CAST: Lew Ayres, Marjorie Steele, Sonny Tufts, Lewis Martin, Charles Cane, Gertrude Michael, Renny McEvoy, Jess Kirkpatrick, James Griffith, Robert Watson.   Ayres is a down-on-his-luck songwriter who ekes out a living as a piano player in a San Francisco bar. When all the clues of the murder of artist Griffith point to Steele, her police detective boyfriend, Tufts, fixes things so that Ayres will be blamed. Steele, feeling guilty, helps Ayres escape, and after dodging the police all over town, they end up in Griffith's apartment. Tufts, the real killer, turns up and is about to do them in, too, but is stopped by the police, who arrive and arrest him.

This film was one of the few made by the immortal Sonny Tufts after 1952. His problem, according to Harry and Michael Medved, authors of *The Golden Turkey*

Awards, "went beyond mere ineptitude. There was a certain magic that took place whenever he walked onto a set that absolutely guaranteed low quality for the resulting film." During the 1940s, Tufts, promoted as a glamor boy, amassed a record of enough celluloid bombs to put an end to his career by the early fifties. Although his film career fizzled, Tufts managed to stay in the public eye through a series of bar brawls and peccadillos. In 1954 he was sued for $250,000 by a stripper named Melody Carol who claimed Tufts had disfigured her by taking a bite out of her left thigh. Carol eventually settled out of court for $600, but a year later, Tufts was picked up by the police for beating up a woman at another bar. The man who some bad movie buffs rate as the worst actor of all time died of pneumonia in 1970 at the age of fifty-four.

Although *No Escape* is of higher quality than most of Tufts's fare, he turns in his usual bad performance, and the rest of the cast, although competent, cannot rescue a movie that is slow paced and wordy.

Nowhere to Go (1959) MGM. (Brit.) 87m. (B&W) P: Michael Balcon. D: Seth Holt. Sc: Holt and Kenneth Tynan, based on a novel by Donald MacKenzie. Ph: Paul Beeson. Ed: Harry Aldous. M: Dizzy Reece. CAST: George Nader, Maggie Smith, Bernard Lee, Geoffrey Keen, Bessie Love, Howard Marion Crawford, Arthur Howard, John Welsh, Margaret McGrath, Harry Corbett.   Canadian burglar Nader escapes from prison and is on the lam. In a flashback, it is revealed that he conned an older woman and, after stealing and selling her rare coin collection, wound up with a nest egg before being arrested. In trying to retrieve the money after his prison escape, he is double-crossed by his partner, unintentionally kills him during a fight, and ends up wanted for murder. Smith takes him in, but his paranoia leads him to think she will turn him in; in his attempt to get away, he is shot to death by the police.

Produced in Britain, this little known but exceptional noir is beautifully realized from start to finish and has a fine jazz score by trumpeter Reece. This was Maggie Smith's film debut.

Open Secret (1948) Eagle Lion. 70m. (B&W) P: Frank Satenstein. D: John Reinhardt. Sc: Henry Blankfort and Max Wilk, from a story by Wilk and Ted Murkland. Ph: George Robinson. Ed: Jason Bernie. M: Herschel Gilbert. CAST: John

Ireland, Jane Randolph, Roman Bohnen, Sheldon Leonard, George Tyne, Morgan Farley, Arthur O'Connell, Ellen Lowe, Anne O'Neal, John Alvin, Bert Conway, King Donovan.   Ireland and his wife come to stay with a wartime buddy who turns up missing. During his stay, Ireland finds that his friend belonged to a secret, anti-Semitic, white supremacist group that has been terrorizing and even murdering Jews in the neighborhood. When the wartime buddy is found murdered, Ireland discovers the motive to be photographs the buddy has taken of the group, which consists of some of the town's respectable businessmen. The group picks up Ireland and is going to kill him, but he is saved by the cops. As a final twist, the leader of the gang turns out to be a sleazy politician who Ireland thought represented an exposé magazine.

The film is above average and memorable because it's one of the few in which Sheldon Leonard appears as a cop and not a criminal. (V)

Paid to Kill (1954) Hammer/Lippert. (Brit.) 72m. (B&W) AKA: *Five Days*. P: Anthony Hinds. D: Montgomery Tully. Sc: Paul Tabori. Ph: Jimmy Harvey. Ed: James Needs. M: Ivor Slaney. CAST: Dane Clark, Thea Gregory, Paul Carpenter, Cecile Chereau, Anthony Forwood, Howard Marion Crawford, Avis Scott, Peter Gawthorne, Hugo Schuster.   When businessman Clark loses all his money, he takes out a large insurance policy and asks his lifelong buddy, Carpenter, to murder him so that his wife, Gregory, will have the insurance money. Carpenter refuses but relents when Clark tells him he knows about a murder Carpenter committed years before. When Clark's financial situation suddenly changes, he desperately tries to find Carpenter to cancel the deal. After he almost gets it a couple of times, Clark decides to go into hiding, but when he tells his wife of his plans, his business partner, Forwood, appears with a gun and tells him that he and Gregory are lovers and have conspired to murder him. When they learned of the murder plan, they kidnapped Carpenter and planned to kill both of them, making it look like a murder-suicide. Clark's secretary arrives, and in an ensuing struggle for the gun, Gregory is killed and Forwood is turned over to the police.

The premise was lifted directly from the original, *The Whistler*, but the movie is not nearly as good.

Parole, Inc. (1948) Eagle Lion. 71m. (B&W) P: Constantin J. David. D: Alfred Zeisler. Sc: Sherman L. Lowe, from the story by Lowe and Royal K. Cole. Ph:

Gilbert Warrenton. Ed: John D. Faure. M: Alexander Laszlo. CAST: Michael O'Shea, Turhan Bey, Evelyn Ankers, Virginia Lee, Charles Bradstreet, Lyle Talbot, Michael Whalen, Charles Williams.   The tale is told in flashback from a hospital bed by federal agent O'Shea, who is badly beaten. At a secret meeting of police officials concerned about corruption within the state parole board, which is releasing dangerous criminals into the population, O'Shea is given the task of infiltrating the underworld and ferreting out the rotten apples. He takes on the identity of a paroled criminal who is out of the country and starts to frequent Ankers's club, a hangout for paroled felons. He works his way into the crooks' confidence and finds out that Bey, Ankers's attorney and lover, is the head honcho for the ring. O'Shea goes to a farm owned by Bey, ostensibly to meet his ex-partner in crime, who is now paroled. He manages to plant a recorder in the house and lures the two crooked parole board members to the farm. His "ex-partner," whom O'Shea originally had put in prison, shows up and uncovers O'Shea as a cop. O'Shea is beaten up, but the police arrive to save him from extinction.

Ultracheap fare even for Eagle Lion, *Parole, Inc.* is a marginal noir and lacks any element of suspense. Ankers and Bey, both competent remnants from Universal horror flicks a few years before, sleepwalk through the film, and O'Shea plays the same role he did in countless other programmers. The shoddiness of the production makes this one hard to watch. (V)

Philo Vance's Gamble (1947) PRC. 62m. (B&W) P: Howard Welsch. D: Basil Wrangell. Sc: Eugene Conrad and Arthur St. Clair, based on a story by Lawrence Edmund Taylor and on characters created by S. S. Van Dine. Ph: Jackson Rose. Ed: W. Donn Hayes. M: Irving Friedman. CAST: Alan Curtis, Terry Austin, Frank Jenks, Tala Birell, Gavin Gordon, Cliff Clark, Toni Todd, James Burke, Francis Pierlot, Grady Sutton.   PI Vance, while on a trip out West, is asked for help by an actress acquaintance who is trying to jump-start her career in Hollywood. It seems the show that's going to make her hinges on the sale of a famous and invaluable emerald currently in the possession of a racketeer. While Vance is visiting the racketeer, the bad guy is snuffed. The corpses begin to pile up after that (the victims always killed by the ubiquitous gun barrel poking from behind a curtain). Vance recovers the emerald and determines that the aspiring actress is the murderer.

The S. S. Van Dine (real name Willard Wright) character of Philo Vance was originally portrayed on the screen by William Powell in 1929 (in a production that began as a silent film and was completed with sound). In the subsequent series of eleven films, which ended in 1940, Vance remained the same urbane, debonair character (portrayed by Basil Rathbone, Warren William, Grant Richards, Paul Lukas, and James Stephenson). In 1947, PRC revived the character in *Philo Vance Returns* with William Wright in the title role and produced two more films starring Alan Curtis. By this time, Philo Vance had changed into a hard-boiled, wise-cracking detective, obviously transformed because Hollywood had embraced the popular, tough-guy writers of the pulps. Of all the PRC entries, however, only *Philo Vance's Gamble* was given the noir treatment, the other two being more whodunits with a lot of cutesy dialogue and large doses of comic relief by Jenks as Vance's sidekick. By this time, Grady Sutton, who played so brilliantly against W. C. Fields in *The Man on the Flying Trapeze* and *The Bank Dick*, was reduced to playing a bit part as secretary to the DA.

Pickup (1951) Columbia. 76m. (B&W) P&D: Hugo Haas. Sc: Haas and Arnold Phillips, based on the novel *Watchman 47* by Joseph Kopta. Ph: Paul Ivano. Ed: Donald W. Bagler. M: Harold Byrns. CAST: Hugo Haas, Beverly Michaels, Allan Nixon, Howland Chamberan, Jo Carroll Dennison, Mark Lowell, Bernard Gorcey.   Haas is a rich and lonely, half-deaf and middle-aged widower who is married by floozy Michaels for his money. She and her lover intend to kill the old nuisance by running him over (see *Hit and Run*, featuring this favorite means of disposal by Haas), but in a fit of conscience, the lover swerves the car and they succeed only in knocking Haas down, restoring his hearing in the process. When he recovers, Haas sees how he's been suckered and tosses Michaels out.

   God knows why Columbia turned Haas loose to do what he wanted, but they did.

Please Murder Me (1956) Distributors Corporation of America. 78m. (B&W) P: Donald Hyde. D: Peter Godfrey. Sc: Al C. Ward and Hyde, based on an original story by E. A. Dupont and David Chantler. Ph: Allen Stensvold. Ed: Kenneth Crane. M: Albert Glasser. CAST: Angela Lansbury, Raymond Burr, Dick Foran, John Dehner, Lamont Johnson, Robert Griffin, Denver Pyle, Alex Sharpe, Lee Miller.   Burr, a whizbang lawyer, goes to his best friend, Foran, who saved his life in the war, and tells him that Foran's wife, Lansbury, and he are in love and that she wants a divorce. Foran tells Burr he'll have to think about it, goes home and confronts Lansbury, who shoots him. She tells the police that it was self-defense, that Foran was going to kill her, but they indict her for murder. Burr defends her, getting her off by providing the reason for Foran's rage—Burr himself. Later, when Burr pushes Lansbury to marry him, he gets a posthumous letter from Foran, telling him that Lansbury is no good and is in love with a young artist, not Burr. Burr locates and makes friends with the artist, who is unaware of Lansbury's duplicity. In a fit of guilty conscience, knowing he has betrayed his best friend and that Lansbury not only doesn't love him but used him to get herself off a murder rap, Burr forces Lansbury to shoot him to death by threatening to wreck her life. The DA, having been called by Burr, arrives on the scene just after the crime, which Burr has secretly recorded to make sure Lansbury gets her just desserts.

Pedestrian material is elevated by the performances of Burr and Lansbury. (V)

Port of New York (1949) Eagle Lion. 82m. (B&W) P: Aubrey Schenck. D: Laslo Benedek. Sc: Eugene Ling, adapted by Leo Townsend from a story by Arthur A. Ross and Bert Murray. Ph: George K. Diskant. Ed: Geraldine Lerner. M: Sol Kaplan. CAST: Scott Brady, Richard Rober, K. T. Stevens, Yul Brynner, Arthur Blake, Lynne Carter, John Kellogg, William Challee, Neville Brand (unbilled).   As a passenger ship arrives in New York, a female passenger witnesses the ship's purser go over the side in a raft. The purser is picked up by a launch, stabbed to death, and dumped into the harbor. The female witness is part of a gang of smugglers headed by Brynner. The purser was killed because he helped the gang steal a shipment of morphine headed for a medical lab. Discovering the narcotics missing, federal agents Brady and Rober are called into the case. Brynner's girlfriend, nervous about being part of a murder, contacts the agents and tells them about part of the shipment that she has stored in a locker. Brynner finds out she is cooperating with the police and kills her. Brady and Rober stake out the locker and tail the messenger who picks it up to a nightclub, where he delivers the package to the club comedian. They arrest the comedian, and the comic's girlfriend goes to Brynner to see if he can help. The comedian tells the agents about Brynner's yacht, and the pair sneak aboard to find incriminating evidence. Brady is caught and murdered by the gang. To get inside the operation, Rober assumes the identity of a Canadian drug dealer. The comedian is inadvertently released by the police and is killed by Brynner's people. Rober meets Brynner aboard his yacht and arranges for a dope purchase, but while he is there, the comedian's girlfriend shows up and reveals Rober as a cop. Before they can kill him, the feds show up and arrest Brynner and his cohorts.

Done in voice-over documentary style, this hard-edged, violent film generates a sinister, brooding atmosphere through its use of New York locations and some nice photography and good direction. The film industry must have noticed the latter, as Laslo Benedek was soon hired to direct some top-notch A films, such as *Death of a Salesman* (1952) and *The Wild One* (1954). *Port of New York* was Yul Brynner's film debut and one of the few movies in which he appeared with hair. (V)

Power of the Whistler (1945) Columbia. 66m. (B&W) P: Leonard S. Picker. D: Lew Landers. Sc: Aubrey Wisberg, based on the radio program *The Whistler*. Ph: L. W. O'Connell. Ed: Reg Browne. M: Wilbur Hatch. CAST: Richard Dix, Janis Carter, Jeff Donnell, Loren Tindall, Tala Birell, John Abbott, Murray Alper. After being hit by a car, Dix becomes amnesiac. He is befriended by Carter, who enlists the aid of her younger sister to help Dix find his identity. The younger sister discovers that Dix is really an escaped homicidal mental patient who intends to kill the judge who committed him and the warden of the hospital where he was confined. Meanwhile, Dix has recovered his memory, and while on his homicidal sojourn to kill the judge, he tries to do in Carter, who kills him while trying to save her own life.

Carter, who played the unforgettable sexual psychopath in the very noir *Night Editor*, reverses roles here as the innocent victim and pulls it off just as well. Dix, who had a tendency to be as wooden as the walking tree in *From Hell It Came*, is convincingly menacing as the nut case.

Price of Fear, The (1956). Universal. 79m. (B&W) P: Howard Christie. D: Abner Biberman. Sc: Robert Tallman, from a story by Dick Irving. Ph: Irving Glassberg. Ed: Ray Snyder. M: Joseph Gershenson. CAST: Merle Oberon, Lex Barker, Charles Drake, Gia Scala, Warren Stevens, Phillip Pine, Mary Field, Dan Riss, Konstantin Shayne, Stafford Repp, Tim Sullivan.   When dog track owner Barker finds out his partner has sold out to gangster Stevens, he goes to Stevens's nightclub to protest. He finds the ex-partner there, threatens to kill him, and is thrown out of the club. Barker takes a cab and is tailed by Pine, who has instructions from his boss, Stevens, to get rid of the pesky partner. In the meantime, Oberon, a successful businesswoman, leaves a dinner club and drives home after having too many. She runs down an old man crossing the street and, in a panic, leaves the scene. When reason catches up with her, she stops at a pay phone to call the police and report the accident. Barker, knowing he's being tailed, bails out of the cab and stumbles onto Oberon's car. He takes her car, and Oberon, seeing an out for herself, reports the car stolen. Across town, Stevens, knowing everyone in his joint heard Barker threaten his ex-partner, shoots the man to death in an attempt to frame Barker for the crime and get the whole track. Barker is picked up by the cops and charged with grand theft auto and hit-and-run. Since the hit-and-run victim is still alive and Barker knows he's being framed for murder, he confesses to the former crime to use it as an alibi. Barker bails himself out of jail and goes to see Oberon to explain what happened, and the two start up an affair. Knowing the cab driver is Barker's alibi, Barker and Stevens both begin a hunt for the man. Stevens, guessing Oberon is really guilty of the hit-and-run, begins to blackmail her. Barker finds the cab driver's address and goes there, but Oberon buys off the man's wife in order to keep her husband under wraps. The hit-and-run victim dies and Scala, the man's daughter, comes to Barker and swears revenge. In a fit of conscience, the cab driver decides to clear Barker but is killed by Pine before he can do so. The driver's widow confronts Oberon in front of Barker, and he finds out about her duplicity; Oberon lies her way out, telling him she loves him and is going to turn herself in. The next day, she phones Barker and tells him she can't go through with it and that she's leaving the country, giving him her train number. Scala, now believing in Barker's innocence and Oberon's guilt, calls Barker's cop-buddy, Drake, and tells him about the train. Barker gets on the train and tries to talk Oberon into facing the music, but she leads him back to the baggage car, where Stevens and Pine are waiting. Barker realizes Oberon has set him up; she responds, "I made one mistake . . . and when I wanted to stop, I was weak." The gangsters are going to throw Barker off the train, but Oberon grabs one of the men's gun arm just as Drake arrives and shoots Stevens to death. Professing her love for Barker, Oberon jumps off the train to her death.

This film depends on even more coincidences than most films noirs, but once you get past the first four, you can forgive the rest. The movie has good production values and decent performances. Barker, most well known for playing Tarzan from 1949 to 1955, puts in a low-key but reasonable acting job, as do Stevens and the rest of the cast. Oberon, a megastar of the late thirties and forties (*Wuthering*

Heights was just one of her starring roles), by the mid-fifties had been reduced to Bo, and she did few films after *The Price of Fear*. Ironically, one of her last screen performances was in the 1967 star-studded film *Hotel*, in which she plays a European aristocrat who breaks the law in trying to save her husband, who is involved in a fatal hit-and-run accident.

Red Menace, The (1949) Republic. 81m. (B&W) P: Herbert J. Yates. D: R. G. Springsteen. Sc: Albert DeMond and Gerald Geraghty, based on a story by De-Mond. Ph: John MacBurnie. Ed: Harry Keller. M: Nathan Scott. CAST: Robert Rockwell, Hanne Axman, Shepard Menken, Barbara Fuller, Betty Lou Gerson, James Harrington, Lester Luther, William J. Lally, William Martel, Duke Williams. Rockwell (Mr. Boynton of *Our Miss Brooks*), a disillusioned GI, is sucked into the Communist movement and falls in love with Axman, a "teacher" of Marxism. The two of them make it into the elite inner circle of the Party, but after witnessing the murder of one dissenter and the suicide of another, they become disillusioned and decide to get out. They become objects of extermination by the Party higher-ups and take off together, fearing for their lives. They eventually turn themselves in, realizing they are not the bad guys but merely stupid.

This film is an absolute must-see classic, the *Attack of the 50-Foot Woman* of the Red-scare films. The story is told in flashback in the documentary style popularized by such noirs as *The Naked City*, narrated by "Lloyd G. Davis, member of the Los Angeles City Council." Notable are the scenes in which a priest, delivering a lecture about the evils of communism, steals a fifty-cent piece from a Party member for the poor box and Gerson's going-nuts scene in front of the cops. It is also never explains why a simple worker who walks out of an indoctrination meeting is beaten to death, whereas Menken, a member of the inner circle who resigns from the Party, is merely designated for the cold shoulder by his former Party colleagues; depressed, he finally commits suicide by jumping out of a window. The moral apparently seems to be: "The farther up you get in the organization and learn the secrets that could send everyone to prison, the safer you are."

Return of the Whistler, The (1948) Columbia. 60m. (B&W) P: Rudolph C. Flothow. D: Ross Lederman. Sc: Edward Bock and Maurice Tombragel, based on the story "All At Once, No Alice" by Cornell Woolrich. Ph: Philip Tannura. Ed: Dwight Campbell. M: Mischa Bakaleinikoff. CAST: Michael Duane, Lenore Aubert, Richard Lane, James Cardwell, Ann Shoemaker, Wilton Graff, Olin Howlin, Eddy Waller, Ann Doran, Emmett Keane.   On the eve of their marriage, Duane's fiancée, Aubert, disappears. He sets out to find her, but the task is difficult because he knows almost nothing about her past aside from her claim that she was the French widow of an American flyer. She had come to America and moved in with her dead husband's in-laws, but when one of them made a pass at her, she ran away. Private detective Lane offers to help, and when Duane finds out the in-laws are the Barclays, a rich local family, Lane KOs Duane. Lane, it turns out, is working for the Barclays and was hired to find her and bring her home. Duane tracks down the house of the in-laws and is informed that Aubert was never married to the American flyer but is still married to someone else. Suspicious, Duane does some investigating and finds that the family is lying, that they are trying to seize the estate of the dead flyer and intend to commit Aubert. Posing as a mental patient, Duane goes to the sanitorium where Aubert is confined and frees her just as Lane, who figures he has been duped, shows up with the cops.

The last and weakest of the *Whistler* series, this entry is of note primarily because it was based on a story by Cornell Woolrich and also because it was the only film in the series that did not star Richard Dix. NOTE: Richard Lane, a veteran actor of many B movies, would a few years later change his vocation to wrestling announcer, going by the name Dick Lane and making famous his trademark exclamation "Whhoooa, Nellie!" as wrestlers were slammed into the mat.

Revolt in the Big House (1958) Allied Artists. 79m. (B&W) P: David Diamond. D: R. G. Springsteen. Ph: William Margulies. Ed: William Austin. CAST: Gene Evans, Robert Blake, Timothy Carey, John Qualen, Sam Edwards, John Dennis, Walter Barnes, Frank Richards, Arlene Hunter.   While serving a stretch, Evans, a superracketeer, manipulates his Mexican cellmate, Blake, into planning a bustout. They plan a riot that will allow Evans to get away during the ado, but at the last minute, Blake changes his mind after he realizes that Evans has rigged it that some of Blake's friends will be killed by the guards to provide the distraction. Before he can warn his friends not to riot, Blake is knifed by Evans. Evans escapes but meets his fate in the subway when he is gunned down by police.

This taut film is exceptional for its meager budget and has good performances by Evans and Blake.

Riff Raff (1947) RKO. 80m. (B&W) P: Nat Holt. D: Ted Tetzlaff. Sc: Martin Rackin. Ph: George E. Diskant. Ed: Philip Martin. M: Roy Webb. CAST: Pat O'Brien, Walter Slezak, Anne Jeffreys, Percy Kilbride, Jerome Cowan, George Givot, Jason Robards, Marc Krah.   O'Brien is a private eye in Panama City who is hired by Krah to protect him. Although O'Brien doesn't know it, Krah murdered a man to get a valuable map showing the location of rich oil deposits in South America. Slezak is a villain who also wants the map. Cowan, an oil company executive, not knowing Krah has hired O'Brien, also hires O'Brien to locate Krah and get the map, but Slezak gets to Krah first and kills him. Jeffreys, a nightclub singer and Cowan's girlfriend, is ordered by Cowan to get close to O'Brien to find out what he knows, but she gets too close and the two start up an affair. After Slezak murders Cowan and his hoods give O'Brien a good beating, O'Brien finds the map (which Krah stashed in plain sight in O'Brien's office—the old purloined-letter gag) and gets even by turning Slezak and his crew over to the cops.

This all-around entertaining film has snappy dialogue, a breezy characterization by O'Brien, and exceptional cinematography. In the first five minutes of the movie, one of filmdom's absolute classic beginnings, not a word of dialogue is spoken! Tetzlaff, a former cinematographer who had done the camera work for Hitchcock's *Notorious* a year before, went on to direct other noir films such as *A Dangerous Profession* (1946), *Gambling House* (1951), and the Cornell Woolrich classic *The Window* (1949), all for RKO. (V)

Rio (1939) Universal. 75m. (B&W) D: John Brahm. Sc: Stephen Morehouse Avery, Frank Partos, Edwin Justus Mayer, and Aben Kandel, based on a story by Jean Negulesco. Ph: Hal Mohr. Ed: Phil Cahn. M: Charles Previn. CAST: Basil Rathbone, Victor McLaglen, Sigrid Gurie, Robert Cummings, Leo Carrillo, Billy Gilbert, Maurice Moscovitz, Samuel S. Hinds.   Rathbone, a ruthless banker who has been sentenced to a ten-year prison stretch for cheating people out of their money, busts out with the aid of his wife, Gurie, and faithful servant, McLaglen. When Rathbone finds out that his wife has fallen for Cummings, he plans to kill the man, but McLaglen, siding with Gurie, kills Rathbone instead.

One of the few early noir entries by Universal, *Rio* is prosaic on some levels but succeeds on others with good direction by Brahm and a believably obsessive performance by Rathbone. Rumanian Jean Negulesco, who wrote the original story, would go on to become one of the most famous directors in Hollywood, directing four A noirs—*The Mask of Dimitrios* (1944), *Nobody Lives Forever* (1946), *Road House* (1948), and *Deep Valley* (1947)—before turning to big-budget dramas and comedies in the 1950s, for example, *Titanic* (1953), *How to Marry a Millionaire* (1953), and *Daddy Long Legs* (1955).

Road to the Big House (1947) Screen Guild. 74m. (B&W) P: Selwyn Levinson and Walter Colmes. D: Colmes. Sc: Aubrey Wisberg. Ph: Walter Strenge. Ed: Jason Bernie. CAST: John Shelton, Ann Doran, Guinn Williams, Dick Butler, Joe Allen Jr., Rory Mallinson, Eddy Fields, Walden Boyle, Keith Richards. Shelton, trying to get himself out of the hole, embezzles $200,000 from the bank where he works. He hides the cash and is caught but doesn't mind, figuring he will do his time and live the rest of his life a rich man. His plans are foiled when a group of prisoners forces him into a prison break, during which he is caught and more years are added on to his sentence. At the end of the movie, Shelton, still in prison, learns that his wife has found the money and returned it to the police.

This film is extremely depressing.

Second Chance (1947) Twentieth Century Fox. 62m. (B&W) P: Sol W. Wurtzel. D: James S. Tinling. Sc: Arnold Belgard, based on a story by Lou Breslow and John Patrick. Ph: Benjamin Kline. Ed: Frank Baldrige. M: Dale Butts. CAST: Kent Taylor, Louise Currie, Dennis Hoey, Larry Blake, Ann Doran, John Eldredge, Paul Guilfoyle, William Newell, Guy Kingsford. Taylor and Currie pull off a jewel robbery and decide to team up. They are caught by the police, who are unable to pin anything on them. After an attempt to sell the stolen jewels back to the insurance company is broken up by the police, the pair decide to combine forces with a big gang. The gang plans to heist $1 million worth of diamonds by having Currie model the jewels and be kidnapped by the gang. Taylor and Currie have by this time fallen for each other. She tries to talk him out of the caper, but they find they are in too deep to get out. Whatever moves they make, however, the cops always seem to have the jump on them. Eventually, Currie reveals she's an insurance company detective and has been telling the cops of their moves. She tries to convince Taylor to turn himself in, but he refuses and she sends him over, telling him she'll wait for him.

Well crafted for its type, with a script reminiscent of something Hammett would write, this film packs a lot in a little over an hour. One can see in it the germ from which sprang Steve McQueen's smash hit *The Thomas Crown Affair*.

Secret of the Whistler (1946) Columbia. 68m. (B&W) P: Rudolph C. Flothow. D: George Sherman. Sc: Raymond L. Shrock, based on a story by Richard H. Landau. Ph: Allen Siegler. Ed: Dwight Caldwell. M: Mischa Bakaleinikoff. CAST: Richard Dix, Leslie Brooks, Marry Currier, Michael Duane, Mona Barrie, Ray Walker, Claire DuBrey, Charles Trowbridge, Arthur Space.   In this sixth entry in the series, Dix plays an artist married to a rich wife with a heart ailment. He becomes infatuated with cold-hearted artist's model Brooks, who plays him for a sucker. Dix's wife recovers enough to make a surprise visit to Dix at his studio and witnesses Dix making love to Brooks. Shattered, she makes her way home. Later, she confronts Dix and threatens to cut him out of her will. Dix tries to poison her before she can do that, but she sees him. She writes the incident down in her diary. Later, she dies of a heart attack, but Dix thinks she died from the poison and orders the body cremated. He marries Brooks but continues to have fits of conscience. Learning about his wife's diary, he searches frantically and finds it but, as there is nothing incriminating in it, starts to relax. When he learns that Brooks has possession of the incriminating page and intends to turn him over to the cops, Dix kills her. Ironically, after the diary is discovered, he is arrested not for the murder of Brooks but for the murder of his first wife.

This is another solid entry in the series and Dix's last role in it.

Shack Out on 101 (1955) Allied Artists. 80m. (B&W) P: Mort Millman. D: Edward Dein. Sc: Dein and Mildred Dein. Ph: Floyd Crosby. Ed: George White. M: Paul Dunlap. CAST: Terry Moore, Frank Lovejoy, Keenan Wynn, Lee Marvin, Whit Bissell, Jess Barker, Donald Murphy, Frank DeKova.   Lovejoy is a government agent posing as a professor willing to sell top secret information to Marvin, who is a short-order cook working in a greasy spoon owned by Wynn. Lovejoy's main goal is to find out who is the head of the spy ring Marvin works for. At the same time, Lovejoy is romantically involved with Moore, who is a waitress at the diner. When Moore finds out to her disenchantment that Lovejoy is a Commie, she threatens to tell, but Marvin finds out and stops her. When Marvin's identity as the head of the ring comes out, he holds everyone hostage at the diner. He intends to get out of the country but is killed by a speargun as government agents move in. Moore, of course, is relieved that her love, Lovejoy, is an okay guy.

Among the last of the Red-scare movies, this is also one of the most hilarious. It's in the so-bad-it's-great category. In what other genre could a grease-stained, lecherous cook named "Slob" also serve as Mr. Big in the Communist Party? (V)

Shed No Tears (1948) Eagle Lion. 70m. (B&W) P: Robert Frost. D: Jean Yarbrough. Sc: Brown Holmes and Virginia Cook, based on the novel by Don Martin. Ph: Frank Redman. Ed: Norman A. Cerf. M: Ralph Stanley. CAST: Wallace Ford, June Vincent, Robert Scott, Johnstone White, Dick Hogan, Frank Albertson.   At the urgings of his wife, Ford fakes his own death to collect the insurance money. The wife collects the dough but has been having an affair on the side for some time and double-crosses Ford. Ford's son from a previous marriage smells a rat and hires a detective to investigate, but the detective is bought off. When Ford finds out about his wife's infidelity, he commits suicide.

This downer is saved only by veteran actor Ford's performance.

Shoot to Kill (1947) Screen Guild. 64m. (B&W) P&D: William Berke. Sc: Edwin V. Westrate. Ph: Benjamin Kline. Ed: Arthur A. Brooks. M: Darrell Calker. CAST: Russell Wade, Edmund MacDonald, Susan Walters, Douglas Blackley, Vince Barnett, Nestor Paiva, Douglas Trowbridge, Harry Brown.   MacDonald, scheduled to take over as a big-city district attorney the following morning, is killed in a car wreck while fleeing the police. In the car with him were escaped convict Dixie Logan (Blackley), whom MacDonald sent up for twenty years on a murder beef, and MacDonald's wife, Walters. Walters is still alive, so intrepid reporter Wade questions her in an attempt to piece together what happened. Walters recalls in flashback how she went to work for MacDonald as a secretary and learned he was in cahoots with the town's political and gangster underworld. It was they who railroaded Blackley in order to take over the town. When MacDonald asked Walters to marry him, she agreed, knowing full well he was doing it solely to prevent her from testifying against him. Once married, she revealed herself to be a cynical opportunist, telling MacDonald she hated his guts and married him only for power.

She convinced him to pit the mob bosses against one another and take over the town, which he proceeded to do. In the end, it turns out that the justice of the peace who married her and MacDonald was Dixie Logan in disguise and that Walters is really Mrs. Dixie Logan. When Blackley and MacDonald decide to cooperate to take over the town, Walters, who was only trying to clear her framed husband, sees him for what he is and threatens to blow the whistle. The two bad guys decide she has to go, but before they can kill her, they get in a car wreck and die. Wade, who always had a soft spot for Walters, destroys her testimony to save her.

This film has a lot of plot twists for 64 minutes and is not without merit, at least for a Lippert film. (V)

Short Cut to Hell (1957) Paramount. 87m. (B&W) P: A. C. Lyles. D: James Cagney. Sc: Ted Berkman and Raphael Blau, based on a screenplay by W. R. Burnett from the novel *This Gun for Hire* by Graham Greene. Ph: Haskell Boggs. Ed: Tom McAdoo. M: Irvin Talbot. CAST: Robert Ivers, Georgann Johnson, William Bishop, Jacques Aubuchon, Peter Baldwin, Yvette Vickers, Murvyn Vye, Milton Frome, Jacquelin Beer.   Ivers is a hit man who murders two men for a friend. When he discovers that his buddy has paid him off with hot money and the cops know the serial numbers, he sets out to even the score with the cops hunting him for the killings. In order to protect himself, Ivers kidnaps Johnson, the girlfriend of the detective in charge of the case. In the end, he lets her go and is gunned down by the police.

A cheaply made version of *This Gun for Hire* (1942), this film is the only directorial effort by actor James Cagney, who appears in the prologue. The film is generally taut and well executed, and it is a mystery why Cagney never directed another film. Perhaps part of the reason was that Cagney agreed to take minimum scale for his salary and a percentage of the profits, which were not that great.

Sign of the Ram, The (1948). Columbia. 88m. (B&W) P: Irving Cummings Jr. D: John Sturges. Sc: Charles Bennett, based on the novel by Margaret Ferguson. Ph: Burnett Guffey. Ed: Aaron Stell. M: Morris Stoloff. CAST: Susan Peters, Alexander Knox, Phyllis Thaxter, Peggy Ann Garner, Ron Randell, Dame May Whitty, Allene Roberts, Ross Ford, Diana Douglas.   Wheelchair-bound Peters (whose birth sign is the ram, symbolic of trouble) lives in an English home with her husband, Knox, and his three grown children. Using her physical ailment to maliciously manipulate those around her, Peters comes to dominate everyone in the household. After breaking up the romance of one of Knox's daughters, she tries and nearly succeeds in driving the son's fiancée to suicide. Isolated in her own home as those around her become aware of her evil intentions, Peters becomes more and more emotionally and mentally unbalanced and eventually takes her own life by wheeling her chair off a cliff.

Peters had lost the use of her own legs in a hunting accident years before, and this was her first and only film. This was also one of the first directorial efforts by Sturges, who later directed superior films noirs such as *Mystery Street* (1950) and *The People Against O'Hara* (1951), as well as many high-budget productions for MGM, Warners, and Paramount.

Spectre of the Rose (1946) Republic. 90m. (B&W) P,D&Sc: Ben Hecht. Ph: Lee Garmes. Ed: Harry Keller. M: George Antheil. CAST: Judith Anderson, Michael Chekhov, Ivan Kirov, Viola Essen, Lionel Stander, Charles (Red) Marshall, George Shdanoff, Billy Gray, Juan Panalle, Lon Hearn, Ferike Boros, Bert Hanlon, Constantine.   Young ballerina Essen is swept off her feet by Chekhov, the lead dancer of her ballet troupe. Chekhov's earlier love, Nicki, had died on the stage of a heart attack, and Essen is warned by members of the troupe, in particular by Anderson, who was at one time a great ballerina herself, that Chekhov is teetering on the verge of insanity. Anderson tells her that Chekhov went crazy and attacked Nicki with a knife in her dressing room the night she died and that her heart attack was brought on by the attack. Love-bitten Essen won't listen, however, and marries Chekhov. The ballet troupe embarks on a successful international tour, but Essen's happiness is clouded by the fact that Chekhov is going slowly insane. Convinced she can nurse him back to health, Essen ditches the troupe and checks herself and Chekhov into a high-rise hotel. She takes some pills to help her sleep, and Chekhov, totally mad now, takes out a knife and performs his dance of death. To keep himself from killing Essen, Chekhov jumps out of the window to his death. Essen goes back to the ballet troupe and resumes her career.

This fascinating and truly strange film is by one of the greatest American writers of the twentieth century. (V)

Spider, The (1945) Twentieth Century Fox. 61m. (B&W) P: Ben Silvey. D: Robert Webb. Sc: Jo Eisinger and W. Scott Darling, based on a play by Charles Fulton Oursler and Lowell Brentano. Ph: Glen MacWilliams. Ed: Norman Colbert. M: David Buttolph. CAST: Richard Conte, Faye Marlowe, Kurt Kreuger, John Harvey, Martin Kosleck, Mantan Moreland, Walter Sande, Cara Williams, Charles Tannen, Margaret Brayton, Ann Savage.   New Orleans ex-cop-turned-PI Conte is approached by Marlowe to retrieve an envelope from his partner, Savage. Conte calls Savage, and she comes to his apartment, where she is murdered by a shadowy figure of a man who sneaks in and strangles her. Knowing things look bad, Conte and his assistant, Moreland, move the body to Savage's own apartment, but Conte finds himself a prime suspect by the cops anyway. In searching for Savage's killer, Conte discovers that his client, Marlowe, is really a stage mentalist called the Spider Woman. He also discovers that Asther, her stage manager, among others, are also looking for the mysterious envelope. Marlowe tells Conte that she hired Savage to find out what happened to her twin sister, who disappeared five years earlier. Savage told Marlowe she had proof that the sister was murdered (the contents of the envelope). Conte, whose moves are being watched by the same shadowy figure who murdered Savage, returns to Savage's apartment and finds the envelope. The contents reveal that the sister was murdered in a hotel and that after the murder, her unidentified boyfriend vanished. Conte talks to the manager of the hotel, who claims he could identify the boyfriend if he saw him again. Conte gives him a ticket to the theater where the Spider Woman is playing, but before the manager can get there, he is murdered. Conte is arrested for the murder of Savage but breaks out of jail and goes to the theater. He is about to reveal to Marlowe that the killer-boyfriend is her stage partner when the murderer gets the drop on them. Before he can kill them, the police arrive and foil his plans.

Set in the New Orleans French Quarter, this is a so-so remake of the 1931 film of the same name and another example of the fact that Fox was not really comfortable making B noirs.

Spin a Dark Web (1956) Columbia. (Brit.) 76m. (B&W) P: M. J. Frankovich and George Maynard. D: Vernon Sewell. Sc: Ian Stuart Black, from the novel *Wide Boys Never Work* by Robert Westerby. Ph: Basil Emmott. Ed: Peter Rolfe Johnson. M: Mark Paul and Paddy Roberts. CAST: Faith Domergue, Lee Patterson, Rona Anderson, Martin Benson, Robert Arden, Joss Ambler, Peter Hammond, Peter Burton.   Patterson is a Canadian vet in London, trying to make it as a boxer without much success. He meets Domergue, the sister of a Sicilian London mob kingpin who specializes in fixing races, and is seduced by her feminine wiles and promise of easy money into joining the gang. When murder becomes part of the deal, he tries to back out; Domergue won't let him, and he finds himself getting in deeper and deeper. The film ends with a dash for a waiting boat during which the gang leaders are killed and Patterson is wounded. He ends up with Anderson, the "good girl" of the piece.

Domergue was handpicked by Howard Hughes in the late forties to be an RKO vamp (and, presumably, to take on other roles in his personal life) and starred with Robert Mitchum as the nutso femme fatale in the noir *Where Danger Lives*. She was later dropped by Hughes and became a screamer in sci-fi films like *This Island Earth* and *It Came from Beneath the Sea* before her career in the States started to wane. In 1956, she journeyed to Britain, where she starred in this film and sci-fi *The Atomic Man* with Gene Nelson, whose American career had also started to fizzle (see *The Way Out*). Soon after that, she married an Argentinian businessman and moved to Switzerland.

Spiritualist, The (1948) Eagle Lion. 79 min. (B&W) AKA: *The Amazing Mr. X.* P: Ben Stoloff. D: Bernard Vorhaus. Sc: Muriel Roy Bolton and Ian McLellan Hunter, from an original story by Crane Wilbur. Ph: John Alton. Ed: Norman Colbert. M: Alexander Laszlo. CAST: Turhan Bey, Lynn Bari, Cathy O'Donnell, Richard Carlson, Donald Curtis, Virginia Gregg, Harry Mendoza.   Emotionally unbalanced and rich Bari is haunted by the voice of her dead husband, who allegedly drowned in a boating accident. When she "accidentally" runs into spiritualist Bey while walking on the beach, she enlists him to get in touch with her husband on "the other side." Bey is a con man, and once he gets Bari's confidence through some slick trickery, the "dead" husband (Curtis) shows up and blackmails Bey into continuing his charade. The husband's plan is to kill Bari, then show up and inherit the estate. In the meantime, Bari's younger sister, O'Donnell, falls for Bey, who has a change of heart and thwarts the murder plan by using his flimflammery on Curtis, getting killed himself in the process.

Everything in this superior small film is well done, from writing to photography to acting. The original story was penned by talented writer, director, photographer, and actor Crane Wilbur, who went on to write the screenplays for the noir films *Phenix City Story* and *I Was a Communist for the F.B.I.* and the classic 3-D horror film *House of Wax.* (V)

Split Second (1953) RKO. 85m. (B&W) P: Edmund Grainger. D: Dick Powell. Sc: William Bowers and Irving Wallace, from a story by Chester Erskine and Irving Wallace. Ph: Nicholas Musuraca. Ed: Robert Ford. M: Roy Webb. CAST: Stephen McNally, Alexis Smith, Jan Sterling, Keith Andes, Paul Kelly, Arthur Hunnicutt, Robert Paige, Richard Egan, Frank deKova.   Killer McNally and his wounded mentor, Kelly, bust out of a Carson City, Nevada, prison and are picked up by gang member deKova. Andes, a reporter assigned to cover the story, meets cynical out-of-work dancer Sterling in a Nevada café and gives her a lift. The gangsters, in a search for a new car, take over a desert gas station after McNally brutally kills the attendant. Smith, the wife of doctor Egan, and Paige, with whom she is having an adulterous affair, pull in for some gas. McNally and company take them and their car. Running into a roadblock, they are forced to take a dirt road. McNally, seeking help for his wounded pal Kelly, calls Egan and tells him that if he wants to see his wife alive again, he must meet him at a ghost town in the desert. The gang runs out of gas, and when Andes and Sterling show up, McNally takes them and their car to a desert ghost town, where he knows he will be safe because it is to be the site of an atomic test blast the next morning at 6:30. Smith, perfidious and sexually aroused by the animalistic McNally, starts up an affair with the gangster and begs him to take her with him when he goes. Prospector Hunnicutt pops in and adds to the hostage count. McNally, attracted to the hard-boiled Sterling, now shows disdain for Smith and offers to take Sterling along when he leaves. Playing the chivalrous role to protect Smith, Paige is mercilessly gunned down by McNally. Although disgusted by his wife's behavior and aware of her infidelity, Egan shows up to save her life and operates on Kelly, saving his life. Andes tries to get the drop on McNally and is beaten up by the gangster, who slaps Sterling around when she tries to stop it. Smith, who is willing to let her husband and everyone else die, begs McNally to take her with him, but he rejects her. McNally is going to tie up all the hostages, but Kelly, having a fit of conscience because of his near-death experiences, pulls a gun on McNally and tells him to leave them alone. Just then, the five-minute warning blows; the atomic test, to McNally's surprise, has been moved up an hour. As McNally and Kelly dash for the car, followed by Smith, deKova is overpowered by the hostages. McNally drives the wrong way, and the trio is killed by the nuclear explosion. The hostages, who have taken refuge in an abandoned mine shaft, survive.

Sort of an atomic *The Desperate Hours*, this film was actor Dick Powell's directorial debut. Well paced with a good script, direction, and cinematography by Nicholas Murusaca, who shot such classic noirs as *Stranger on the Third Floor* (1940), *Out of the Past* (1947), and *The Hitch-Hiker* (1953), *Split Second* is a superior suspense film.

Stakeout on Dope Street (1958) Warner Brothers. 83m. (B&W) P. Andrew Fenady. D: Irvin Kershner. Sc: Kershner, Irwin Schwartz, and Fenady. Ph: Mark Jeffrey. Ed: Melvin Sloan. M: Richard Markowitz. CAST: Yale Wexler, Jonathon Haze, Morris Miller, Abby Dalton, Allen Kramer, Herman Rudin, Philip Mansour, Frank Harding, Bill Shaw, A. J. Fenady, Herschel Bernardi. While being arrested, a dope dealer kills a couple of cops and loses his briefcase containing a can of uncut heroin in the process. The briefcase is found by three teenagers (Wexler, Haze, and Miller), who throw away the can and hock the briefcase. When they read the papers and find out what they've thrown away, they go to the city dump to look for it. When they find it, they decide to go into the dope-selling business, but not knowing how to do that, they recruit a junkie to sell it for them. Wexler, in the meantime, has begun to have reservations about what they are doing, but his two pals like the easy money. The gangsters trace the dope to the junkie and, interrogating him, kill him. Miller, making a visit to the junkie, is beaten to a pulp by the thugs, and Haze is forced at gunpoint to tell them where the stash is after Wexler threatens to take the junk to the cops. Wexler, in possession of the heroin, flees the gangsters, and Haze alerts the police. Wexler is chased into an industrial yard, where he climbs a high tower. When the gangsters try to climb up after him, he empties the can of heroin on the head of one of them. The cops arrive in the knick of time, shooting the gangster off the tower and arresting his partner. Wexler and company, having seen the error of their ways, are taken into custody by the cops.

Done documentary style with narrative voice-overs, this bad and extremely cheap film has some memorable lines, including a complaint by one of the investigating detectives about the lack of information on the street: "There isn't a whisper of a rumble out there." Writer-director Fenady went on to write books as well as movies such as *The Man with Bogart's Face*. This was the directorial debut of Kershner, who directed *The Empire Strikes Back*.

Strange Impersonation (1946) Republic. 68m. (B&W) P: William Wilder. D: Anthony Mann. Sc: Mildred Lord, from a story by Anne Wigton and Louis Herman. Ph: Robert W. Pittack. Ed: John F. Link. M: Alexander Laszlo. CAST: Brenda Marshall, William Gargan, Hillary Brooke, George Chandler, Ruth Ford, H. B. Warner, Lyle Talbot, Mary Treen, Cay Forrester, Dick Scott.   Marshall is a research scientist who knocks a drunk woman (Ford) down while backing her car out of a garage. Ford is not seriously hurt, and the accident was her fault, but an ambulance-chasing attorney tries to solicit her business. Marshall drives Ford home and gives her a few dollars and thinks that is that. Returning to her own apartment, she meets her sweetheart, Gargan, a medical colleague. He proposes to her and tells her she has to make a decision tonight, as he is leaving in the morning to take an important post overseas. She turns him down, as she is in the midst of experimenting with a new anesthetic. When her research assistant, Brooke, arrives, Marshall decides to speed up the experimental process by experimenting on herself. She puts herself out, and while she is asleep, Brooke, who wants Gargan for herself, causes a fiery explosion that disfigures Marshall's face. Brooke inserts herself between the recovering Marshall and Gargan, making Marshall think Gargan wants nothing to do with her now that she's ugly. When she gets home from the hospital, Marshall is confronted by Ford, who has been convinced by the ambulance chaser that her case is worth $25,000. She pulls out a gun and demands the money, and when Marshall tells her she doesn't have it, Ford starts looking around for what she can take. She takes Marshall's engagement ring, after which the two struggle and Ford falls out of the window on her face, obliterating her features. Marshall flees New York and goes to LA, where she has plastic surgery to make her look like the dead woman. Assuming Ford's identity, she returns to New York, where she angles a job with Gargan, who doesn't recognize her. She now knows Brooke disfigured her intentionally and tells Brooke she is going to take Gargan away from her, which she does. As Marshall and Gargan are at the airport waiting to go away to Paris together, the shyster lawyer, angry with his "client" for not paying him, appears with the cops, who arrest Marshall for her own murder. She tries to convince the cops of her true identity, but Gargan can't truthfully identify her as her old self, and Brooke, knowing the truth, refuses to. At that point, Marshall awakens to find it has all been only a dream induced by the anesthetic.

   Probably the most interesting thing about *Strange Impersonation*, aside from its out-and-out oddity, is that it was directed by Anthony Mann and that it was probably the cheapest film he ever made. From a cinematographic standpoint, *Strange Impersonation* is flat and exhibits little of Mann's later brilliant work. And although the story could have been truly dark, the ending leaves the viewer feeling robbed.

Strange Mr. Gregory, The (1945) Monogram. 63m. (B&W) P: Louis Berkoff. D: Phil Rosen. Sc: Charles S. Belden, based on the story by Myles Connolly. Ph: Ira Morgan. Ed: Seth Larson. CAST: Edmund Lowe, Jean Rogers, Don Douglas, Frank Reicher, Majorie Hoshelle, Robert Emmett Keane, Jonathon Hale, Frank Mayo.   Lowe, a stage mentalist and magician, is an expert in Tibetan meditation practices that allow him to go into a state of suspended animation simulating death. During a performance, he meets and becomes obsessed with the wife of another man and, to get her, frames the man for his own "murder" as well as for the cold-blooded murder of his longtime and devoted servant, the only man who knew Lowe's secret. The husband is convicted and sent to prison. Lowe returns as his own twin brother and charms the wife into falling for him. A friend of the woman smells a rat, and after the cops find Lowe's coffin empty, the wife learns the truth. Mentally unbalanced and knowing the cops are closing in, Lowe decides that if he can't have the woman, nobody can. The police arrive in time to shoot Lowe and save the woman.

This noir is totally off-beat but nicely done with Lowe playing his part as the crazed magician to the hilt.

Strangers in the Night (1944) Republic. 56m. (B&W) P: Rudolph E. Abel. D: Anthony Mann. Sc: Bryant Ford and Paul Gangelin, based on a story by Phillip MacDonald. Ph: Reggie Lanning. Ed: Arthur Roberts. M: Morton Scott. CAST: William Terry, Virginia Grey, Helen Thimig, Edith Barrett, Anne O'Neal. Thimig is a lonely woman who, for lack of a real daughter, makes up a fictitious one, "Rosemary Blake," who writes to Terry, a Marine sergeant stationed in the South Pacific. When Terry comes home, he tries to look up Blake but is told by Thimig that his pen pal has gone away. Barrett tells Terry the truth, and Thimig kills her in a rage. To preserve her insane fantasy, she tries to kill Terry, too, but is herself killed when a painting of the imaginary daughter falls on her head.

This was one of Mann's first efforts and has his creative fingerprints all over it, from the deep-focus photography to creative lighting schemes. The film is a study in insanity and packs more in less than an hour than most modern films do in two.

Sudden Danger (1955) Allied Artists. 85m. (B&W) P: Ben Schwalb. D: Hubert Cornfield. Sc: Daniel B. Ullman and Elwood Ullman, based on a story by Daniel Ullman. Ph: Ellsworth Fredericks. Ed: William Austin. M: Marlin Skiles. CAST: Bill Elliott, Tom Drake, Beverly Garland, Dayton Lummis, Helene Stanton, Lucien Littlefield, Minerva Urecal, Lyle Talbot, Frank Jenks, Pierre Watkin, John Close.   When a female sportswear manufacturer's death is determined to be a suicide, police lieutenant Elliott is dissatisfied and begins to conduct his own investigation. His suspicions begin to settle on the dead woman's son, Drake, who was blinded by his mother's carelessness years before. His suspicions become stronger when he interviews a next door neighbor who heard the young man arguing loudly with his mother the night of the murder; he finds out that the kid is the beneficiary of a large insurance policy. Drake uses the insurance money to get an operation that restores his sight, but only his doctor and fiancée, Garland, know he can see. Drake sets out to find the real killer. When the attorney for his mother's former business partner, Lummis, is found murdered, both Elliott and Drake focus on Lummis. Drake finds out that Lummis was carrying on a hot and heavy affair with a model at the company and goes to see her. She gives him evidence that implicates Lummis in the double murders, and he is subdued by Drake after nearly doing in Garland.

This film is the first and best in the Lt. Doyle series starring "Wild" Bill Elliott. In this initial entry he is without his sidekick, Don Haggerty, who would costar in the rest of the films in the series. This film has much better production values than the rest of the series, which was done on a shoestring budget.

Sun Sets at Dawn, The (1950) Eagle Lion. 71m. (B&W) P: Helen H. Rathvon and Paul H. Sloane. D: Sloane. Sc: Sloan, from his story. Ed: Sherman Todd. M: Leith Stevens. CAST: Walter Reed, Phillip Shawn, Sally Parr, Lee Fredericks, Houseley Stevenson, Charles Arnt, Howard St. John, Percy Helton, King Donovan.   Shawn is a former cub reporter about to be executed for the murder of a notorious gangster, for which he was framed. Efforts by his girlfriend, Parr, and the sympathetic prison warden to get a stay of execution have come to no avail. At a nearby diner, the cynical members of the press who have come to witness the execution wisecrack even though Shawn is one of their own. On the first execution try, the electric chair malfunctions and everybody goes back to the diner to wait for the next attempt. While the reporters jabber, a truck pulls up carrying the head of the trucking firm. A janitor working at the diner recognizes the big boss as a supposedly dead gangster who caused him to be sent to prison years ago. When he confronts the man, all hell breaks out, and the truck boss is arrested and taken to the prison. Even though he has had plastic surgery and doesn't look anything like he used to, his fingerprints identify him as the gangster. Knowing he's wanted for six other killings, the gangster confesses to the murder of which Shawn is accused, saving him from the chair.

Allegedly based on a true story, the film is talky and plodding, and the scenes with the reporters' cynical tale-swapping are bad imitations of similar scenes in Ben Hecht's *Our Girl Friday*. (V)

Teenage Doll (1957) Allied Artists. 68m. (B&W) P&D: Roger Corman. Sc: Charles B. Griffith. Ph: Floyd Crosby. Ed: Charles Gross. M: Walter Greene. CAST: June Kenney, Fay Spain, John Brinkley, Collette Jackson, Barbara Wilson, Ziva Rodann (Shapir), Sandy Smith, Barboura Morris, Richard Devon, Jay Sayer. Kenney, a relatively innocent teen who has been flirting with the Vandalettes (the female counterpart of the male Vandals), kills the member of a rival gang, the Black Widows (the female counterpart of the Vandal-rival Tarantulas). Spain, the Black Widowette, leads her girls in a hunt for Kenney to kill her for her transgression, and Kenney takes refuge with the Vandals, whose head honcho, Brinkley, has fed her a line in an effort to seduce her. She tells him what she has done and informs him that the Widows and Tarantulas intend to invade the Vandals' turf and rumble. Brinkley is more than willing to oblige, and both male and female gangs get into a huge gang fight that is broken up by the cops. Brinkley tells Kenney he is splitting to Phoenix and she can come with him, but she refuses and turns herself in to the police. Several of the Black Widows follow her lead; the hard-core members of the gang continue their criminal ways under Spain's leadership.

This bleak, dark film is one of the first outings by Corman, who went on to direct some decent, but mostly awful, horror and science-fiction cheapies for Allied Artists and American International. Given the body of his work, it is hard to understand why Corman is revered by many top-notch Hollywood directors as a master of his craft. Perhaps their admiration is based on the fact that he gave many of them—including Francis Ford Coppola, Martin Scorsese, and Ron Howard—their first breaks after they graduated from film school. (V)

Terror Street (1953) Hammer/Lippert. 83m. (B&W) AKA: *36 Hours*. P: Anthony Hinds. D: Montgomery Tully. Sc: Steve Fisher, from his story. Ph: Jimmy Harvey. Ed: James Needs. M: Ivor Slaney. CAST: Dan Duryea, Elsy Albiin, Ann Gudron, Eric Pohlmann, John Chandos, Kenneth Griffith, Harold Lang, Jane Carr, Michael Golden, Marianne Stone.   In London on a thirty-six-hour layover, American pilot Duryea pays a visit to his estranged wife, Albiin, only to find that she has moved to a plush West End flat. He goes there and is knocked out by Chandos, who then kills Albiin with Duryea's gun. Duryea awakens to find the cops at the door and takes refuge with next door neighbor Gudron, who believes his story. Duryea traces Chandos to his estate and learns that he is the head of a ring that uses unwitting people to smuggle diamonds and then blackmails them and that Albiin was his accomplice. When Albiin set up her own scheme to blackmail Chandos, he killed her. Needless to say, Duryea straightens out the entire mess satisfactorily for the authorities before his pass runs out.

Screenwriter Steve Fisher built his reputation as a hard-boiled writer for *Black Mask* and other mystery pulp magazines, as the author of such novels as the noir *I Wake Up Screaming,* and as a screenwriter for such noir films as *Lady in the Lake* (1947), *Dead Reckoning* (1947), and *City That Never Sleeps* (1953). His favorite theme throughout, as in *Terror Street,* was "the wrong man on the run."

They Made Me a Killer (1946) Paramount. 64m. (B&W) P: William Pine and William Thomas. D: Thomas. Sc: Geoffrey Homes, Winston Miller, and Kae Salkow, based on a story by Owen Francis. Ph: Fed Jackman. Ed: Henry Adams. M: Alexander Laszlo. CAST: Robert Lowery, Barbara Britton, Frank Albertson, Lola Lane, James Bush, Edmund MacDonald, Byron Barr, Elisabeth Risdon, Paul Harvey.   Lowery, whose brother has been killed in an accident, quits his job and takes off across the country. He picks up a girl who gets him and another innocent man, Barr, involved in a bank robbery pulled off by the girl's cohorts. Barr is killed during the robbery, and during the getaway, Lowery crashes his car, knocking himself out. The crooks get away, but Lowery is arrested for the crime. Despite his claims of innocence, the cops think he and Barr were in on it. Lowery escapes and manages to convince Barr's sister, Britton, that he and her brother were innocent victims. The two set out to find the real gang, the trail ending up at a diner run by a crooked Ma Barker type. Britton gets a job there as a waitress to try to find out what she can. In the meantime, Lowery is again snagged by the gang; he tries to convince them to take him in, since they made him a fugitive, but they are suspicious. Britton and Lowery manage to alert the cops and everybody's reputation is saved, but not before the gang gets all shot up.

This marginal and cheap noir is notable solely for being one of the few noirs made by Pine-Thomas, the B unit of Paramount. (V)

13th Hour, The (1947) Columbia. 65m. (B&W) P: Rudolph Flothow. D: William Clemens. Sc: Edward Bock and Raymond L. Shrock, based on a story by Leslie Edgley. Ph: Vincent Farrar. Ed: Dwight Caldwell. M: Wilbur Hatch. CAST: Richard Dix, Karen Morley, Mark Dennis, John Kellogg, Bernadene Hayes, Jim Bannon, Regis Toomey, Nancy Saunders, Lillian Wells, Michael Towne. Dix is the head of a successful trucking company that consistently undercuts his competition. The head of the competing firm does everything he can to foul up Dix's operation until Dix is framed for killing a cop. Sought by the police, Dix goes on the run in a hunt for the real killer. The plot escalates from trucking to diamond theft, and in the end, the least likely member of the cast is revealed to be the real killer.

This tightly made, suspenseful little film was the last for Dix, who made ninety-seven films during his career.

This Side of the Law (1950) Warner Brothers. 74m. (B&W) P: Saul Elkins. D: Richard L. Bare. Sc: Russell Hughes, based on a story by Richard Sale. Ph: Paul Guthrie. Ed: Frank Magee. M: William Lava. CAST: Viveca Lindfors, Kent Smith, Janis Paige, Robert Douglas, John Alvin, Monte Blue, Frances Morris, Nita Talbot. The story is told by Smith in flashback from the inside of a cistern, where he has been thrown. Smith, a vagrant, is bailed out of jail by lawyer Douglas, who hires him to impersonate a missing millionaire for whom he is a dead ringer. The hitch is that the missing man's estate needs protecting before the man is declared legally dead. Smith moves into the millionaire's mansion and soon regrets his acquiescence after finding that the missing man's wife, Lindfors, and brother both hate him and his sister-in-law, trampy Paige, wants to seduce him. When Douglas, who has been plundering the estate, gets everything in place, he shoves Kent into the cistern to die, as he did the missing millionaire. Douglas plots to arrange the deaths of the other principals to cover his financial misdeeds, but Smith manages to escape from his prison and save Lindfors, who is about to be done in by Douglas. Douglas tries to get away but is driven into the cistern by the family police dog and captured by the police.

Exemplifying a common noir theme, that of the doppelgänger-impersonator who, because of his masquerade, finds himself embroiled in circumstances he did not foresee, *This Side of the Law* manages some measure of suspense and some decent performances from an able cast. The tricky beginning, in which the trapped Smith relates how he got into his predicament, is handled well. The film as a whole, however, is hampered by a hokey script and perhaps demonstrates Warner Brothers's half-haltered interest in producing B fare. The fact the Big Four—Warners, Fox, MGM, and Paramount—produced not only fewer B noirs but fewer notable B movies in general seems to reflect the view of the majors' moguls that Bs were strictly to fill the bottom half of the theater bill and had little merit on their own. The author of the original story for *This Side of the Law*, Richard Sale, became a noted director-writer who went on to do the screenplay for the superior Frank Sinatra B noir *Suddenly* (1954) and collaborated on such big-budget screenplays as *Around the World in 80 Days* (1956). He also authored several novels blasting the Hollywood studio system, such as *Lazarus #7* and *The Oscar*. The studio execs immortalized Sale's view of them when they made an absolutely abominable movie of the latter in 1966.

Timetable (1956) United Artists. 79m. (B&W) P&D: Mark Stevens. Sc: Aben Kandel, from an original story by Robert Angus. Ph: Charles Van Enger. Ed: Kenneth Crane. M: Walter Scharf. CAST: Mark Stevens, King Calder, Felicia Farr, Marianne Stewart, Wesley Addy, Alan Reed, Rudolpho Hoyos, Jack Klugman, John Marley.   A train is robbed of $500,000 through an elaborate plan involving a fake doctor, a sick polio victim, and his wife. The crime seems to have been perfect, based precisely on the train's timetable. Stevens, who is about to go on vacation in Mexico with his wife, is called onto the case as the insurance company's top investigator. He and his partner, Calder, manage to track down a stolen ambulance and a helicopter that were used as part of the plot. The strain of solving the crime seemingly starts to take its toll on Stevens's relationship with his wife, but the reality is that Stevens, fed up with his low-paying job and his devoted wife, masterminded the robbery and is involved in a relationship with Farr, one of the robbers. She also happens to be married to the fake doctor Addy, who had his license revoked for alcoholism and is submitting phony insurance claims. The perfect crime starts to fall apart when one of the gang is accidentally killed, throwing off "the timetable" and preventing all from escaping to Mexico. As head of the investigation, Stevens tries to guide the clues away from himself and the others, but his relentless partner keeps the pursuit on track. Things really begin to get complicated when they nab the wheelman, Klugman, and Stevens is forced to murder the owner of the stolen helicopter to prevent the man from turning state's evidence. Addy, panicked, tries to run away with Farr to Mexico but is shot to death trying to cross the border at Tijuana. Farr manages to get away, but Stevens and Calder are sent to Tijuana to ferret her out. Stevens's wife, who meets Stevens across the border, finds out the ugly reality—that Stevens is a thief and doesn't love her. Stevens asks her for a few hours head start, planning to leave the country with Farr. Stevens tracks down Farr through underworld connections and arranges to leave the country, but things go wrong and he is forced to kill a gangster to acquire false passports. Calder finally manages to get the truth out of Stevens's wife and regretfully goes after Stevens. In an atttempt to escape, Farr is shot to death and Stevens's partner is forced to kill him. He dies saying, "This wasn't on the timetable, either."

This is a neatly done, tight little film with Stevens nicely juggling two noir themes—the straight-arrow insurance-agent-gone-wrong and the man fed up with the cozy emptiness of his middle-class existence—without getting heavy-handed. The other actors handle their parts with similar restraint, giving this sleeper a feeling of stark realism absent from many fifties noirs. Stevens is notable both as a noir actor, playing leading roles in such seminal films as *The Dark Corner* (1946) and *The Street with No Name* (1948), and as a director-actor in later B noirs such as *Timetable* and *Cry Vengeance* (1954). This movie marked Jack Klugman's film debut.

Time Without Pity (1957) Astor. (Brit.) 88m. (B&W) P: John Arnold and Anthony Simmons. D: Joseph Losey. Sc: Ben Barzman, based on the play *Someone Waiting* by Emlyn Williams. Ph: Freddie Francis. Ed: Alan Obiston. M: Marcus Dods. CAST: Michael Redgrave, Ann Todd, Leo McKern, Peter Cushing, Alec McCowen, Renee Houston, Pal Daneman, Lois Maxwell, Richard Wordsworth, George Devine, Joan Plowright.   Drying-out alcoholic Redgrave learns his son, McCowen, is about to be executed for the murder of an automobile bigwig's wife. Convinced his boy is innocent and having only twenty-four hours to prove it, Redgrave goes to the house of bigwig McKern, where the son had been living. He learns that McKern's neurotic wife, Todd, had a thing for the son and that McKern was the real killer. Redgrave forces McKern to kill him in order to save his son.

This is a fine film by Losey, who cut his directorial teeth on noirs in the early fifties, among them M (a remake of the Fritz Lang German classic), *The Big Night*, *The Prowler*, and *The Lawless*. He proved himself to be a masterful director, but his career in America was ended by the McCarthy hearings when he was branded as a Commie and blacklisted. He was forced to emigrate to England, where he fortunately went on to reconstruct his career. (V)

Two of a Kind (1951) Columbia. 75m. (B&W) P: William Dozier. D: Henry Levin. Sc: Lawrence Kimble and James Grunn, from a story by James Edward Grant. Ph: Burnett Guffey. Ed: Charles Nelson. M: George Duning. CAST: Edmond O'Brien, Lizabeth Scott, Terry More, Alexander Knox, Griff Barnet, Robert Anderson, Virginia Brissac, J. M. Kerrigan, Claire Carleton.   Con artist partners Scott and Knox are privy to the fact that a wealthy couple are desperate to find their missing son, who was lost at the age of two. They hire O'Brien, a carnival barker, to play the part of the son in order to get at the older couple's money. Greedy O'Brien, to cement the performance, smashes his fingers in a car door to match an accident the kid had before his disappearance. He moves into the house and strikes up a romance with Moore, the couple's ditzy niece, but Barnett, the father, makes known his intentions to exclude O'Brien from his will. Knox decides to kill the old geezer before the plan can be consummated, but Scott and O'Brien refuse to go along. Knox tries to kill O'Brien, who has had enough and confesses everything to Barnett. Barnett tells O'Brien that he knew all along about his identity but said nothing because of his wife's happiness at seeing her son again. Knox's evil is uncovered; he is sent on his way, and O'Brien and Scott go off on theirs.

Although the script is verbose, *Two of a Kind* manages to hold viewer interest and is interesting from several aspects. First, it teams two noir icons, O'Brien and femme fatale Scott, and second, the story is yet another example of the noir impersonator-in-trouble theme.

Unholy Wife, The (1957) RKO. 94m. (C) P&D: John Farrow. Sc: Jonathon Latimer, based on a story by William Durkee. Ph: Lucien Ballard. Ed: Eda Warren. M: Daniele Amfitheatrof. CAST: Diana Dors, Rod Steiger, Tom Tryon, Beulah Bondi,

Marie Windsor, Arthur Franz, Luis Van Rooten, Argentina Brunetti, Tol Avery, James Burke. The story is told in flashback by Dors, who is confessing her perfect crime to priest Franz as she awaits execution. After marrying Franz's brother, wealthy wine grower Steiger, for his money, she soon starts carrying on an affair with rodeo star Tryon. When her elderly mother-in-law, Bondi, reports a prowler to the cops (the prowler is in reality Tryon making adulterous visits to the house), Dors hatches a plan to kill Steiger and claim she thought the victim was the prowler. Things go awry when she kills a buddy of Steiger's by mistake, but using her wiles, she talks Steiger into taking the blame for the shooting, convincing him he will surely be acquitted. Dors seals his fate by writing an incriminating letter and testifying against him in court. Steiger is sentenced to death. By this time, he knows who is behind it all, but he won't talk; he married Dors for her son, as he is incapable of having a son of his own, and doesn't want the kid to grow up thinking his mother is a murderess. Franz and the cops have their doubts about Steiger's guilt. When Dors tells the truth to Tryon to make him an accessory and therefore unable to testify against her, Bondi overhears and has a stroke that leaves her speechless. The doctor gives Dors medicine to administer to the old woman, who overdoses, knowing Dors will be blamed. The police arrest Dors for killing the old woman to shut her up, and Dors is convicted and sent to the gas chamber for a crime she didn't commit. Steiger is freed and gets the son he always wanted.

It would be hard to get together a more noir moviemaking crew than director John Farrow (*The Big Clock*, *Where Danger Lives*, *His Kind of Woman*), writer Jonathon Latimer (*The Glass Key*, *The Accused*, *Nocturne*), and cinematographer Lucien Ballard (*Laura*, *Berlin Express*, *The Killing*), although in this case, Ballard was working in Technicolor rather than black-and-white. Latimer and Farrow worked together on two other noirs, *The Big Clock* and *Night Has 1000 Eyes*. Before succumbing to the lures and money of Hollywood, Latimer penned a series of wonderful hard-boiled novels, two of which, *Lady in the Morgue* and *Headed for a Hearse*, were made into movies. Tom Tryon acted in a few more films, including the sci-fi cult classic *I Married a Monster from Outer Space*, before giving up acting for a career as a best-selling novelist. (He was one of the few actors-turned-writers who actually did write books.)

Unmasked (1950) Republic. 60m. (B&W) P: Stephen Auer. D: George Blair. Sc: Albert DeMond and Norman S. Hall, based on a story by Manuel Seff and Paul

Yawitz. Ph: Ellis W. Carter. Ed: Robert M. Leeds. M: Stanley Wilson. CAST: Robert Rockwell, Barbara Fuller, Raymond Burr, Hillary Brooke, Paul Harvey, Norman Budd, John Eldredge, Russell Hicks, Emory Parnell.   Burr is the editor of a scandal sheet and has borrowed heavily from Brooke, the young wife of once-famous theater producer Harvey, to keep the paper going. Burr has promised to marry Brooke when she gets a divorce. During an argument, Harvey refuses to give her a divorce and takes the jewelry he has given her. Burr sees Harvey leave the apartment and kills her, stealing back his IOUs and framing Harvey for the crime. Harvey goes into hiding and gives the jewels to Budd, a crooked pal of Burr's, to sell so he can hire an attorney. Police detective Rockwell makes friends with Harvey's daughter, Fuller, in an attempt to locate her father. Fuller locates her dad but is tailed by the cops, and as they close in, Harvey commits suicide. Budd takes the jewelry to fence Eldredge, who kills Budd. Eldredge plans to clean up everything by getting rid of Fuller and Burr and lure the pair to his place. Rockwell, after breaking down Burr's alibi by working on his secretary, rushes to the scene, and during a shootout, all the heavies are killed.

Burr, one of film noir's most frequently cast heavies, has a chance to play the bad guy to the hilt and steals the show in this solidly done flick.

Vicious Circle (1948) United Artists. 77m. (B&W) AKA: *The Woman in Brown.* P&D: W. Lee Wilder. Sc: Guy Endore and Heinz Herald, based on the play *The Burning Bush* by Herald and Geza Herczeg, adapted by Noel Langley. Ph: George Robinson. Ed: Asa Boyd Clark. M: Paul Dessau. CAST: Conrad Nagel, Lyle Talbot, Fritz Kortner, Reinhold Schunzel, Frank Ferguson, Edwin Maxwell, Michael Mark, Rita Gould, Eddie LeRoy, Ben Welden.   A mute is dying in an American boarding house. As a doctor is summoned, he speaks, shocking everyone. Ferguson, a boarder who knew the man, reveals that the man actually chose not to speak and tells his story in flashback. In Hungary, where the dying man came from, an evil and rich baron discovers there is oil beneath nearby properties. He manages to buy out all the farms in the area except a few, owned by Jews. When they refuse to move, the baron uses the local corrupt constabulary to try the men for the murder of a woman who actually committed suicide. Ferguson, the prosecutor, sensing a railroad job, resigns in disgust. During the trial, the baron corrupts the son of one of the men into testifying against his own father. The men are eventually found innocent, but the son, the mute boarder, never speaks another word after that. In the end, the mute dies.

This film, dubbed noir by some critics and a period piece-courtroom drama by others, is included here for those buffs of the genre whose primary criterion for inclusion is cinematographic. This has to be one of the darkest films ever made, as every scene was lighted with ten-watt bulbs. It is never explained why Ferguson, the prosecutor, came to America to live with the fink son, but then, nobody cares, as the movie packs every frame of its 77 minutes with boredom. This is truly one of the oddball films of all time, as it is hard to envision for what commercial audience it was aimed. (V)

Violated (1953) Panther. 78m. (B&W) P: Wim Holland. D: Walter Strate. Sc: William Paul Mishkin. Ph: Pat Rich. M: Tony Mottola. CAST: Wim Holland, Lili Dawn, Mitchell Kowal, Vicki Carlson, William Martel, Jason Niles, Michael Keene, Fred Lambert.   When six women are found murdered in New York City, a police psychiatrist is called in. All the women were stabbed with scissors, and locks of their hair had been cut off. The psychiatrist concludes the killings are the work of a deranged mind. One of the suspects is Holland, a photographer who had photographed one of the dead women. Carlson, a model, is infatuated with Holland, but he has eyes for a nightclub dancer. When the dancer rejects him, Holland kills her, revealing himself to be the murderer. Carlson, in the meantime, has begun to have fearful doubts about Holland, but before he can do her in, he is apprehended by the police. The psychiatrist concludes that Holland's murderous compulsions are rooted in his childhood experiences but nevertheless declares him sane. The film ends with another pickup in the street, intimating the possibility of another cycle of killings.

A police procedural à la the noir *The Tattooed Stranger*, this alleged exposé of the seedier side of urban life merely exposes the incompetence of the police and the actors who portray them.

Violence (1947) Monogram. 72m. (B&W) P: Jack Bernhard and Bernard Brandt. D: Bernhard. Sc: Stanley Rubin & Lewis Lantz. Ph: Henry Sharp. Ed: Jason Bernie. M: Edward J. Kay. CAST: Nancy Coleman, Michael O'Shea, Sheldon Leonard, Peter Whitney, Emory Parnell, Pierre Watkin, Frank Reicher, Cay Forrester, John Hamilton, Richard Irving, Jimmy Clark.   Coleman, an undercover op for an exposé magazine, is working as a secretary for United Defenders, an organization that recruits disgruntled World War II vets under the guise of patriotism but is really a Fascist front out to spread civil discord. She is informed by her publisher that the story is going to break on the Defenders and to get out. She takes a taxi, and fearing she is being followed by Leonard, who is one of the heads of the organization and is in love with her, she tells the driver to speed up. In reality, she is being tailed by FBI agent O'Shea. Her taxi crashes, resulting in Coleman losing her memory. O'Shea shows up, claiming to be her fiancé, and takes her back to the United Defenders, where he gets a job. Coleman, still unaware of her identity, turns on O'Shea but regains her memory when she falls, hitting her head. A wife shows up at the outfit's headquarters to search for her husband, who has been murdered. There is a struggle between the Defenders and loyal GIs, resulting in a falling-out between Parnell, the other head of the organization, and his aide; they are both killed.

Well directed with plenty of action and convincing acting, this is one of those transitional movies between the Nazi and Communist cycles of social conspiracy films such as *Jigsaw* and *Open Secret*.

Voice in the Wind (1944) United Artists. 85m. (B&W) P: Rudolph Monter and Arthur Ripley. D: Ripley. Sc: Frederick Torberg, based on a story by Ripley. Ph: Dick Fryer. M: Michael Michelet. CAST: Francis Lederer, Sigrid Gurie, J. Edward Bromberg, J. Carroll Naish, Alexander Grandach, David Cota, Olga Fabian, Howard Johnson.   Lederer is a concert pianist who has been tortured by the Nazis for playing a banned song. He is trying to regain his memory on the island of Guadalupe. He has also become a refugee to try to save the life of his girlfriend, Gurie, whom the Nazis also dislike. He is unsuccessful because in the end, everybody dies.

Originally scheduled for Poverty Row studio PRC, *Voice in the Wind*, which was shot on a shoestring in twelve days, was released through UA. The UA publicity department tried to use the cheapness of the production as a plus, putting out numerous stories in the trades about how an artistic masterpiece had been made on a very low budget. The UA push managed to get the film a Broadway opening to big fanfare, but the critics didn't bite and the film went on to artistic obscurity. Perhaps the strangest thing about *Voice in the Wind* (and perhaps why it doesn't work) is that this dark, brooding, slow film was the product of Arthur Ripley, who started out as a gagman for Mack Sennett.

Voice of the Whistler (1945) Columbia. 60m. (B&W) P: Rudolph C. Flothow. D: William Castle. Sc: Castle and Wilfred H. Petit, based on a story by Allan Rader from the radio program. Ph: George Meehan. Ed: Dwight Caldwell. M: Mischa Bakaleifikoff. CAST: Richard Dix, Lynn Merrick, Rhys Williams, James Cardwell, Tom Kennedy, Donald Woods, Egon Brecher, Gigi Perreau.   Dix, a ruthless industrialist, collapses and is sent away to recuperate. Not knowing Dix's true identity, taxi driver and ex-pugilist Williams befriends Dix and takes him to a neighborhood clinic, where Dix realizes his sickness is loneliness. He becomes enamored with a nurse, Merrick, who is engaged to a poor doctor. Dix reveals his true identity to Merrick and lies to her, telling her he has only six months to live; if she marries and goes away with him, she will inherit all his money. She blows off her fiancé for the money, and she, Dix, and Williams go to live in a lighthouse in Maine. Dix falls in love with Merrick and confesses he is not terminal. Merrick, who cannot stand the isolation of the lighthouse, wants to break off their arrangement, but Dix convinces her to go away with him. Before they can leave, her old fiancé, the doctor, comes calling, and he and Merrick pick up their affair again. The doctor tries to convince her to leave Dix, but Merrick is determined to stick it out for the money. Dix, who knows about his wife's feelings for the doctor, plans to get rid of the man. He plants murderous thoughts in the doctor's mind to incite him to make an attempt on Dix's life. The doctor falls for it and tries to kill Dix, but Dix is one step ahead of him and kills the doctor. Dix tries to make the murder look like an accident but is caught by Merrick. Dix is executed for the crime, and Merrick inherits the money she coveted. In the end, she lives alone in the lighthouse she hates and pines for her true love.

This film is a haunting entry in the *Whistler* series.

Way Out, The (1956) RKO. (Brit.) 90m. (B&W) P: Alec Snowden. D: Montgomery Tully. Sc: Tully, based on a story by Bruce Graeme. Ph: Philip Grindrod. Ed: Geoffrey Miller. M: Richard Taylor. CAST: Gene Nelson, Mona Freeman, John Bentley, Michael Goodliffe, Sydney Tafler, Charles Victor, Arthur Lovegrove, Cyril Chamberlain.   Nelson comes to his wife, Freeman, and tells her he is being hunted by police for the murder of a bookie while in an alcoholic haze. Convinced of his innocence, she and her brother hide him out and set out to reconstruct the events of the evening in order to clear Nelson, but as they collect more and more evidence, it becomes clear Nelson did it and did it with malice. Knowing his whining about his innocence has nobody fooled and pursued by the cops, Nelson tries to escape but gets run down and killed by a truck in the street.

Plodding and clumsy, this film accomplishes nothing except to set Nelson up as a manipulative piece of garbage and Freeman as a sucker. Nelson, who had a varied career, started out as an ice-skater in Sonja Henie films and graduated as an accomplished dancer in lavish Hollywood musicals including *Oklahoma!* (1955). Freeman was competent as both a child and an adult actress. Freeman and Nelson were two of a number of stars whose American careers were on the wane and who continued as leads abroad. In the same year *The Way Out* was released, Freeman starred in the British-produced noir *Shadow of Fear* (1956), and Nelson headlined in the low-budget sci-fi flick *The Atomic Man*. After his British star began to dim, Nelson returned to the U.S. to direct films, among which were several movies starring Elvis Presley. (V)

Whip Hand, The (1951) RKO. 82m. (B&W) P: Lewis J. Rachmil. D: William Cameron Menzies. Sc: George Bricker and Frank L. Moss, based on a story by Roy Hamilton. Ph: Nicholas Musuraca. Ed: Robert Golden. M: Paul Sawtell. CAST: Carla Balenda, Elliott Reid, Edgar Barrier, Raymond Burr, Otto Waldis, Michael Steele, Lurene Tuttle, Peter Brocco, Lewis Martin.   Reid, a vacationing journalist on a fishing trip, injures himself and wanders into the town of Winoga. Once a flourishing fishing spot, Winoga is now a near ghost town because all the fish in the lake mysteriously died years before. He finds the few people left there either strangely afraid to talk or downright hostile. He meets and falls for Balenda, the town doctor's sister, who also seems strangely skittish. His curiosity leads him to discover that the entire town has been taken over by Communists who are conducting germ warfare experiments in a fortresslike lodge across the lake. The group's head is the ex-Nazi-now-Commie doctor Waldis, who is being sought for war crimes. Reid manages to get a message out to his magazine before he and Balenda are taken prisoner and taken to the lodge. They learn that Waldis and company intend to spread all kinds of terrible diseases across the U.S. and that they are going to be used as guinea pigs in Waldis's experiments. Before that can happen, however, Balenda's brother, who is in on the plot, has a change of heart and shoots the lab assistant as he is about to inject his sister; the brother, in turn, is mortally wounded. The feds arrive and blast their way in, but Waldis, who has locked himself in a room with the zombielike results of his experiments, threatens to blow up the building, killing everyone and spreading the germs across the U.S. in a deadly cloud. Reid pulls the plug on his device, and Waldis is set upon and beaten to death by his zombie guinea pigs.

One of Howard Hughes's Red-scare movies, *The Whip Hand* was originally shot as *The Man He Found* and was about Adolph Hitler, who hadn't really died in Berlin but had escaped and was living in a small American town, again plotting the conquest of the world. After the production was ready for release, Hughes decided Communists were a hotter topic than Hitler, so he ordered Menzies to reshoot the picture. Despite being shot twice, the picture still cost the studio only $376,000. All in all, the picture is not bad for a propaganda film, certainly twenty steps up from *The Red Menace*.

Whispering City (1947). Eagle Lion. 89m. (B&W) P: George Marton. D: Fedor Ozep. Sc: Rian James and Leonard Lee, from a story by George Zuckerman and Michael Lennox. Ph: William Steiner. Ed: Douglas Bagier and Richard J. Jarvis. M: Jean Deslauriers. CAST: Helmut Dantine, Mary Anderson, Paul Lukas, John Pratt, Joy Lafleur, George Alexander, Arthur Lefebvre, Mimi de'Este, Henri Poitras. Set in Quebec, the story is told by a sleigh driver to two visitors. Reporter Anderson gets word that a famous actress is dying in the hospital after being hit by a car. She visits the actress, who tells the reporter that her wealthy fiancé, who was allegedly killed in an accident years before, was actually murdered. Anderson goes to see Lukas, a prominent attorney who represented the dead fiancé. At the same time, Lukas is being visited by Dantine, a tormented composer who is married to a nagging, neurotic virago and whom Lukas is trying to convince to get a divorce. Lukas tells Anderson that the dying actress is delusional and was institutionalized after the death of her fiancé. The actress dies, and Anderson goes to her apartment and finds her diary, all the while being shadowed by Lukas. After a row with his wife, Dantine gets drunk and shows up on Lukas's doorstep. Dantine passes out, and Lukas goes to Dantine's apartment, intending to kill his wife. He finds she has already committed suicide by overdosing on sleeping medicine. He takes the suicide note, and when Dantine wakes up, he convinces him that he, Dantine, killed his wife. Lukas tells Dantine that he will hang without his help and that the price of that help is for Dantine to murder Anderson. Dantine reluctantly agrees, but when he meets Anderson, he can't go through with it. Anderson finds out Dantine's true identity and, believing him innocent, sets out to clear him. The two go to a waterfall, and the next day the papers carry the story that the reporter accidentally plunged to her death. Lukas gives Dantine the suicide note, absolving him of guilt. Lukas begins to see the dead reporter everywhere and is on the road to a breakdown. In reality, Anderson is alive, and she and Dantine are working with the police to entrap Lukas. Lukas goes to Anderson's apartment, finds her alive, and confesses that he killed the actress's fiancé years before in order to get access to his money as executor of his will. Lukas is about to kill her when Dantine and the police break in and shoot him.

Well put together, this was the first of the films noirs produced by Eagle Lion shortly after its conversion from PRC. Lukas is competent as usual, and Dantine plays the composer with his typical brooding flair. The one weak spot in the film is Anderson's performance, probably why she was shortly thereafter consigned to oblivion. (V)

Whispering Footsteps (1943) Republic. 54m. (B&W) P: George Blair. D: Howard Bretherton. Sc: Gertrude Walker, based on her story. Ph: Jack Marta. Ed: Ralph Dixon. M: Morton Scott. CAST: John Hubbard, Rita Quigley, Joan Blair, Charles Halton, Cy Kendall, Juanita Quigley, Mary Gordon, Billy Benedict.   Hubbard is a bank clerk who returns home from a vacation in Indianapolis to hear a radio report of a girl found murdered in that city. The radio description of the killer fits him to a tee, and the other inhabitants of the boarding house where he lives begin to view him with suspicion. The murders of two more girls make him look even guiltier. He has no alibi for the times of the killings, and soon everyone—including his own fiancée—is convinced he is the murderer. The only person in town who does not turn against him is the town's "fast lady," but when she is murdered, the townspeople are truly convinced and are about to lynch him. Before they can, the real killer confesses.

This very good movie manages to expose the hypocrisies and petty sanctimoniousness of Smalltown, U.S.A., in less than an hour. Director Bretherton had previously worked on Rin Tin Tin flicks and Hopalong Cassidy westerns at Monogram but did a bang-up job on this one.

Whistler, The (1944) Columbia. 60m. P: Rudolph C. Flothow. D: William Castle. Sc: Eric Taylor, based on a story by J. Donald Wilson, suggested by the radio program *The Whistler*. Ph: James Brown. Ed: Jerome Thoms. M: Wilbur Hatch. CAST: Richard Dix, J. Carroll Naish, Gloria Stuart, Alan Dinehart, Joan Woodbury, Cy Kendall, Trevor Bardette, Don Costello, Clancy Cooper, Robert E. Keane.   Dix, despondent over the death of his wife, wants to kill himself but can't get up the nerve. He hires a man to hire a hit man to kill him. When Dix finds out his wife is not really dead and that the man he hired to hire an assassin has been killed, he tries desperately to find out the identity of his would-be assassin (Naish) and cancel the contract but is unsuccessful. Dix is pursued relentlessly by Naish, but Dix's secretary manages to get Dix to a police station before he is harmed. Naish, desperate to complete his contract, tries to shoot Dix through the window but is himself gunned down.

This film is the first in the unusual and highly original mystery series of films based on the popular thirties and forties radio program *The Whistler*. Each program was kicked off by a shadowy narrator who would whistle the same weird tune and, before setting the scene for the story to come, would intone: "I am the Whistler, and I know many things. For I walk by night. I know the tales of many men and women who have stepped into the shadows." Richard Dix starred in all but one of the eight films but played different characters in each film, alternating from hero to villain.

Wicked as They Come (1957) Columbia. (Brit.) 94m. (B&W) AKA: *Portrait in Smoke*. P: Maxwell Setton and M. J. Frankovich. D: Ken Hughes. Sc: Hughes, Robert Westerby and Sigmund Miller, based on the novel *Portrait in Smoke* by Bill S. Ballinger. Ed: Max Benedict. M: Malcolm Arnold. CAST: Arlene Dahl, Phil Carey, Herbert Marshall, Michael Goodliffe, David Kossoff, Marvin Kane, Sidney James, Gilbert Winfield, Patrick Allen, Faith Brook.   Dahl, a guttersnipe, sets her aims on a better life. When a beauty contest is fixed so that she wins, she parlays her success by having an affair with a wealthy executive, then marrying the head of a big corporation. She "accidentally" shoots him and goes to jail but is released for lack of evidence and continues her evil social climbing.

This British-produced noir stars Americans Dahl, who makes a good femme fatale, and competent Carey, who was probably most famous for playing Philip Marlowe in the short-lived TV series.

Wicked Woman (1954) United Artists. 77m. (B&W) P: Clarence Greene. D: Richard Rouse. Sc: Greene and Rouse. Ph: Edward Fitzgerald. Ed: Chester Schaeffer. M: Buddy Baker. CAST: Beverly Michaels, Richard Egan, Percy Helton, Evelyn Scott, Robert Osterloh, William Phillips, Frank Ferguson, Bernadene Hayes, Herb Jeffries.   Femme fatale Michaels is a waitress who sets her scheming sights on her employer, bar owner Egan. She convinces him to ditch his nagging wife, Scott, and split with her to Mexico, using the money from the bar to finance the trip. Their plans go awry when Helton, a local tailor, finds out and threatens to spill the beans to Scott. Michaels seduces Helton in an attempt to keep his mouth shut, but the pair are caught by Egan, who sees Michaels's perfidious ways and goes back to his wife. Michaels takes a bus out of town, apparently on to her next male victim.

Richard Rouse wrote and directed several interesting noirs, such as *The Well* (1951), an insightful look at crowd violence and race relations; *The Thief* (1952), a Cold War noir known primarily for its gimmick of not having one word of dialogue spoken through the entire film; and *New York Confidential* (1955), one of the better "confidential" movies inspired by U.S. senator Estes Kefauver's public investigation of organized crime. *Wicked Woman* is Rouse's cheapest and seediest work, and although the dialogue keeps the script from being hackneyed, there is nobody to like in the film. By the end, you wish they would all go to Mexico and stay there. Although the movie is tame by modern standards, some critics jumped on it for its blatant sexual content.

Without Honor (1949). United Artists. 69m. (B&W) P: Robert and Raymond Hakim. D: William Nigh. Sc: Harry P. Christ (Harry Fraser) and Lee Sage, based on a story by Sage. Ph: Edward Linden. M: Max Steiner. CAST: Laraine Day, Dane Clark, Franchot Tone, Agnes Moorehead, Bruce Bennett, Frank Marlowe, Harry Lauter, Peter Virgo, Margie Stapp, Patricia Ann Ewing.   Housewife Day is visited at home by Tone, with whom she has had an adulterous affair. He threatens to make trouble, and to protect her home, she sticks a barbecue skewer in his chest. She drags him into the laundry room and spends the rest of the day terrified someone will discover the body. Clark, Day's unpleasant brother-in-law, who had been rejected by Day before her marriage to Clark's brother, Bennett, spills the beans about Day's illicit affair with Tone to Bennett and to Tone's wife, Moorehead. Day, overcome by guilt, confesses to her murder of Tone and tries to kill herself. After she is rushed to the hospital, Day finds that Tone is not really dead but is also in the hospital after he wandered, wounded, into the street. As in *Mildred Pierce*, Bennett finds it in his heart to forgive his wife and tells off his nasty brother for his maliciousness.

A top-notch cast is wasted in a total clunker. The film takes an award, however, for the movie with the shortest performance by a top-billed star: Leading man Tone, after his brief initial appearance, spends most of the picture as the "corpse" in the laundry room.

Without Warning (1952) United Artists. 75m. (B&W) AKA: *The Story Without a Name*. P: Arthur Gardner and Jules Levy. D: Arnold Laven. Sc: Bill Raynor. Ph: Joseph F. Biroc. Ed: Arthur H. Nadel. M: Herschel Burke Gilbert. CAST: Adam Williams, Meg Randall, Edward Binns, Harlan Warde, John Maxwell, Angela Stevens, Byron Kane, Charles Tannen, Robert Shayne. Williams plays a deranged serial killer whose blond wife ran out on him. To exact revenge on her, he picks up look-alikes in bars and stabs them to death with garden shears. Detectives Binns and Warde use blond undercover policewomen in an attempt to catch the killer, but he does not fall for the bait. Williams is finally undone by forensic evidence left at a crime scene and is captured by the police.

Done in semidocumentary style, *Without Warning* was one of the first noirs to deal with a serial killer, a theme all too common on the screen and in today's newspapers. Although the film suffers in comparison to Stanley Kramer and Edward Dymytrk's *The Sniper*, a film noir with a similar theme released the same year, it is a taut little film with good performances; an understated script; good photography by Biroc, a veteran of many B films noirs; and tight editing by Nadel (who in 1950, at the age of eighteen, was the youngest solo film editor in history when he edited the film noir classic *D.O.A.*). Presumably for all those reasons, Sol Lesser, who in the early 1940s had been production head at RKO (he broke away to form his own production company, which became best known for cranking out the Tarzan series), acquired an interest in the film and made arrangements with United Artists for its release.

Woman's Devotion, A (1956) Republic. 88m. (C) AKA: *Battleshock*. P: John Bash. D: Paul Henreid. Sc: Robert Hill. Ph: Jorge Stahl Jr. Ed: Richard L. Van Enger. M: Les Baxter. CAST: Ralph Meeker, Janice Rule, Paul Henreid, Rosenda Monteros, Fanny Schiller, Jose Torvay, Yerye Beirute, Tony Carbajal.   Meeker, an artist and World War II vet still suffering mental problems from his wartime experiences, is on his honeymoon in Acapulco with Rule. While having a beer alone in a beachside café, he sketches a young woman who shills drinks for the place and ends up going with her to her place, seemingly to do more sketching. He wanders home the next morning, not remembering anything from the night before. When the girl is found beaten to death and he finds one of the sketches he made of her, he starts to wonder about himself. He hides the sketch, which is found by a maid. The principal police suspect is the dead girl's boyfriend, a sleazeball boxer known as a woman abuser, but as he was in another city fighting the night of the murder, the cops let him go. The maid takes the sketch to the boxer, and the two of them decide to blackmail Meeker and Rule. The maid talks to Rule, who agrees to pay, but Meeker finds out and tells her that he will deliver the money. When he does, he finds the boxer passed out drunk and the maid there. A loud noise puts Meeker back into battleshock, and he has one of his fits and begins punching the girl in a violent rage. When she is found dead, the boxer is again blamed. Henreid, the police captain, suspects Meeker, but his efforts to keep the couple in the country are overruled by his superior, and Meeker and Rule are allowed to leave. At the airport, the loud noise of the airplane engines sets off Meeker again, and he has one of his fits. He knocks down a cop, takes his gun, and starts firing it into the air at imaginary German airplanes. Despite Henreid's efforts to stop them (he realizes Meeker is sick), the police shoot Meeker to death.

This is a disturbing little film, especially because the audience never gets to know for sure whether Meeker really did kill the two women. Competently directed by actor Henreid of *Casablanca* fame, *A Woman's Devotion* suffers more from the washed-out color photography than anything else. (V)

EPILOGUE

Film noir had its origins in the B crime film, graduated to more lavish A productions of the major studios in the 1940s, then returned to its B roots in the 1950s.

Throughout the 1960s, film noir production fell off sharply as the big-picture mentality took over Hollywood, and in the 1970s, the few noirs that were produced tended to be bigger-budget productions, such as *Dirty Harry* and *The French Connection* (1971), *Chinatown* and *The Conversation* (1974), *Farewell, My Lovely* and *Night Moves* (1975), and *The Driver* (1978). Some low-budget and independent films noirs did manage to get made, such as *The Nickel Ride* (1974) and *Mikey and Nicky* and *The Killing of a Chinese Bookie* (1976).

During the 1980s, however, after writings about film noir began to find increased publication and the proliferation of video and cable TV created a greatly increased demand for low-budget film product, film noir once again found itself in favor with independent and younger filmmakers enamored with the style.

Such independent companies as Miramax, Polygram, New Line, and Fine Line have shown an eagerness to finance films noirs with budgets up to $4 million. Direct-to-video companies Vestron, Promark, Concorde, and Vidmark have found noir to be a natural for their $1 million plus budgets, as have cable companies such as Showtime, which showed forty made-for-cable movies in 1995, half of which were noir. Showtime even produced its own anthology of films noirs, *Fallen Angels*, based on the works of such classic hard-boiled writers as Raymond Chandler and Cornell Woolrich as well as modern noir writers such as James Ellroy. Films in this anthology were directed by such talents as Tom Cruise, Tom Hanks, and Steven Sonderbergh. Finally, the French, originators of the term film noir, have not diminished in their enthusiasm for the themes and style of noir. Such companies as Lumiere, Gaumont, UGC, and PFG Entertainment have demonstrated a willingness to finance or cofinance noir projects. Examples include *Reservoir Dogs* (1992), *Killing Zoe* (1994), and *The Doom Generation* (1995).

The 1990s, like the 1940s, brought a sharp demarcation between mainstream studio fare and the works of such directors as James Foley, Joel and Ethan Coen, Quentin Tarantino, John Dahl, Bill Duke, Martin Scorsese, and Dennis Hopper. Just as the earlier directors and producers drew on the work of pulp writers of the thirties, the new noir is coming from the pens of modern hard-boiled writers such as James Ellroy, Carl Hiassen, and Gerald Petievich, as well as from the rediscovered works of neglected fifties authors such as David Goodis and Jim Thompson. As with those noir gems of the 1940s, these new filmmakers have sought to bring high production values; punchy, pop dialogue; and intricate plots to films with relatively meager budgets.

The examples of such modern films constitute a long list: *Thief* (1981); *Blood Simple* and *Mike's Murder* (1984); *Trouble in Mind* (1985) and *Positive I.D.* (1987); *Mortal Passions* (1990); *Bulletproof Heart* (1994); *To Live and Die in L.A.* (1995); *Manhunter* (1986); *Slamdance, House of Games, The Killing Time,* and *Tough Guys Don't Dance* (1987); *Cop* and *Stormy Monday* (1988); *Kill Me Again, Relentless,* and *Hit List* (1989); *The Grifters, After Dark, My Sweet,* and *Body Chemistry* (1990); *Delusion, Dead Again,* and *Liebestraum* (1991); *Deep Cover, In the Heat of Passion, Reservoir Dogs, Diary of a Hitman, Storyville, The Public Eye, One False Move, Desire and Hell at Sunset Motel,* and *Guncrazy* (1992); *Red Rock West, Boiling Point,* and *Romeo Is Bleeding* (1993); *The Last Seduction, Pulp Fiction, Killing Zoe, Shallow Grave, China Moon,* and *The Underneath* (1994); *Things to Do in Denver When You're Dead, Clockers,* and *The Doom Generation* (1995); *Fargo* and *2 Days in the Valley* (1996); *City of Industry, U-Turn,* and *Jackie Brown* (1997); *Suicide Kings and Palmetto* (1998); and *Best Laid Plans* (1999).

Film noir has once again achieved popularity as well as legitimacy and brought artistry to the moderate-to-low-budget feature. In fact, in this modern era of runaway production costs—expensive action sequences can push movie budgets through the roof—film noir has become the darling of low-budget filmmakers, even more so than in the forties and fifties. Hip dialogue, references to modern rock and movie stars and popular products, and sound tracks filled with modern rock songs have been freely used in modern film noir to replace car chases and appeal to younger audiences. In *Pulp Fiction*, for example (the title itself is an homage to the roots of film noir), hit men John Travolta and Samuel L. Jackson spend five minutes discussing what McDonald's hamburgers are called in France. *Reservoir Dogs*, a film about a robbery gone awry, takes place on one set, in a warehouse. "In the 40s," says producer Don Murphy, "*The Usual Suspects* would have been about a big caper, *Reservoir Dogs* would have been about a bank job. In the 90s, you don't even see the job—all you hear about is what went wrong. They're saying, you may have plans, you may have grand ambitions, but you're screwed no matter what you do." Talk, in other words, is cheap.

It is not just screen texts that the new low-budget filmmakers have experimented with in showing their reverence for film noir. Because of technological advancements within the movie industry itself, such as the development of more sensitive color stock that allows more contrast between light and shadow, the new directors and photographers have been able to economically duplicate the look of film noir of the 1930s.

But is economics the sole reason for the resurgence in film noir? Some sociologists and film critics would argue no, pointing to social changes within America as the principal cause. They see the renewal of interest as a reaction to the Reagan materialism of the 1980s, the loss of identity and meaningful sense of values among the "me generation," unstable economic times brought on by corporate dislocations and layoffs, a feeling of nihilism in the young, and the seemingly insatiable interest by the public and media in crime and violence. Perhaps there is some truth in all of that, just as there undoubtedly was some truth in the view that the social dislocations brought on by World War II were in part responsible for the popularity of film noir in the late 1940s.

In the final analysis, we must ask whether film noir was a "true cultural reflection of the nation's mental dysfunction of a nation in uncertain transition," as posited by Silver and Ward, or whether these films were and continue to be popular because they provide escape, entertainment, and vicarious thrills and are artistically interesting and different. Geoffrey O'Brien argues, and correctly, I think, that those films noirs of the forties (and the modern films noirs of the eighties and nineties) are examples of flamboyance and "hip self-parody" rather than nihilistic desperation or national mental dysfunction. "Noir might more realistically be considered not so much a 'universe' or a 'sensibility,' and certainly not a 'movement' as one writer calls it—as a particular sheen, a slick new variety of packaging, faddish at the time and subsequently much prized by connoisseurs."

I hope you connoisseurs prize these lost B noirs as much as I do.

B NOIRS LISTED BY YEAR AND BY STUDIO

B Noirs Listed by Year

The following abbreviations are used to denote the releasing studios.

(A) Astor
(AA) Allied Artists
(Ain) Ainsworth
(AIP) American International Pictures
(Alex) Alexander
(Col) Columbia
(DCA) Distributors Corporation of America
(EL) Eagle-Lion
(F) Filmakers
(FC) Film Classics
(Fox) Twentieth Century Fox
(How) Howco
(Lip) Lippert
(MGM) Metro Goldwyn Mayer
(Mon) Monogram
(Pan) Panther

(Par) Paramount
(PI) Pacific International
(PRC) Producers Releasing Corporation
(Rep) Republic
(RKO) RKO Radio Pictures
(SG) Screen Guild
(Tem) Tempean
(U) Universal
(UA) United Artists
(VD) Visual Drama
(WB) Warner Brothers

1939

Blind Alley (Col)
Let Us Live (U)
Rio (U)

1940

Angels over Broadway (Col)
Stranger on the Third Floor (RKO)

1941

Among the Living (Par)
Ladies in Retirement (Col)
Out of the Fog (WB)

1942

Moontide (Fox)
Street of Chance (Par)

1943

Journey into Fear (RKO)
The Seventh Victim (RKO)
Whispering Footsteps (Rep)

1944

Bluebeard (PRC)
Destiny (U)
Lady in the Death House (PRC)
The Lodger (Fox)
Mark of the Whistler (Col)
Phantom Lady (U)
Strangers in the Night (Rep)
Voice in the Wind (UA)
When Strangers Marry (Mon)
The Whistler (Col)

1945

Apology for Murder (PRC)
Bewitched (MGM)
Circumstantial Evidence (Fox)
Danger Signal (WB)
Dangerous Intruder (PRC)
Detour (PRC)
Escape in the Fog (Col)
The Great Flamarion (Rep)
Hangover Square (Fox)
Jealousy (Rep)
Johnny Angel (RKO)
The Lady Confesses (PRC)
My Name Is Julia Ross (Col)
Power of the Whistler (Col)
The Spider (Fox)
The Strange Affair of Uncle Harry (U)
The Strange Mr. Gregory (Mon)
The Suspect (U)
Two o'Clock Courage (RKO)
The Unseen (Par)

1946

Accomplice (PRC)
Black Angel (U)

The Chase (UA)
Criminal Court (RKO)
Deadline at Dawn (RKO)
Decoy (Mon)
Fear (Mon)
The Glass Alibi (Rep)
Her Kind of Man (WB)
Inside Job (U)
The Locket (RKO)
The Mask of Diijon (PRC)
Mysterious Intruder (Col)
The Mysterious Mr. Valentine (Rep)
Night Editor (Col)
Nocturne (RKO)
Secret of the Whistler (Col)
Shadow of a Woman (WB)
Shock (Fox)
So Dark the Night (Col)
Spectre of the Rose (Rep)
Strange Impersonation (Rep)
Strange Triangle (Fox)
They Made Me a Killer (Par)
The Verdict (WB)
Whistle Stop (UA)

1947

Backlash (Fox)
Blackmail (Rep)
Blind Spot (Col)
Born to Kill (RKO)
The Brasher Doubloon (Fox)
Bury Me Dead (PRC)
Desperate (RKO)
The Devil Thumbs a Ride (RKO)
Fall Guy (Mon)
Fear in the Night (Par)
The Flame (Rep)

Framed (Col)
The Gangster (AA)
The Guilty (Mon)
High Tide (Mon)
I Love Trouble (Col)
The Invisible Wall (Fox)
Key Witness (Col)
Love from a Stranger (EL)
Moss Rose (Fox)
Philo Vance's Gamble (PRC)
The Pretender (Rep)
Railroaded! (PRC)
Riff Raff (RKO)
Road to the Big House (SG)
Second Chance (Fox)
Shoot to Kill (SG)
Singapore (U)
The 13th Hour (Col)
Violence (Mon)
The Web (U)
Whispering City (EL)
Woman on the Beach (RKO)

1948

Behind Locked Doors (EL)
Blonde Ice (FC)
Bodyguard (RKO)
Canon City (EL)
The Dark Past (Col)
Escape (Fox)
For You I Die (FC)
He Walked by Night (EL)
Hollow Triumph (EL)
The Hunted (AA)
I, Jane Doe (Rep)
I Wouldn't Be in Your Shoes (Mon)
Incident (Mon)

Inner Sanctum (FC)
Kiss the Blood off My Hands (U)
Larceny (U)
Money Madness (FC)
Open Secret (EL)
Parole, Inc. (EL)
Race Street (RKO)
Raw Deal (EL)
Return of the Whistler (Col)
Ruthless (EL)
Shed No Tears (EL)
The Sign of the Ram (Col)
The Spiritualist (EL)
T-Men (EL)
Vicious Circle (UA)

1949

Abandoned (U)
Act of Violence (MGM)
The Big Steal (RKO)
Border Incident (MGM)
C-Man (FC)
City Across the River (U)
The Clay Pigeon (RKO)
The Crooked Way (UA)
A Dangerous Profession (RKO)
Follow Me Quietly (RKO)
The Hidden Room (EL)
Illegal Entry (U)
Impact (UA)
Jigsaw (UA)
Johnny Stool Pigeon (U)
The Judge (FC)
Manhandled (Par)
Port of New York (EL)
The Reckless Moment (Col)
Red Light (UA)

The Red Menace (Rep)
The Set-Up (RKO)
Shockproof (Col)
Strange Bargain (RKO)
Tension (MGM)
Thieves' Highway (Fox)
The Threat (RKO)
Too Late for Tears (UA)
Trapped (EL)
The Undercover Man (Col)
Undertow (U)
The Window (RKO)
Woman in Hiding (UA)
Woman on Pier 13 (RKO)
A Woman's Secret (RKO)

1950

Armored Car Robbery (RKO)
Between Midnight and Dawn (Col)
The Capture (RKO)
Convicted (Col)
D.O.A. (UA)
Destination Murder (RKO)
Dial 1119 (MGM)
Guilty Bystander (FC)
Gun Crazy (UA)
Highway 301 (WB)
House by the River (Rep)
Hunt the Man Down (RKO)
The Killer That Stalked New York (Col)
A Lady Without Passport (MGM)
The Lawless (Par)
Once a Thief (UA)
One Way Street (MGM)
Outside the Wall (U)
Quicksand (UA)
Scene of the Crime (MGM)

Shadow on the Wall (MGM)
Shakedown (U)
The Sleeping City (U)
Southside 1–1000 (AA)
The Sun Sets at Dawn (EL)
The Tattooed Stranger (RKO)
This Side of the Law (WB)
Try and Get Me (UA)
Under the Gun (U)
The Underworld Story (UA)
Union Station (Par)
Unmasked (Rep)
Walk Softly, Stranger (RKO)
Where Danger Lives (RKO)
Without Honor (UA)
Woman on the Run (U)

1951

The Big Night (UA)
Cause for Alarm (MGM)
Cry Danger (RKO)
Fugitive Lady (Rep)
Gambling House (RKO)
Girl on the Bridge (Fox)
He Ran All the Way (UA)
Hollywood Story (U)
The Hoodlum (UA)
I Was a Communist for the F.B.I. (WB)
Iron Man (U)
M (Col)
The Man Who Cheated Himself (Fox)
The Man with My Face (UA)
The Mob (Col)
No Questions Asked (MGM)
Pickup (Col)
The Prowler (UA)
The Raging Tide (U)

Roadblock (RKO)
The Scarf (UA)
The Second Woman (UA)
The Strip (MGM)
Three Steps North (UA)
Tomorrow Is Another Day (WB)
Two of a Kind (Col)
The Unknown Man (MGM)
The Well (UA)
The Whip Hand (RKO)

1952

Another Man's Poison (UA)
Beware, My Lovely (RKO)
Captive City (UA)
The Gambler and the Lady (Lip)
The Green Glove (UA)
Hoodlum Empire (Rep)
Kansas City Confidential (UA)
Loan Shark (Lip)
Man Bait (Lip)
Narrow Margin (RKO)
Night Without Sleep (Fox)
On Dangerous Ground (RKO)
Scandal Sheet (Col)
The Sellout (MGM)
The Sniper (Col)
The Steel Trap (Fox)
Strange Fascination (Col)
Talk about a Stranger (MGM)
The Thief (UA)
Without Warning (UA)

1953

Bad Blonde (Lip)
The Big Frame (RKO)

A Blueprint for Murder (Fox)
City That Never Sleeps (Rep)
Dangerous Crossing (Fox)
The Glass Wall (Col)
The Glass Web (UA)
The Hitch-Hiker (RKO)
I, the Jury (UA)
Jennifer (AA)
Jeopardy (MGM)
Man in the Attic (Fox)
Man in the Dark (Col)
Marilyn (A)
Murder Without Tears (AA)
99 River Street (UA)
No Escape (UA)
Split Second (RKO)
Stolen Identity (Ain)
Stranger on the Prowl (UA)
The System (WB)
Terror Street (Lip)
Vicki (Fox)
Violated (Pan)

1954

Bait (UA)
Black Tuesday (UA)
Blackout (Lip)
Crime Wave (WB)
Cry Vengeance (AA)
Drive a Crooked Road (Col)
Forbidden (U)
Heat Wave (Lip)
Hell's Half Acre (Rep)
Highway Dragnet (AA)
The Human Jungle (AA)
Jailbait (How)
The Long Wait (UA)

Loophole (AA)
Make Haste to Live (Rep)
Naked Alibi (U)
The Other Woman (Fox)
Paid to Kill (Lip)
Playgirl (U)
Private Hell 36 (F)
Pushover (Col)
Riot in Cell Block 11 (AA)
Shield for Murder (UA)
The Sleeping Tiger (A)
Suddenly (UA)
Wicked Woman (UA)
Witness to Murder (UA)
World for Ransom (AA)

1955

Accused of Murder (Rep)
The Big Bluff (UA)
The Big Combo (AA)
Cast a Dark Shadow (A)
Crashout (F)
The Crooked Web (Col)
Female on the Beach (U)
Finger Man (AA)
Gangbusters (VD)
Hell's Island (Par)
Illegal (WB)
Impulse (Tem)
Killer's Kiss (UA)
Kiss Me Deadly (UA)
Mr. Arkadin (Alex)
Murder Is My Beat (AA)
The Naked Street (UA)
New York Confidential (WB)
The Night Holds Terror (Col)
The Phenix City Story (AA)

Queen Bee (Col)
Shack out on 101 (AA)
Sudden Danger (AA)
Women's Prison (Col)

1956

Behind the High Wall (U)
Beyond a Reasonable Doubt (RKO)
Blonde Sinner (AA)
The Come-On (AA)
Crime Against Joe (UA)
Crime in the Streets (AA)
A Cry in the Night (WB)
The Deadliest Sin (AA)
Female Jungle (AIP)
The Houston Story (Col)
The Killer Is Loose (UA)
The Killing (UA)
The Man in the Vault (RKO)
The Man Is Armed (Rep)
Nightmare (UA)
Please Murder Me (DCA)
The Price of Fear (UA)
Shadow of Fear (UA)
Spin a Dark Web (Col)
The Steel Jungle (WB)
Storm Fear (UA)
Terror at Midnight (Rep)
Timetable (UA)
The Way Out (RKO)
A Woman's Devotion (Rep)

1957

Affair in Havana (AA)
Baby Face Nelson (UA)
The Brothers Rico (Col)

The Burglar (Col)
Chain of Evidence (AA)
Chicago Confidential (UA)
Crime of Passion (UA)
Footsteps in the Night (AA)
Four Boys and a Gun (UA)
The Garment Jungle (Col)
Hellbound (UA)
Hit and Run (UA)
House of Numbers (MGM)
My Gun Is Quick (UA)
The Night Runner (UA)
Nightfall (Col)
Plunder Road (Fox)
Shadow on the Window (MGM)
Short Cut to Hell (Par)
The Tattered Dress (U)
Teenage Doll (AA)
Time Without Pity (A)
The Unholy Wife (RKO)
Wicked as They Come (Col)

1958

Appointment with a Shadow (U)
Kill Her Gently (Col)
The Lineup (Col)
The Man Who Died Twice (Rep)
Murder by Contract (Col)
Revolt in the Big House (AA)
Screaming Mimi (Col)
Stakeout on Dope Street (WB)

1959

The Beat Generation (MGM)
City of Fear (Col)
The Crimson Kimono (Col)

Cry Tough (UA)
Date with Death (PI)
The Last Mile (UA)
The Louisiana Hussey (How)
Nowhere to Go (MGM)
Odds Against Tomorrow (UA) .
Step down to Terror (U)

B Noirs Listed by Studio

Ainsworth

Stolen Identity (1953)

Alexander

Mr. Arkadin (1955)

Allied Artists

Affair in Havana (1957)
The Big Combo (1955)
Blonde Sinner (1956)
Chain of Evidence (1957)
The Come-On (1956)
Crime in the Streets (1956)
Cry Vengeance (1954)
The Deadliest Sin (1956)
Finger Man (1955)
Footsteps in the Night (1957)
The Gangster (1947)
Highway Dragnet (1954)
The Human Jungle (1954)
The Hunted (1948)
Jennifer (1953)
Loophole (1954)
Murder Is My Beat (1955)
Murder Without Tears (1953)
The Phenix City Story (1955)

Revolt in the Big House (1958)
Riot in Cell Block 11 (1954)
Shack out on 101 (1955)
Southside 1-1000 (1950)
Sudden Danger (1955)
Teenage Doll (1957)
World for Ransom (1954)

American International Pictures

Female Jungle (1956)

Astor

Marilyn (1953)
The Sleeping Tiger (1954)
Cast a Dark Shadow (1955)
Time Without Pity (1957)

Columbia

Angels over Broadway (1940)
Between Midnight and Dawn (1950)
Blind Alley (1939)
Blind Spot (1947)
The Brothers Rico (1957)
The Burglar (1957)
City of Fear (1959)
Convicted (1950)
The Crimson Kimono (1959)
The Crooked Web (1955)
The Dark Past (1948)
Drive a Crooked Road (1954)
Escape in the Fog (1945)
Framed (1947)
The Garment Jungle (1956)
The Glass Wall (1953)
The Houston Story (1956)

I Love Trouble (1947)
Key Witness (1947)
Kill Her Gently (1959)
The Killer That Stalked New York (1950)
Ladies in Retirement (1941)
The Lineup (1958)
M (1951)
Man in the Dark (1953)
Mark of the Whistler (1944)
The Mob (1951)
Murder by Contract (1958)
My Name Is Julia Ross (1945)
Mysterious Intruder (1946)
Night Editor (1946)
The Night Holds Terror (1955)
Nightfall (1957)
Pickup (1951)
Power of the Whistler (1945)
Pushover (1954)
Queen Bee (1955)
The Reckless Moment (1949)
Return of the Whistler (1948)
Scandal Sheet (1952)
Screaming Mimi (1958)
Secret of the Whistler (1946)
Shockproof (1949)
The Sign of the Ram (1948)
The Sniper (1952)
So Dark the Night (1946)
Spin a Dark Web (1956)
Strange Fascination (1952)
The 13th Hour (1947)
Two of a Kind (1951)
The Undercover Man (1949)
The Whistler (1944)
Wicked as They Come (1956)
Women's Prison (1955)

Distributors Corporation of America

Please Murder Me (1956)

Eagle Lion

Behind Locked Doors (1948)
Canon City (1948)
He Walked by Night (1948)
The Hidden Room (1949)
Hollow Triumph (1948)
Love from a Stranger (1947)
Open Secret (1948)
Parole, Inc. (1948)
Port of New York (1949)
Raw Deal (1948)
Ruthless (1948)
Shed No Tears (1948)
The Spiritualist (1948)
The Sun Sets at Dawn (1950)
T-Men (1948)
Trapped (1949)
Whispering City (1947)

Filmakers

Crashout (1955)
Private Hell 36 (1954)

Film Classics

Blonde Ice (1948)
C-Man (1949)
For You I Die (1948)
Guilty Bystander (1950)
Inner Sanctum (1948)
The Judge (1949)
Money Madness (1948)

Howco

Jail Bait (1954)
The Louisiana Hussey (1959)

Lippert

Bad Blonde (1953)
Blackout (1954)
The Gambler and the Lady (1952)
Heat Wave (1954)
Loan Shark (1952)
Man Bait (1952)
Paid to Kill (1954)
Terror Street (1953)

Metro Goldwyn Mayor

Act of Violence (1949)
The Beat Generation (1959)
Bewitched (1945)
Border Incident (1949)
Cause for Alarm (1951)
Dial 1119 (1950)
House of Numbers (1957)
Jeopardy (1953)
A Lady Without Passport (1950)
No Questions Asked (1951)
Nowhere to Go (1959)
One Way Street (1950)
Scene of the Crime (1950)
The Sellout (1952)
Shadow on the Wall (1950)
Shadow on the Window (1957)
The Strip (1951)
Talk about a Stranger (1952)
Tension (1949)
The Unknown Man (1951)

Monogram

Decoy (1946)
Fall Guy (1947)
Fear (1946)
The Guilty (1947)
High Tide (1947)
I Wouldn't Be in Your Shoes (1948)
Incident (1948)
The Strange Mr. Gregory (1945)
Violence (1947)
When Strangers Marry (1944)

Pacific International

Date with Death (1959)

Panther

Violated (1953)

Paramount

Among the Living (1941)
Fear in the Night (1947)
Hell's Island (1955)
The Lawless (1950)
Manhandled (1949)
Short Cut to Hell (1957)
Street of Chance (1942)
They Made Me a Killer (1946)
Union Station (1950)
The Unseen (1945)

Producers Releasing Corporation

Accomplice (1946)
Apology for Murder (1945)
Bluebeard (1944)

Bury Me Dead (1947)
Dangerous Intruder (1945)
Detour (1945)
The Lady Confesses (1945)
Lady in the Death House (1944)
The Mask of Diijon (1946)
Philo Vance's Gamble (1947)
Railroaded! (1947)

RKO Radio Pictures

Armored Car Robbery (1950)
Beware, My Lovely (1952)
Beyond a Reasonable Doubt (1956)
The Big Frame (1953)
The Big Steal (1949)
Bodyguard (1948)
Born to Kill (1947)
The Capture (1950)
Clay Pigeon (1949)
Criminal Court (1946)
Cry Danger (1951)
A Dangerous Profession (1949)
Deadline at Dawn (1946)
Desperate (1947)
Destination Murder (1950)
The Devil Thumbs a Ride (1947)
Follow Me Quietly (1949)
Gambling House (1951)
The Hitch-Hiker (1953)
Hunt the Man Down (1950)
Johnny Angel (1945)
Journey into Fear (1943)
The Locket (1946)
Man in the Vault (1953)
Narrow Margin (1952)
Nocturne (1946)
On Dangerous Ground (1952)

Race Street (1948)
Riff Raff (1947)
Roadblock (1951)
The Set-Up (1949)
The Seventh Victim (1943)
Split Second (1953)
Strange Bargain (1949)
Stranger on the Third Floor (1940)
The Tattooed Stranger (1950)
The Threat (1949)
Two o'Clock Courage (1945)
The Unholy Wife (1957)
Walk Softly, Stranger (1950)
The Way Out (1956)
Where Danger Lives (1950)
The Whip Hand (1951)
The Window (1949)
Woman on the Beach (1947)
Woman on Pier 13 (1949)
A Woman's Secret (1949)

Republic

Accused of Murder (1955)
Blackmail (1947)
City That Never Sleeps (1953)
The Flame (1947)
Fugitive Lady (1951)
The Great Flamarion (1945)
Hell's Half Acre (1954)
Hoodlum Empire (1952)
House by the River (1950)
I, Jane Doe (1948)
Jealousy (1945)
Make Haste to Live (1954)
The Man Is Armed (1956)
The Man Who Died Twice (1958)
The Mysterious Mr. Valentine (1946)

The Pretender (1947)
The Red Menace (1949)
Spectre of the Rose (1946)
Strange Impersonation (1946)
Strangers in the Night (1944)
Terror at Midnight (1956)
Unmasked (1950)
Whispering Footsteps (1943)
A Woman's Devotion (1956)

Screen Guild

Road to the Big House (1947)
Shoot to Kill (1947)

Tempean

Impulse (1955)

Twentieth Century Fox

Backlash (1947)
A Blueprint for Murder (1953)
The Brasher Doubloon (1947)
Circumstantial Evidence (1945)
Dangerous Crossing (1953)
Escape (1948)
Girl on the Bridge (1951)
Hangover Square (1945)
The Invisible Wall (1947)
The Lodger (1944)
Man in the Attic (1953)
The Man Who Cheated Himself (1951)
Moontide (1942)
Moss Rose (1947)
Night Without Sleep (1952)
The Other Woman (1954)
Plunder Road (1957)

Second Chance (1947)
Shock (1946)
The Spider (1945)
The Steel Trap (1952)
Strange Triangle (1946)
Thieves' Highway (1949)
Vicki (1953)

United Artists

Another Man's Poison (1952)
Baby Face Nelson (1957)
Bait (1954)
The Big Bluff (1955)
The Big Night (1951)
Black Tuesday (1954)
Captive City (1952)
The Chase (1946)
Chicago Confidential (1957)
Crime Against Joe (1956)
Crime of Passion (1957)
The Crooked Way (1949)
Cry Tough (1959)
D.O.A. (1950)
Four Boys and a Gun (1957)
The Glass Web (1953)
The Green Glove (1952)
Gun Crazy (1950)
He Ran All the Way (1951)
Hellbound (1957)
Hit and Run (1957)
The Hoodlum (1951)
I, the Jury (1953)
Impact (1949)
Jigsaw (1949)
Kansas City Confidential (1952)
The Killer Is Loose (1956)

Killer's Kiss (1955)
The Killing (1956)
Kiss Me, Deadly (1955)
The Last Mile (1959)
The Long Wait (1954)
The Man with My Face (1951)
My Gun Is Quick (1957)
The Naked Street (1955)
The Night Runner (1957)
Nightmare (1956)
99 River Street (1953)
No Escape (1953)
Odds Against Tomorrow (1959)
Once a Thief (1950)
The Prowler (1951)
Quicksand (1950)
The Scarf (1951)
Shadow of Fear (1956)
Shield for Murder (1954)
Storm Fear (1956)
Stranger on the Prowl (1953)
Suddenly (1956)
The Thief (1952)
Three Steps North (1951)
Timetable (1956)
Too Late for Tears (1949)
Try and Get Me (1950)
The Underworld Story (1950)
Vicious Circle (1948)
Voice in the Wind (1944)
The Well (1951)
Whistle Stop (1946)
Wicked Woman (1954)
Without Honor (1950)
Without Warning (1952)
Witness to Murder (1954)
Woman in Hiding (1949)

Universal

Abandoned (1949)
Appointment with a Shadow (1958)
Behind the High Wall (1956)
Black Angel (1946)
City Across the River (1949)
Destiny (1944)
Female on the Beach (1955)
Forbidden (1954)
Hollywood Story (1951)
Illegal Entry (1949)
Inside Job (1946)
Iron Man (1951)
Johnny Stool Pigeon (1949)
Kiss the Blood off My Hands (1948)
Larceny (1948)
Let Us Live (1939)
The Naked Alibi (1954)
The Night Runner (1957)
One Way Street (1950)
Outside the Wall (1950)
Phantom Lady (1944)
Playgirl (1954)
The Price of Fear (1956)
The Raging Tide (1951)
Rio (1939)
Shakedown (1950)
Singapore (1947)
The Sleeping City (1950)
Step down to Terror (1959)
The Strange Affair of Uncle Harry (1945)
The Suspect (1945)
The Tattered Dress (1957)
Under the Gun (1950)
Undertow (1949)
The Web (1947)
Woman on the Run (1950)

Visual Drama

Gangbusters (1955)

Warner Brothers

Crime Wave (1954)
Cry in the Night (1956)
Danger Signal (1945)
Her Kind of Man (1945)
Highway 301 (1950)
I Was a Communist for the F.B.I. (1951)
Illegal (1955)
New York Confidential (1955)
Out of the Fog (1941)
Shadow of a Woman (1946)
Stakeout on Dope Street (1958)
The Steel Jungle (1956)
The System (1953)
This Side of the Law (1950)
Tomorrow Is Another Day (1951)
The Verdict (1946)

FILM NOIR SOURCES

Available on Video

Eddie Brandt's Saturday Matinee
5006 Vineland Ave.
North Hollywood, CA 91601
(818) 506-4242 506-7722
FAX (818) 506-6649

By far the best source for film noir or any kind of film on video, Eddie Brandt's has a
library of 52,000 videos. In addition to its regular cataloged films, it also has a lending
library of films not available on video that can be checked out for free with the
checkout of a certain number of regularly listed titles. Eddie Brandt's also has a mail
order rental service. For researchers and collectors of memorabilia, Eddie Brandt's also
has available for purchase one of the largest collections of film photographs in the
world.

Movies Unlimited
3015 Darnell Rd.
Philadelphia, PA 19154
1-800-4-MOVIES e-mail: movies@moviesunlimited.com

Movies Unlimited is a clearing house for many different video companies and has a
huge number of titles of all types of movies available, including a section on film
noir. The catalog is available for a price upon request.

Sinister Cinema
P.O. Box 4369
Medford, OR 97501-0168
(503) 773-6860

Sinister Cinema specializes in old forgotten and cult horror and sci-fi films as well as cheap westerns but does have a "Mystery-film noir" selection of videos, some of which are not available elsewhere.

Englewood Entertainment
10917 Winner Rd.
Independence, MO 64052
(888) 573-5490 FAX (816) 836-3400
http://www.englewd.com

Englewood has a beautifully packaged video line titled Hollywood Noir. Quite a few of the titles it lists as noir, however, are not, such as *The Bigamist* and *Not Wanted*, so caveat emptor. It does have several hard-to-find B titles, such as *The Louisiana Hussey* and *Date with Death.*

Unavailable on Video

Films in this book not available on video tend to be the property of either the studios that produced them or companies that have purchased a defunct studio's library. Until the library owners release the films to video or to television, there are limited sources available for viewing them. There are, however, two sources that do screenings for researchers and have archives available to the public.

The Academy of Motion Pictures Arts and Sciences
Center for Motion Picture Study
333 S. La Cienega Blvd.
Los Angeles, CA 90211
(310) 247-3020

Although the academy does have archives, they are in general inferior to Eddie Brandt's. The academy library does, however, have a wealth of printed information (reviews, plot summaries, etc.). Researchers can access the library at the phone number above. Phone requests for information must be limited to questions that can be answered within three to five minutes.

UCLA Film Archives Research and Study Center
Powell Library, Room 46
UCLA Campus
Los Angeles, CA
(310) 206-5388

Screenings are available, but requests have to be made in advance.

NOTES

Introduction

p. 1   At least one writer on the subject... Spencer Selby. *The Dark City: The Film Noir*, Jefferson, NC: McFarland, 1984, p. 3.

3   As writer and director Paul Schrader puts it... Paul Schrader. "Notes on Film Noir," reprinted in Alain Silver and James Ursini, eds., *Film Noir Reader*, New York: Limelight Editions, 1996, p. 62.

4   That's what makes it attractive... Andrew Olsten. "It's the End of the World . . . Smiling Through the Apocalypse with the Noir Generation," *Los Angeles Magazine*, October 1995.

5   "High-budget trash is considered..." Schrader, op. cit., p. 62.

Chapter 1

p. 8   Director tastes and techniques have nothing... Interview with the author.

8   "What I like about film noir is that..." Todd R. Erickson. *Evidence of Film Noir in the Contemporary American Cinema*, thesis for Master's Degree, presented to the Department of Theatre and Film, Brigham Young University, 1990, p. 56.

10   "You can make one mistake..." Andrew Olstein. "It's the End of the World: Smiling Through the Apocalypse with the Noir Generation," *Los Angeles Magazine*, October 1995, p. 58.

12   "We are all constrained, because of contioning..." Erickson, op. cit., p. 55.

Chapter 2

p. 16   As one writer put it, "Humanity was still..." David Madden. *Tough Guy Writers of the Thirties*, Carbondale: Southern Illinois University Press, 1968, p. 73.

18   It marks the first time that Hollywood has... Frank Krutnik. *In a Lonely Street: Film Noir, Genre, Masculinity*, London: Routledge, 1991, p. 37.

20 "These novels, and the covers that illustrate..." Geoffrey O'Brien. *Hardboiled America,* New York: Van Nostrand, 1981, p. 14.

Chapter 4

p. 39 "They made films cheaply, but obscuring..." Don Miller. *B Movies,* New York: Ballantine, 1987, pp. 123–4.

40 "Nevertheless, the curiously cross-generic quality..." Paul Kerr. "Out of What Past? Notes on the Film Noir", in Alain Silver and James Ursini, eds., *Film Noir Reader,* New York: Limelight, 1998, p. 117.

40 In a later interview, Robson recalled that... *Ibid.,* p. 114.

Epilogue

p. 165 "They're saying, you may have plans, you may..." Andrew Olstein. *op. cit.,* p. 60.

165 In the final analysis, we must ask whether... Alain Silver, and Elizabeth Ward, (eds.), *Film Noir: An Encyclopedic Reference to the American Style,* Woodstock, NY: Overlook Press, 1992, p. 6.

166 "Noir might more realistically be considered..." Geoffrey O'Brien. "The Return of Film Noir!" *New York Review,* August 15, 1991, p. 45.

BIBLIOGRAPHY

Anger, Kenneth. *Hollywood Babylon*. New York: Bell, 1981.

Anger, Kenneth. *Hollywood Babylon II*. New York: Plume, 1985.

Crowther, Bruce. *Reflections in a Dark Mirror*. New York: Ungar, 1989.

Erickson, Todd R. *Evidence of Film Noir in the Contemporary American Cinema*. Thesis for Master's Degree presented to the Department of Theatre and Film, Brigham Young University, 1990.

Hannsberry, Karen Burroughs. *Femme Noir: Bad Girls of Film*. Jefferson, NC: McFarland, 1998.

Hirsch, Foster. *The Dark Side of the Screen*. Da Capo, 1983.

Johnson, Tom, and Del Vecchio, Deborah. *Hammer Films: An Exhaustive Filmography*. Jefferson, NC: McFarland, 1996.

Karimi, Amir Nassourd. *Toward a Definition of the American Film Noir*. New York: Arno Press, 1970.

Krutnik, Frank. *In a Lonely Street: Film Noir, Genre, and Masculinity*. London: Routledge, 1991.

Madden, David. *Tough Guy Writers of the Thirties*. Carbondale: Southern Illinois University Press, 1968.

Martin, Len D. *The Allied Artists Checklist*. Jefferson, NC: McFarland, 1993.

Martin, Len D. *The Republic Pictures Checklist*. Jefferson, NC: McFarland, 1998.

Martin, Richard. *Mean Streets and Raging Bulls: The Legacy of Film Noir in Contemporary American Cinema*. Lanham, MD, and London: Scarecrow Press, 1997.

Medved, Harry, and Medved, Michael. *The Golden Turkey Awards*. New York: Perigree, 1980.

Miller, Don. *B Movies*. New York: Ballantine, 1987.

Nash, Jay Robert, and Ross, Stanley Ralph. *The Motion Picture Guide*. Chicago: Cinebooks, 1985.

O'Brien, Geoffrey. *Hardboiled America*. New York: Van Nostrand, 1981.

O'Brien, Geoffrey. "The Return of Film Noir!" *New York Review*, August 15, 1991.

Okuda, Ted. *Grand National, Producers Releasing Corporation, and Screen Guild/Lippert: Complete Filmographies with Studio Histories*. Jefferson, NC: McFarland, 1989.

Okuda, Ted. *The Monogram Checklist*. Jefferson, NC: McFarland, 1987.

Olstein, Andrew. "It's the End of the World . . . Smiling Through the Apocalypse with the Noir Generation." *Los Angeles Magazine*, October 1997.

Ottoson, Robert. *A Reference Guide to the American Film Noir: 1940–1958*. Metuchen, NJ, and London: Scarecrow Press, 1981.

Selby, Spencer. *Dark City: The Film Noir*. Jefferson, NC: McFarland, 1984.

Silver, Alain, and Ursini, James. *Film Noir Reader*. New York: Limelight Editions, 1998.

Silver, Alain, and Ward, Elizabeth. *Film Noir: An Encyclopedic Reference to the American Style*. Woodstock, NY: Overlook Press, 1998.

Stephens, Michael L. *Film Noir: A Comprehensive Illustrated Reference to Movies, Terms, and Persons*. Jefferson, NC: McFarland, 1995.

Telotte, J. P. *Voices in the Dark: The Narrative Patterns of Film Noir*. Urbana: University of Illinois Press, 1989.

INDEX

Bold page numbers indicate location in
Filmography.